The State and the
Non-Public School
1825–1925

Lloyd P. Jorgenson

The State and the Non-Public School

1825–1925

University of Missouri Press
Columbia, 1987

Copyright © 1987 by
The Curators of the University of Missouri
University of Missouri Press, Columbia, Missouri 65211
Printed and bound in the United States of America
All rights reserved

Library of Congress Cataloging-in-Publication Data
Jorgenson, Lloyd P.
The state and the non-public school, 1825–1925.
Bibliography: p.
Includes index.
1. State aid to private schools—United States—
History—19th century. 2. Educational law and
legislation—United States—History—19th century.
3. Education and state—United States—History—
19th century. I. Title.
LB2828.J67 1987   379.3'0973   86–30776
ISBN 0–8262–0633–6 (alk. paper)

♾™This paper meets the minimum requirements of
the American National Standard for Permanence of Paper
for Printed Library Materials, Z39.48, 1984.

To Virginia, Ann, and Chuck

Preface

In a narrow sense, this is a history of the origins of the political and legal principles that non-public schools are ineligible to receive public funds and that Bible reading and prayer are forbidden in the public school. During the nineteenth century, the often bitter controversies over these issues were commonly referred to as the "School Question." This study is not an account of laws and judicial decisions, which in fact are given only passing attention, but rather of the social, political, and economic conditions that brought such laws and decisions into existence. In a broader sense, this is a history of the bifurcation of education into public and non-public sectors, and of the ensuing struggles between the proponents of the two sectors.

Colonial and early national schools were neither wholly public nor wholly private. There were at the time no terms to distinguish between public and private schools as we now know them. Our present public school systems have their origins in the Common School Movement of about 1830–1860. ("Common schools" were primary schools "common"—or at least open—to all white children of all classes and religious persuasions. Public secondary schools were a later development.) Important as the Common School Movement was, there were other concurrent developments that profoundly influenced the course of American public education. Prime among them were the great religious movement known as the Second Awakening, the vast increase of immigration and the subsequent rise of nativist and anti-Catholic agitation, and the dominant role of the Protestant clergy in the school movement.

Transferring the theme of "non-sectarianism" so vigorously promoted by the Second Awakening to the field of education, the Common School leaders insisted that schools should be "common" to all children, non-sectarian, and hence necessarily under the jursidiction of the state. A small minority of Protestant denominational bodies were unwilling to accept as adequate the non-sectarian religious instruction of the common schools, and they withheld their support for the movement. This was a disappointment for the leaders of the Common School Movement, but they agreed that the major obstacle to the development of schools common to all children was the existence and growth of Catholic schools. Accordingly, and making it abundantly clear that their target was the Catholic schools, common school leaders pressed vigorously for abolition of the traditional policy of granting public aid to non-public (including church-related) schools. In the 1850s the Native American (Know-Nothing) party seized the momentum generated by the common school leaders. Portraying themselves as the champions and defenders of the common schools, the Know-Nothings promised to keep the (Protestant) Bible in the schools and to abolish public aid to non-public schools. Although the Know-Nothings soon collapsed as a party, their goals in education were to a large extent achieved. Bible reading was safeguarded, often by law, and by 1860 most states had enacted legislation denying financial aid from public sources to non-public schools. Catholic leaders responded to these developments by rejecting the common schools, by increasing their emphasis on the need for more Catholic schools, and by demanding what they considered to be their fair share of public funds for such schools.

Although the common school leaders, in league with the Know-Nothings, had succeeded in pushing the Catholic and other non-public schools to the periphery of the educational scene, they were not yet satisfied. In the late 1880s compulsory school-attendance bills, so worded as to make attendance at non-public schools non-compliance and therefore legally punishable, were introduced in several states. Such bills were enacted in two states, but soon repealed because of the furious opposition they engendered. The controversies subsided for a time, but nationalistic ardor aroused by World War I moved many patriots to resume the campaign against the non-public schools. Bills very similar to those of 1888–1890 were introduced in a few states, and one was enacted in Oregon. The striking down of the Oregon law by the U.S. Supreme Court in 1925 ended this threat. However, in spite of high court rulings, no one would pretend that any consensus of opinion has been reached on the School Question.

* * *

Although I had earlier published a few articles on some of the topics discussed in this volume, most of the work has been done since my retirement. Were it not for the generous help provided by several people, the work might yet be unfinished. My heaviest indebtedness is to Professors Emeriti Daniel D. McGarry of Saint Louis University, Charles T. Dougherty of the University of Missouri–St. Louis, and Wilbur H. Glover, my undergraduate major professor and, later, Director of the Buffalo Historical Society. If the weaknesses they found in the original manuscript have not been adequately remedied, the fault lies wholly with me. Over a period of many years, Robert F. Huffman of the Elmer Ellis Library at the University of Missouri–Columbia saved me countless hours by locating sources and providing needed items of information. Janet Ann Thornton, of the College of Education, University of Missouri–Columbia, found time in her already busy schedule to type the original version of the manuscript.

The indexing of this book was funded by a grant from the Research Council of the University of Missouri–Columbia.

To my wife a special tribute is due. Too often when we should have been on vacation in parts near or far (as proper retirees), I was engrossed in this work. If the book contributes toward a better understanding of the troubled church-state relationships in education in this country, we will be amply repaid.

L. P. J.
Columbia, Missouri
November 1986

Contents

1

The American State-Aided
Voluntary School

Schoolmen Search for the Roots of Public Education

American schools of the colonial and early national periods were neither wholly public nor wholly private, as we now use those terms. They were in large part the product of voluntary efforts, aided sporadically by governmental grants. The campaign to extend educational opportunities in the United States at the primary-school level and to bring them increasingly under civil control—the so-called Common School Movement—was set into vigorous motion during the years 1830–1860 and consolidated in the decades after the Civil War. The custom of flying the flag over public schoolhouses, rarely seen before the war, became common in the postbellum period, and the school, like the flag, became a symbol of nationalism.[1] By 1900 the non-public school share of primary school enrollments had shrunk to about 8 percent of the total. It was a striking victory for the champions of public (in the nineteenth century called "common school") education, and they frequently reminded their countrymen that the "sectarian interests," as they called the sponsors of church-related schools, had stubbornly tried to retard this development.

Those who yearned to see the public school movement in perspective and, in a sense, to legitimize it, now began to search for the origins of public education. It was a welcome task for George H. Martin, who as agent for the Massachusetts State Board of Education could trace his official lineage back to Horace Mann, generally re-

---

1. Merle Curti, *The Growth of American Thought* (New York: Harper and Brothers, 1943), p. 413. A note on my use of terminology: in this work, schools are classified into two major categories: (1) public, and (2) non-public or voluntary. No fine distinctions are made among the many subgroups included in the non-public category, because all of them were adversely affected by the determined nineteenth-century campaigns to abolish the policy of granting public funds to such schools. The term *the state* is used in a generic sense to denote legally constituted public authority at all levels. Hence, on matters within their jurisdiction, local or state boards of education speak and act for the state.

garded as the primary figure in the Common School Movement. In 1891 Martin elaborated the thesis that public education in all its essentials was a heritage from the Puritan fathers.[2]

To those who regarded New England as the nursery of all learning and virtue—and they were many—this conclusion seemed almost self-evident. But Andrew S. Draper was not impressed. As state superintendent of public instruction in New York, Draper had come to be an admirer of the early Dutch colonists in that state. New England's claims to primacy in public education were vastly overrated, said Draper. What the New Englanders had done, he said, was to follow the English tradition of establishing secondary grammar schools and a college for an elite class, leaving elementary education to parents and masters. "The whole fact is," concluded Draper, "that for certainly more than sixty years of Massachusetts colonial life, and probably much longer, elementary instruction was held to be only a family duty for the attainment of religious ends."

In New York, argued Draper, it was much different. They were an impressive lot, these pioneering Dutchmen. To be sure, they were "few in numbers, poor in pocket, quaint in manner." But they paid for the land they occupied, and "The shotgun was not their chief instrument for converting Indians to the Christian faith." Quite as much as the Puritans, they prized piety and public worship, but they "*did* things without so much talk about them." As early as possible, they set up churches and schools and brought over pastors and schoolmasters. Then Draper confronted Martin with a bold conclusion: "America is indebted to the Dutch rather than to the English for the essential principles of the great free school system of the country and . . . New York, and not Massachusetts, has led the way."[3]

It was a sharp challenge, and Martin replied tartly: who was Draper, but a modern Van Tromp? "Flying Dutch colors and with broom nailed to his masthead, he sails triumphantly over all the Massachusetts seas, and returns in triumph to hear the plaudits of the Bowery . . . . Had he gone a step further and denied the existence of Massachusetts altogether, he would have done no more violence to history . . . ." The school started by Adam Roelandsen in New Amsterdam in 1633, continued Martin, was "never a public school in the American sense." Roelandsen himself, a pathetic character, had to take in washing to supplement his beggarly income as schoolmaster. Surely he could not be compared with Headmaster Ezekiel Cheever of the

2. "Compulsory Education in Massachusetts," National Education Association *Journal of Proceedings* 30 (1891): 403–12. Martin later developed his work more fully in a book, *The Evolution of the Massachusetts School System* (Boston: D. Appleton & Co., 1894).

3. "Public School Pioneering in New York and Massachusetts," *Educational Review* 3 (April 1892): 313–30.

Boston Latin Grammar School, a classmate of John Milton at St. Paul's School, a graduate of Cambridge, a scholar, and an author. Published in the prestigious *Educational Review*, the debate continued through 1892 and well into 1893.[4]

In spite of their bold assertions about the public nature of colonial schools, the early school historians were forced to make concessions that diluted their claims. Martin was certain that the early Massachusetts experiments "contained in embryo the whole school system of Massachusetts as we know it today." Yet he did not find it inconsistent to say at the same time that the civil organization of Massachusetts was one "in which the ministers had a controlling influence," and that the schools themselves were "under the constant and vigilant supervision of the ministers."[5]

When Professor Kilpatrick later made his thorough investigation of the New Netherland schools, he struggled with the same dilemma. He was forced to admit that "The elementary school of New Amsterdam was the joint concern of church and state," essentially a reproduction of the "Holland parochial system." In spite of this, Kilpatrick insisted, "enough was done by the secular authorities to present a remarkable anticipation of the American public school . . . . It seems proper to call such an institution a public school yet if this school was public, it none the less had peculiar relations with the church." In fact, the colonial church-state school was as much a forebear of the later parochial school as of the later public school. But the argument was stilled in 1920 when the dean of the early school historians placed his imprimatur on the thesis of New England primacy. The Massachusetts laws of 1642 and 1647, said Professor Cubberley, were the "foundations upon which our American state public school systems have been built."[6] This became the conventional wisdom.

Searching for the first public school was a consuming passion of the early school historians. And well they might be engrossed in such an inquiry. By the time they began their work, in the 1890s, there was already a strong tide of opinion that only public schools could adequately serve the republic and that non-public schools were somehow at variance with the genius of American institutions. Indeed, just at the time Martin and Draper were waging their lengthy debate, bitter campaigns were underway in several states to abolish non-public

4. Martin, "Public School Pioneering, A Reply," *Educational Review* 4 (June 1892): 34–39; continued in the *Review* 4 (October 1892): 241–52; 5 (March 1893): 232–42; 5 (April 1893): 345–62, 406–7.

5. "The Evolution of the Massachusetts Public School System," *Journal of Education* 37 (26 January 1893): 57.

6. William H. Kilpatrick, *The Dutch Schools of New Netherland and Colonial New York*, U.S. Bureau of Education *Bulletin*, no. 12, 1912, pp. 71, 84–93, 199–200; Ellwood P. Cubberley, *The History of Education* (Boston: Houghton Mifflin, 1920), p. 366.

schools altogether. This was a daring proposal, calling for complete reversal of the traditional view that schooling was primarily a responsibility of the family and the church and that the proper role of the state was to assist them.

If now the public school was to be presented as deserving of the support and affection that formerly had been extended to the church-related school, it would have to be endowed with historical respectability. Its origins, even if only in embryonic form, would have to be located in an early stage of the country's development. Its development and eventual flowering would have to be the logical and inevitable result of beneficent forces at work in American society. It was not an impossible task; there was indeed a sense in which the early schools had a public dimension. But the consequence of making other considerations subordinate to the emphasis on public control was a distorted view. American educational history became, as Professor Butts aptly described it, a "pietistic" vision of the "public school triumphant."[7]

Early American School Terminology

Governmental financial support for voluntary (including denominational) schools, so common during the colonial period, continued well into the national period. Far from prohibiting such support, the early state constitutions and statutes actively encouraged this policy. In his massively documented work, too long neglected by educational historians, Richard J. Gabel demonstrates that such aid actually increased until about 1820 and persisted in diminishing but still-significant amounts until well after the Civil War.[8] The same blending of state and denominational resources was present in the founding and support of the early colleges. They were creatures of the state as well as of the denominations they were designed to serve, and "whether they should be thought of as state colleges or as church colleges is a problem in semantics that is perhaps best resolved by calling them state-church colleges."[9] During the first half of the nineteenth century, denominational colleges vigorously opposed the claims of the

7. R. Freeman Butts, "Public Education and Political Community," *History of Education Quarterly* 14 (Summer 1974): 167.

8. *Public Funds for Church and Private Schools* (Washington, D.C.: Catholic University of America Press, 1937), pp. 147–262. Bernard Bailyn effectively points out the fallacy of trying to make a distinction between the denominational and public aspects of colonial education in his *Education in the Forming of American Society* (Chapel Hill: University of North Carolina Press, 1960), pp. 10–11. Essentially the same point had been made much earlier by Charles A. and Mary R. Beard in *The Rise of American Civilization*, 2 vols. (New York: Macmillan, 1927), 1:52.

9. Frederick Rudolph, *The American College and University, a History* (New York: Knopf, 1962), p. 13.

new state institutions for a share of the public funds they had come to consider as rightfully their own. Even after the Civil War, the tradition of public support for denominational colleges was still strong enough to permit six states to assign the revenues from the first Morrill Act land grants to church-affiliated institutions.[10]

A more striking reminder of the mingling of public and voluntary efforts in education is the fact that the terminology of colonial and early national education made no provision for differentiating between the schools that much later came to be classified separately as "public" or "private." Cubberley was determined to identify the New England town schools as public schools. But Ezra Stiles and Timothy Dwight, who as presidents of Yale (1778–1795 and 1795–1817 respectively)—and in their capacities as Congregationalist clergymen as well—had shown a deep solicitude for the New England town schools, referred to them affectionately as "our parochial schools."[11]

Similarly, the school later to be known as the William Penn Charter School was described in its charter of 1701 as a "public school" although it was actually a private corporation, founded at the "request, cost and charges of the People of God called Quakers." Much later instances of the casual use of the term *public* in education are also to be found. One church-sponsored school titled itself the New York Protestant Episcopal Public School after 1826. A Congregationalist secondary school was styled the Hartford (Connecticut) Public High School as late as 1871. The "public" schools of Washington and Georgetown, D.C., were under essentially private control until the middle of the nineteenth century.[12]

One of the most comprehensive public/private efforts in education existed in the secondary-level schools in the state of New York. Here, until about 1850, the voluntary academies were looked upon as an integral part of the state system of education, and the policy of the state was to contribute to their support. Thereafter, although the schools underwent little modification, they came increasingly under

10. The institutions aided were Yale and Dartmouth, Congregationalist; Brown, Baptist; Rutgers, Reformed; and Claflin and Corvallis, Methodist. Brown and Yale sued when the states later tried to transfer the funds to new public institutions, and both collected damages (U.S. Office of Education *Bulletin*, no. 9, 1930, pp. 17–18).

11. Stiles, *The Literary Diary of Ezra Stiles*, ed. F. B. Dexter, 3 vols. (New Haven: Yale University Press, 1901), 3:528; Dwight, *Travels in New England and New York*, ed. Barbara M. Solomon, 4 vols. (1821; rpt. Cambridge: Harvard University Press, 1969), 1:171, 4:294–301.

12. Thomas Woody, *Early Quaker Education in Pennsylvania*, Columbia University, Contributions to Education, no. 105 (New York: Teachers College, 1920), p. 50; Clifton H. Brewer, *A History of Religious Education in the Episcopal Church to 1835* (New Haven: Yale University Press, 1924), pp. 267–68; U.S. Commissioner of Education, *Report for the Year 1871* (Washington, D.C.: Government Printing Office, 1872), p. 614; J. Ormond Wilson, "Eighty Years of the Public Schools of Washington, 1805–1885," in U.S. Commissioner of Education, *Report*, 1894–1895, 2:1673–98.

criticism as sectarian institutions by the state superintendent of public instruction and by local school officials as well. Even so, when general state aid was withdrawn in 1850 they continued to serve, with state approval, as the principal vehicle for the training of elementary school teachers until late in the century, and were aided by the state for this purpose.[13]

In the more sparsely populated West, as the entire trans-Appalachian region was then called, the line between voluntary and public efforts in education was often imperceptible. The breaking of the land and the building of homes necessarily took first priority, and schools were usually a product of improvisation, without any nice regard for the relative claims of public and voluntary bodies. The first state superintendent of schools in Ohio, Samuel Lewis, was by personal conviction and legal obligation strongly committed to the promotion of public (common) schools. Yet he conceded freely in his first annual report in 1837, "It is certain that many of those reported as public are, in fact, private schools."[14] In 1836, a year after it was founded, the village of Kenosha in Wisconsin erected a building to be used as a schoolhouse and a church, "free to all denominations." Two years later a larger structure was built to house an academy, and it also was to be available without charge to any congregation desiring to worship there. In neighboring Racine, both the Methodist and Episcopal ministers conducted worship services in the village schoolhouse, and a "union" Sunday school was also conducted there. This arrangement continued until Roman Catholic newcomers objected to it as a misuse of public property. A number of the Protestants then undertook to erect a church building at their own expense, open to all but independent of any one denomination. Reminiscing years later, a Wisconsin pioneer expressed the prevailing view in a casual manner: "Public and private schools were all one in those days." The Texas legislature in 1856 designated any and all schools to which parents might choose to send their children as "free public schools," and therefore entitled to receive their pro rata share of the state school fund, and this law remained in effect until after the Civil War.[15]

In time, the courts were asked to help in clarifying school terminology, but even beyond midcentury their verdicts showed as many

13. George F. Miller, *The Academy System of the State of New York*, University of the State of New York *Bulletin*, no. 750, 1922, pp. 36–47, 64, 78–80, 131ff.

14. Ohio Superintendent of Common Schools, *First annual report of the Superintendent of Common Schools, made to the thirty-sixth general assembly of the state of Ohio, January 1838*, by Samuel Lewis (Columbus, Ohio: S. Medary, 1838), p. 46.

15. Timothy L. Smith, "Protestant Schooling and American Nationality, 1800–1850," *Journal of American History* 53 (March 1967): 688–89; Lloyd P. Jorgenson, *The Founding of Public Education in Wisconsin* (Madison: State Historical Society of Wisconsin, 1956), p. 36; Frederick Eby, *Education in Texas: Source Materials*, University of Texas *Bulletin*, no. 1824, 1918, p. 291.

variations as those found in common usage. A Massachusetts court in 1866 defined the term *public* or *common* school as a school (1) "supported by general taxation," (2) "open to all free of expense," and (3) "under the immediate control and superintendence of agents appointed by the voters of each town and city." This was to become, with variations, the standard definition of a public school. However, at the other extreme, as late as 1881 a Minnesota court could issue the opinion that a Catholic parochial school, operated not for profit and open to all children, "is, in the legal sense, not only a charity, but one wholly and entirely of public nature, and therefore, a public one."[16] Clearly, we cannot assume that all early American institutions that called themselves *public* schools were *public* in the sense in which that term is now used. Precision in school terminology did not exist during the colonial and early national periods because it was not needed. By the mid-nineteenth century it had become important to be able to differentiate between "public" and "non-public" schools because the former were increasingly considered the only legitimate recipients of public financial support. Clearly, there was no such thing as a typical colonial or early national school, yet a brief glimpse of certain groups of schools can give us some understanding of the sponsorship and financial support of education at that time. It can also show us that the voluntary/public approach to education produced impressive results during the late colonial and early national periods.

The Society for the Propagation of the Gospel

The largest school enterprise in the American colonies under a unified (albeit loose) sponsorship was almost certainly the one conducted by the Society for the Propagation of the Gospel in Foreign

16. *Merrick v. Amherst*, 94 Mass. (12 Allen) 509; *County of Hennepin v. Grace* (27 Minn.) 506. The derivation of the term *public school* is not entirely clear. A student of the evolution of the New York City school system traces the origins of the term back to school practices existing in Renaissance England (Carl F. Kaestle, *The Evolution of an Urban School System: New York City 1750–1850* [Cambridge: Harvard University Press, 1973], p. 16). This interpretation, however, is not used by English students of education, one of whom explains that some of the grammar schools succeeded in attracting pupils from a wider area and thus became known as *public* rather than *local* schools (J. C. Dancy in *Encyclopedia of Education*, ed. Edward Blishen [New York: Philosophical Library, 1970], p. 583). This etymology of the term is also given in *Education in Britain* (London: Central Office of Information, 1974), p. 2: "Certain (of the grammar) schools began to be known as 'public' schools as they outgrew their purely local associations." Similarly, we learn from the historical sketch in *The Public Schools and the General Educational System* (The Fleming Report), issued by the British Board of Education in 1944, that the term *public* was applied to Rugby when the school came to have "nearly a hundred pupils of whom eighty were not local boys," and to Harrow at the same time, as it was changing "from a local school of no great repute into one of the most famous schools in England." The most decisive period in the development of the English public schools was the first half of the nineteenth century.

Parts (SPG), the foreign-missionary arm of the Church of England. Predating both the Industrial Revolution and the French Revolution (it was founded in 1701), the society undertook to maintain an orthodox clergy in the British colonies and to supply schools, books, and religious training for colonists and native inhabitants.

The task of inducing competent clergy to serve in the colonies did not prove to be an easy one. But the educational work of the SPG was impressive, and those who have examined its system describe it admiringly. Its schools, says Kemp, "provided the nearest approach to a public school system that was to be found among the English colonists in New York." Knight uses almost the same words to describe SPG schools in the South, while Edwards and Richey call the society "the most important religious and philanthropic agency operating in the American Colonies" and credit it with achieving "the most conspicuous work in elementary education during the entire colonial era."[17] Reliable information concerning the number of SPG schools in each colony is not available, but the number of missionaries sent to the various colonies is known. These figures would probably indicate fairly well the number of schools. From 1702 until 1785, the society sent 197 men to the southern colonies and 149 to the middle colonies. The society was also active in New England, where in most places Puritans held the upper hand and Anglican clergymen were often threatened, persecuted, and fined. Yet 84 missionaries of the society were there, and schools were established.[18]

Most of the society's revenues were received as donations. Fees were paid by students, although indigent children were admitted free—a centuries-old practice. In New York City the society's schools were for the most part free to all children. Several colonial legislatures came to the aid of the society. For some years during the early eighteenth century, the government of South Carolina authorized annual grants to assist one of the society's schools and provided for the use of certain lands and buildings as well. It also established a quasi-public board of commissioners, including the governor, to supervise the school, and reaffirmed the Church of England requirement that the master "catechise and instruct the youth in the principles of the Christian religion professed by that church . . . ." In this colony, such

17. William Webb Kemp, *The Support of Schools in Colonial New York by the Society for the Propagation of the Gospel in Foreign Parts* (New York: Columbia University Press, 1913), p. 227; Edgar W. Knight, *Public Education in the South* (Boston: Ginn, 1922), p. 27; and Newton D. Edwards and Herman G. Richey, *The School in the American Social Order* (Boston: Houghton Mifflin, 1947), p. 195. Kemp's praise of the SPG schools as the "nearest approach to a public school system" is an interesting touch.

18. Kemp, *Support of Schools*, p. 32; Henry P. Thompson, *Into All Lands: The History of the Society for the Propagation of the Gospel in Foreign Parts, 1701–1950* (London: SPCK, 1951), p. 87n.

public assistance plus fees and other sources of revenue enabled the SPG schools to support themselves, and the society consequently withdrew its assistance in 1759. In New York, the Colonial Assembly assisted the society in the establishment of King's College (later Columbia University). This assistance was provided by authorizing a lottery, establishing a board of trustees, and voting five hundred pounds in aid for seven years. The society itself raised more than six thousand pounds and also contributed a library. In Connecticut a school conducted by the missionaries of this society was financially aided by the General Court on several occasions between 1742 and 1766.[19]

The SPG was a product of its age, an example of the eighteenth-century concept of education, both English and colonial. To be sure, with the coming of independence English support for the state church and its agencies in the former American colonies languished. But the view of education as essentially religious in purpose and as properly funded by philanthropy with the assistance of the state was to remain workable and vigorous well into the nineteenth century.

Proposals for State Intervention in Education

Throughout the Western world, the role of the state was to become increasingly important in every sphere of life in the nineteenth century, and nowhere was this more true than in education. That a struggle should ensue as the state reached out for the control historically exercised by the family and the church was inevitable. The concept of civil control and support of education had first been aired prominently in the discourses of the French Enlightenment and Revolutionary periods, and these proposals were by no means unknown to the early leaders of the new American Republic.

The most eloquent profession of faith in the power of education was no doubt the Marquis de Marie Jean Condorcet's *Sketch for a Historical Picture of the Progress of the Human Mind*, published in 1795. In this work, Condorcet predicted the ultimate perfectibility of man through education. The notion of the perfectibility of man took root in the minds of several later American social reformers, not least among them Horace Mann. But Condorcet's assertions of the right of the state in education brought meager results. The grandiose schemes of the French *philosophes* came to naught; the contribution of the French Revolution to education, said François Guizot, France's first minister of public instruction, was "a deluge of words." France alternated

19. Kemp, *Support of Schools*, pp. 276–77; Gabel, *Public Funds*, pp. 105–6; Thompson, *Into All Lands*, pp. 52, 72–73; George Stewart, Jr., *A History of Religious Education in Connecticut to the Middle of the Nineteenth Century* (New Haven: Yale University Press, 1924), pp. 157, 190.

between state and church control of education until 1871 when the Third Republic, strongly anti-clerical, instituted the principle of the lay or secular school, and almost succeeded in entirely excluding the church from the field of education. Cooperative efforts during World War I brought some measure of rapprochement between church and state.

It may well be that the primary school system developed in the Kingdom of Prussia during the early nineteenth century was the most efficient and comprehensive of its time. Many of its features were admired by educational leaders from all of the Western countries, including the United States. In Prussia, and in the German Empire after its consolidation in 1871, church-state cooperation in education was never seriously challenged, and religious instruction in state-supported schools continues to be the norm. It is of course true that the Prussian system was avowedly designed to form loyal subjects of the crown, not (to use James Madison's phrase) "a people who mean to be their own Governors."

England's approach to public sponsorship of education, like Germany's, produced less friction than occurred in France and the United States. In large part, this was because of the strong reluctance of the Church of England to permit any public encroachment upon a field of work it considered primarily its own. Hence the state's first entrance into education, in 1833, came in the form of parliamentary grants to existing voluntary schools. This policy endured. England's "national system" is still a union of civil and voluntary sponsorship of schools, with financial support for both types provided largely or entirely by the state. In both types, every school day opens with a "collective act of worship." Further religious instruction, in varying degrees, is permitted in the voluntary schools.

In the United States, too, many plans for civil support and control of education appeared during the early national period. A prominent one was proposed for Virginia: Thomas Jefferson's "Bill for the More General Diffusion of Knowledge." Although not adopted, this bill proposed that the state should provide for all children at least three years of free schooling. The best students in these elementary schools were to be sent to public secondary schools at public expense. Finally, the best student in each secondary school was to be sent to the College of William and Mary for a full college course at public expense. There were many other plans, some far more ambitious in scope than Jefferson's.[20]

20. Ray J. Honeywell, *The Educational Work of Thomas Jefferson* (Cambridge: Harvard University Press, 1931), pp. 199–205. For other plans, see Frederick Rudolph, ed., *Essays on Education in the Early Republic* (Cambridge: Harvard University Press, 1965); Wilson Smith, ed., *Theories of Education in Early America 1655–1819* (Indianapolis and New York: Bobbs-Merrill Co., 1973); and Allen O. Hansen, *Liberalism and American Education in the Nineteenth Century* (New York: Macmillan, 1926).

But actual achievements in school reform under public auspices during the early decades of the national period fell far short of the lofty ideals painted by the early theorists. A few states did enact laws to create schools under civil control, Massachusetts first among them in 1795, but the results of these laws, like the results of Danou's Law of 1795 in France, were exceedingly modest. Meanwhile, education under voluntary auspices expanded tremendously during the early national period and was hailed by many as a major boon to mankind.

The Sunday School Movement

Among the major instruments for promoting and providing popular education were the school societies that appeared by the hundreds in all parts of the nation. Among the earliest of these were the Sunday School Societies and the Free School Society of New York. The Sunday School Societies, like the earlier Society for the Propagation of the Gospel, were of English origin. The Industrial Revolution had brought not only increased productivity but also a host of problems, among them child labor, unemployment, poverty, and crime. While the creators of the Sunday schools were mindful of the importance of religion, those schools were designed to serve a secular as well as a religious purpose. The original idea of the Sunday school was not that of a school on the Sabbath for religious instruction, although this was always included, but "the use of the Sabbath for working boys who could attend on no other day, and their instruction in secular learning . . . ."[21]

There had been local and temporary ventures, but it was the work of Robert Raikes that made the Sunday school into an international institution. Raikes, publisher of the *Gloucester Journal*, was deeply concerned about the wretched conditions under which children in the factory sections of Gloucester were growing up, and in 1781 he employed four women to instruct some of these children in reading and the church catechism. Although greeted with distrust and even hostility by many employers and Anglican clergymen, the Sunday school movement developed rapidly in England. Influential people in many parts of that nation became interested in the schools, including the poet William Cowper.[22]

Children attended these schools most of the day on Sunday, taking time out for church services. From the beginning, unpaid volunteers as well as paid teachers served in the Sunday schools, and this was a

21. *History of Public School Education in Delaware*, U.S. Office of Education *Bulletin*, no. 18, 1917, pp. 27–28.

22. Edwin W. Rice, *The Sunday-School Movement and the American Sunday-School Union—1780–1917* (Philadelphia: The American Sunday-School Union, 1917), p. 20; Lewis Pray, *The History of Sunday Schools and of Religious Education from the Earliest Times* (Boston: William Crosby and H. P. Nichols, 1847), p. 153.

basic factor in the remarkable growth of the movement in both Great Britain and America. A special text prepared for the English Sunday schools, *The Sunday Scholar's Companion*, was in use as early as 1783 and went through many editions. The 1794 edition consisted of 120 pages, divided into four parts, and these were graded in an effort to adapt the difficulty of the material to the ability of the students. Religious creeds and confessions were used, but on a limited basis since these were non-sectarian schools.[23]

By the time of Raikes's death in 1811, the Sunday schools had already become an important element of the English educational scene. In 1831, on the fiftieth anniversary of the establishment of Raikes's first school, a celebration honoring the work of this pioneer was held in London. There were at that time in the British Empire, according to one account, one and a quarter million pupils enrolled in Sunday schools and one hundred thousand teachers.[24]

In 1785, only four years after the founding of Raikes's first school, a Sunday school was founded in Virginia. Francis Asbury, the first Methodist bishop in America, organized another such school, also in Virginia. Similar schools were soon opened in Charleston, New York, and Boston. Samuel Slater, father of American cotton manufacturing, founded a Sunday school in 1797 in a room in his factory at Pawtucket, Rhode Island, for the benefit of his employees. In many cases black children attended Sunday schools. They displayed "as much intellect as white children could do in similar circumstances," said one observer.[25]

An important event in the development of the Sunday school movement occurred in Philadelphia in 1790. There was at the time no system of public schools in the city. At a meeting attended by many distinguished citizens, including Dr. Benjamin Rush, "the First-Day or Sunday-School Society" was created. Several schools were soon established by the society, and by 1800 more than two thousand scholars had been admitted. It was reported that many of the citizens of Philadelphia were indebted to the society for most, if not all, of their education. Rush was at the same time active also in the Philadelphia Society for the Free Instruction of Indigent Boys, pressing all the while for state and city support of these and similar ventures.[26]

In 1827 the *Republican* of Springfield, Massachusetts, published a review of the work done by the Sunday schools, both in the United States and elsewhere, since their inception. In this country alone,

23. Rice, *Sunday-School Movement*, pp. 15–18.
24. Pray, *History of Sunday Schools*, pp. 169–70.
25. Vera M. Butler, "Education as Revealed by New England Newspapers Prior to 1850" (Ph.D. diss., Temple University, 1935), p. 247.
26. Pray, *History of Sunday Schools*, p. 207; James P. Wichersham, *A History of Education in Pennsylvania, Public and Private . . .* (Lancaster: J. P. Lippincott Co., 1886), p. 136.

according to this account, two hundred thousand children had bene-fited from the work of these schools. It must be assumed that the large majority of these children had attended Raikes-type schools rather than Sunday schools providing only religious instruction, since only a handful of the latter as yet existed. By 1831, the American Sunday School Union (described below) reported that seven hundred thousand children were enrolled in schools sponsored by societies or denominations affiliated with the union. If this figure seems high when compared with the estimate made four years earlier, it is still clear that the Sunday schools were a major factor in the educational scene during approximately the first three decades of the century.[27]

The ultimate purpose of the Sunday schools had always been to provide religious and moral instruction, but the development of liter-acy in the students had been a necessary precondition for this. As public schools gradually became more numerous during the early decades of the century, it became less necessary for the Sunday schools to provide instruction in secular subjects. The Sunday schools now became more and more closely tied to the various denomina-tions, and their work became more and more exclusively religious. By about 1840, all of the major Protestant denominations recognized the promotion and care of the Sunday school as part of their church activities. The American Sunday School Union, created in 1824 and designed to serve as a coordinating agency for the unions and schools connected with several Protestant denominations, actually predated several of its constituent parts.[28]

The transition from the secular-religious to the purely religious Sunday school came later in the West, where in many areas there were as yet no public schools. Here the American Sunday School Union missionaries were often the only pastors available. They vis-ited the sick, buried the dead, and established hundreds of Sunday schools. "Scores of young people graduated from these little country Sunday schools to enter academies, seminaries, and colleges."[29] Else-where, however, the organization that had begun outside the churches almost half a century earlier had come under their supervision by about 1830.

Although the Sunday school movement was essentially a phi-lanthropic enterprise, it was in many cases aided by public funds. In Delaware, the first public funds provided for education, beginning at least as early as 1818, were those authorized for support of Sunday

27. Pray, *History of Sunday Schools*, pp. 214–15; Butler, "Education," pp. 150–51, 247–49.

28. Frank G. Lankard, *A History of the American Sunday School Curriculum* (New York: Abingdon Press, 1927), p. 66.

29. Marianna C. Brown, *Sunday School Movements in America* (New York: Fleming H. Revell, 1901), p. 173.

schools. The legal authorization for such financial distributions remained in effect, although gradually falling into disuse, for several decades. Sunday schools participated in the apportionment of funds authorized by state action in Virginia in 1810; this act was amended and the appropriations increased in subsequent sessions. In 1833 there were 203 Sunday schools in Virginia, enrolling a total of more than fourteen thousand pupils.[30]

From the beginning, the leaders of the Sunday school movement favored the establishment of public schools for secular instruction. One of the earliest acts of the First Day or Sunday School Society of Philadelphia was to petition the state legislature for the establishment of free schools, but not until 1834 did the state take such action. The leaders of the American Sunday School Union insistently called upon the states to provide free public schools. Their reasoning was obvious; this would permit the Sunday school to concentrate on its major purpose—religious instruction.[31]

The Free School Society of New York

The philanthropic enterprise known as the Free School Society of New York was to all intents and purposes the public school system of the City of New York during the first half of the nineteenth century. In 1805 the New York state legislature granted to a group of civic leaders, including former governor DeWitt Clinton, a charter for "The Society for Establishing a Free School in the City of New York, for the Education of Such Poor Children as Do Not Belong To or Are not Provided For, by Any Religious Society." The trustees declared that they wished to reach those children who were "wandering about the streets, exposed to the influence of corrupt example," and "destitute of all moral and mental culture." They acknowledged that there were already schools conducted by Presbyterian, Episcopalian, Methodist, Quaker, and Dutch Reformed groups, but they foresaw no competition with those because the society would serve only children deprived of educational opportunities by the irreligion of their parents. The society's schools were to be religious, but non-sectarian.[32]

Although the society was a charitable corporation, the trustees in 1807 sought and received from the state legislature $4000 to erect a building and $1000 annually for teachers' salaries, the entire sum to

30. Gabel, Public Funds, pp. 221, 235, 378, 394–95; U.S. Office of Education Bulletin, no. 18, 1917, p. 27.
31. Pray, History of Sunday Schools, p. 206; Rice, Sunday-School Movement, p. 86.
32. Smith, "Protestant Schooling," pp. 681–82. The best available single collection of source materials relating to the society and its work is contained in William Oland Bourne, History of the Public School Society of the City of New York (New York: William Wood Co., 1869).

come from the proceeds of the liquor tax. In 1808 the city granted the trustees a building lot valued at $10,000 and a construction subsidy of $1500. Three years later the state legislature provided $4000 more to help in the construction of a second building. In 1813, when regular distributions from the recently created state school fund began, the city's allotment of about $15,000 was to be divided annually among four charitable organizations, including the Free School Society, and such religious congregations as wished to educate children free of charge. In all cases the allotments were to be proportional to the number of children served. As the society was by far the largest enterprise, such a settlement was very advantageous to it.

The success of the society's work depended, of course, upon the ability of the trustees to persuade various denominations in the city that non-sectarian Protestant education could be thoroughly religious. In 1812 they announced a decision to suspend classes on Tuesday afternoons to allow catechizing the children according to the religious preferences of their parents. Fifty "distinguished ladies" representing various denominations were to perform this service. Two years later the trustees promulgated rules requiring all students to assemble at their schools on Sunday mornings, and to proceed under supervision of a student monitor to the churches of their parents' choice. The sight of these orderly processions must have impressed upon the pious the service provided by Clinton's group, an impression reinforced by the society's frequent emphasis on the merits of virtue, industry, sobriety, and cleanliness. The society's efforts were well received, and all denominations in the city except the Roman Catholic, Dutch Reformed, and Associate Reformed Presbyterian relied increasingly upon it to educate the children of their indigent families.[33]

But the work of the society was not to go unchallenged. In 1820 the Bethel Baptist Church opened a school in its basement, which was in a section of the city not yet served by the Free School Society. The Baptist congregation requested and received from the legislature not only the usual per-student distribution for teachers' salaries, but also the right to use any surplus funds, after payment of salaries, to equip or erect buildings—a right previously reserved for the Free School Society alone. Thereupon, the Baptists started building a large schoolhouse some distance from their church in a section of the city which, they claimed, had been neglected by the society.

Obviously alarmed, the Free School Society proposed a city realestate tax to support its work, appointed the mayor and several city officials as ex-officio trustees, and urged the state legislature to forbid the use of state funds for any denominational school not located

33. Smith, "Protestant Schooling," pp. 682–83.

adjacent to the sponsoring church, or for any instruction to children of non-members of the sponsoring congregation. Aggressive as these proposals were, the ensuing controversy revolved more around the Free School Society's petition to the legislature to repeal the law that had granted the Baptists permission to use surplus funds for buildings and equipment. Permitting this, the society declared, would lead to educational economies as a means of increasing the surplus, and to relaxing regulations to swell enrollments. Even worse, it threatened to destroy the society's non-sectarian "common-school" system and to encourage the growth of "sectarian" schools. Indeed, petitions from Methodist and Roman Catholic groups were almost simultaneously submitted to the legislature, declaring that if the privilege to the Baptists were not withdrawn, it should also be extended to them. The New York secretary of state, who served ex-officio as superintendent of common schools, agreed with the Baptists and urged the legislature to extend the "peculiar privilege" to all denominations. But the legislature ruled in 1824 that no public money would thereafter go to sectarian schools.[34] Throughout the controversy, no question was raised about the legality of public aid to church-related or other voluntary schools. The question was one of equity, not of legality.

Although public monies were now denied, the society continued its distinguished public service until 1853, when a public school system was instituted. From the time of its founding until 1853, the large majority of schools in the city were conducted by this voluntary society, which during its first two decades was continuously aided with public funds. Almost six hundred thousand children were educated in its schools.[35]

Lotteries as a Means of School Support

"It would be difficult to overestimate the lottery's value in the development of the American educational system," says the author of the standard work on the history of the lottery in this country.[36] If this seems to be a startling conclusion, we must remember that in the new republic, institutions for the provision of social services—including schools—were not as yet regarded as a responsibility of government. Moreover, although the land was rich in undeveloped natural resources, liquid capital was in short supply. Such public monies as were devoted to the provision of social services were often the product of improvisation: prizes taken at sea, fines, escheats, and taxes on

34. Ibid., pp. 685–87.
35. John Franklin Reigart, *The Lancastrian System of Instruction in the Schools of New York City* (New York: Teachers College, 1916), pp. 13–15.
36. John H. Ezell, *Fortune's Merry Wheel: The Lottery in America* (Cambridge: Harvard University Press, 1960), p. 143.

furs, liquor, and tobacco. But there was another method—the lottery—by which a governmental unit could lend its approval and authority to sponsors of worthy social causes, enabling them to tap sources of revenue not otherwise available.

There was ample precedent for this. Lotteries authorized by the government had been used in England for more than a century before the time of the first settlements in America. The public interest was well served thereby, said the chancellor of the exchequer, because in the absence of lotteries it would have been necessary to rely more extensively on taxation—an unwise alternative in his view. When the Virginia Company announced its plan to establish a colony in the New World, it explained also that "for the establishing of the Gospell there, and the honour of our King and country, we have published a little standing Lotterie . . . ."[37]

There had been occasional complaints in England that lotteries attracted money away from regular commercial channels, but criticism on moral grounds was rarely heard, either in England or here. A textbook used for many generations at Harvard and Yale assured its readers that lotteries were entirely acceptable if the proceeds were put to some "pious use" and if those participating were motivated not by the "hope of gayning, but . . . of bestowing something."[38] Far from protesting against them, religious groups used lotteries extensively, the only significant exception being the Quakers.

As a form of support for governmental activities, the lottery was employed at all levels for purposes officially designated as beneficial to the public. Following the outbreak of the Revolution, the Continental Congress established a lottery to help finance the war. In 1792 Congress authorized the use of lotteries for civic projects in the new capital city to be established on the Potomac. In 1814 President Madison approved a lottery for funds to build a federal penitentiary and again in 1815 approved one for a city hall in the new capital city. At the state level, lotteries were less frequent, but at the local level, they were extensively used for the building of bridges, roads, turnpikes, street paving, courthouses, jails, marketplaces, hospitals, poorhouses, fire equipment, and water systems. Lotteries were authorized by twenty-three of the thirty-three states by 1860.[39]

One of the most extensive uses of the lottery was for the benefit of churches and schools, and it was used in this manner even after it was abolished for other purposes. During the period from 1790 until the Civil War, forty-seven colleges, approximately three hundred lower schools, and two hundred church groups received funds from

37. Ibid., p. 206.
38. Ibid., p. 10.
39. Ibid., pp. 104–14.

lotteries. Harvard College employed the method on several occasions, and James Madison served as the head of a committee that conducted a lottery for the benefit of William and Mary College in 1804. The widespread acceptance of this means of support was perhaps what led the president of the University of North Carolina to declare in 1832 that any proposal to establish a southern school system supported solely by taxation was doomed to failure. In Rhode Island for some time lotteries were used primarily to augment the state school fund; from 1826 to 1844 they provided the fund with over two hundred thousand dollars. Of all the lotteries held during the pre–Civil War era, New York State conducted the largest and also the most troublesome. This venture was to raise two hundred thousand dollars for Union College and smaller amounts for various other schools. Credit for the passage of this bill was given to the "unwearied exertions of the able and eloquent president of Union College," the Rev. Eliphalet Nott. The large sums expected from this venture, however, did not materialize.[40]

Although the lottery had enjoyed great popularity, after about 1830 it began to decline. The great humanitarian movements of the early nineteenth century, which found expression in the antislavery, temperance, prison reform, and other crusades, also brought a reaction against lotteries. After public opinion had begun to swing against lotteries, organized religious groups also began to express opposition. Perhaps the major factor in the decline of lotteries was the fact that they came to be accompanied by fraudulent practices. As the number of lotteries increased, promoters were employed to manage the sales, and a host of abuses developed. What had been a method of raising money for worthy causes now often became a device for exploitation. By 1860 all but two of the states had prohibited lotteries. Finally, the only one remaining was the infamous Louisiana Lottery, governed by a New York gambling syndicate. Reportedly, the lottery controlled every state legislature from the time of its creation until 1892, when it was outlawed by a referendum vote.[41]

During the early decades of the century, while the states were able to hold lotteries in rein, they made a valuable contribution to many socially useful enterprises. At no time, apparently, was any objection raised to using the power and authority of the state to confer financial benefits upon church-related schools (as most of them were) or for that matter upon churches themselves. There were good reasons for the demise of the lottery, but the presumed existence of a wall of separation between church and state was not one of them.

40. Ibid., pp. 140, 144–60.
41. Ibid., pp. 204–22, 243–45.

In retrospect, the voluntary school experiments of the late colonial and early national periods may seem naive. Yet, in a society with scant provisions for schooling under public auspices, even the very modest education then provided for hundreds of thousands of children under largely voluntary sponsorship must command some respect. Clearly, the voluntary tradition in education possessed a high degree of vitality and resourcefulness; just as clearly, it was not equal to the task at hand. Yet, the leaders of the Common School Movement, when they appeared on the scene about 1830, railed against the "sectarian" schools, persuaded state legislatures to revoke the traditional policy of granting financial aid to such schools, and eventually sought to achieve state monopoly in education. A public school law, including a prohibition of public aid to non-public schools (to be discussed below), was enacted in Illinois in 1855. Two years later the state superintendent of public instruction rejoiced that thousands of "old feudal and anti-American" private schools had been nearly swept from the field. Voluntarism in education, prized and sustained in many other Western nations, was an unwelcome intrusion in the eyes of nineteenth-century public school leaders in the United States.

2

The Protestant Common
School Movement

Middle-Class Reformers

The prohibition of aid to non-public schools and of religious observances in the public schools constitutes our basic public policies on church-state relationships in education. The former directly and the latter indirectly were by-products of the Common School Movement of the antebellum decades. The leaders of the Common School Movement regarded non-public schools (most of which were, and are, church-related) as a major obstacle to the full development of public schools. (Cubberley devoted one section of his classic work on the history of American education to "The Battle Against Sectarian Schools.") Hence, to understand our policies on non-public schools, we must first understand the dynamics of the powerful Common School Movement and its determination to achieve a public monopoly in education.

The Common School Movement was a series of state movements occurring roughly during the period 1830–1860 that looked toward the expansion and improvement of education at the elementary level. More specifically, its goals were to provide schooling for all white children, partially or wholly at public expense; to encourage or require school attendance; to create training programs for teachers; and to establish some measure of state control over these processes.[1] Virtually all leaders of the Common School Movement accepted Horace Mann's lead in insisting that religious instruction was an indispensable part of the work of the common school. They agreed, further, that the inclusion of doctrines unique to any one sect would alienate all other sects, so the public schools would have to be non-sectarian. As Mann and others of like mind often expressed it, the great "common truths" of Christianity should be taught—but anything more than this would be sectarianism and hence inadmissible. Non-sectari-

1. Robert L. Church and Michael W. Sedlak, *Education in the United States, An Interpretation* (New York: The Free Press, 1976), p. 59.

anism, one of the most fundamental assumptions of the school reformers, was to become the movement's greatest source of divisive-
ness—and the major reason that the ideal of schools common to all
children was never fully realized.

For the purposes of this study, three aspects of, or closely related
to, the Common School Movement must be singled out for closer
attention. First, in this section we will look at the social and economic
views of the school reformers. Then, in the following sections of the
chapter we will examine two other developments occurring simultaneously with the school reforms: the Second Awakening and the
nativist movement.

The majority of the school reformers identified with the Whig party. The Whig party came together in large part as an anti-Jackson
party; it won some states in the 1830s and came into power nationally
in the 1840s, bridging the gap between the Federalists of the early
national period and the Republican party, which appeared in the
1850s. Horace Mann and Henry Barnard were Whig politicians before
they assumed their roles of leadership in the school movement. Common school laws in the states were most often enacted by Whig
legislatures and opposed by Jacksonian Democrats, who objected
mainly to the centralizing features of the proposed plans. Broadly
speaking, the leadership of the Whig party came from the established
middle and upper classes: industrialists, bankers, large landholders.
The traditional professions—law, medicine, and the ministry—were
heavily Whig, and the party had close ties with organized Protestant
religion.[2]

Although there was some diversity within each party, it is fair to
say that the Whigs favored an active role for the government in stimu-
lating and directing economic activity, while the Democrats were
more sympathetic to a policy of laissez-faire. The Democrats believed
that a maximum of freedom for the individual would lead to the
greatest improvement of society. The Whigs, although certainly not
opposed to individual freedom, would subordinate it to the higher
concerns of social good and economic growth. Hence, they supported
a high tariff to protect the products of American industry from foreign
competition, nationally financed internal improvements such as the
construction of canals and roads, and a central (national) bank.[3]

The school reformers responded positively to Whig policies by explaining that more and better schooling would lead to economic progress. Education, said Horace Mann, "can raise more abundant har-
vests and multiply the conveniences of domestic life; . . . it can build
. . . [and] is often worth more to an individual than a hundred work-

2. Ibid., pp. 61–62.
3. Ibid., pp. 63–66.

men—and to a nation than the addition of provinces to its territory . . . ."[4] This claim was as vague as it was extravagant, but in one
respect it was explicit. Education would foster industrialization by
teaching future workers to respect property, to work hard, and to
accept their lot in life. This current of thought was a leitmotif of the
stories in school readers during much of the nineteenth century; Rev.
William McGuffey's readers provide an excellent example.

More important than such claims for the benefits of schooling was
the establishment of patterns of faith and aspirations that persisted
virtually unchallenged until at least the middle of the present century. Of these the most important was the concept of education as the
basic instrument for achieving social control and (as the school reformers defined it) social progress. This emphasis on schooling as a
means for achieving social ends goes far to explain the schoolmen's
insistence on getting all children, and especially urban children, into
school. The need for an educated electorate, so important in the
thinking of the early leaders of the republic, was still echoed in the
speeches of the leaders of the Common School Movement, to be sure.
But there was a new urgency in the rhetoric of the school reformers,
and sometimes it went so far as to demand that all children be compelled to attend school, an idea that was anathema to many in the
laissez-faire atmosphere of nineteenth-century America. But the reformers argued that many poor parents kept their children away from
school to increase the family income. Industrial states, beginning in
the late 1830s, adopted attendance laws that applied only to children
working in the factories, requiring them to attend school for three
months each year. Such laws did not touch middle-class parents, who
no doubt would have regarded them as interference with parental
prerogatives. There was in the middle-class mentality of the antebellum period a dark foreboding about the growth of an industrial
working class, and it was fanned by the increasing demands for universal male suffrage.

The capstone of the reformers' efforts to enroll all children, and
especially those of the "lower classes," was the free school. Regarded
by the early school historians as the reformers' supreme goal, the free
school is better understood as a means of securing universal attendance so that common values could be instilled in all children. Formerly, many poor children had been kept out of school because their
parents could not pay even the small "rate-bill" involved. (The "rate-
bill," widely used, was a tax on parents only, in proportion to the
number of children they had in school.) In the growing cities and

4. *Fifth Annual Report to the Board of Education together with the Fifth Annual Report of the
Secretary of the Board* (1842), pp. 82–83 (hereafter cited as *Annual Report*).

manufacturing and port towns, poverty was widespread—and visible. Earlier, philanthropists had tried to deal with this problem by financing charity schools or free places in the regular schools, but well-to-do parents had shunned such schools. As the reformers saw it, free schools, supported by public funds, would solve these problems. Everyone would go to school "free," so no child would be identified as unable to pay. There would be no charity scholars to offend the sensibilities of middle- and upper-class parents. The last barrier to prevent the poor from attending school would be removed.[5]

The Second Awakening and the Common School Movement

When the Unitarian Horace Mann tried to express his deepest convictions about the nature and meaning of the Common School Movement, he felt constrained to borrow a term from evangelical Protestantism: "I have long been accustomed to look at this great movement of education as a part of the Providence of God, by which the human race is to be redeemed." The millennial tone of the rhetoric of American education has not gone unnoticed, although it has come into the mainstream of historical writing only recently. In the late part of the last century one observer noted, "We have made a sort of God of our common school system. It is treason to speak a word against it."[6] More recently, some clergymen have commented about the "messianic complex" of the public schools. Dean Roscoe Pound expressed a similar intuition when he compared the American faith in education to the medieval faith in religion. John Dewey had commented on the subject much earlier.[7]

The theme of public education as an agent of moral and social redemption (to be achieved in large part through "non-sectarian" religious instruction) was perhaps the most fundamental assumption underlying the Common School Movement. To be sure, non-sectarianism (or, more properly, pan-Protestantism) was not an invention of either the Second Awakening or the Common School Movement; its origins can be traced well back into the colonial period. But the tremendous impetus given to it by the Awakening vastly strengthened the appeal of non-sectarianism. Without this support from the larger

5. Church and Sedlak, *Education*, pp. 60–61.

6. "Industrial Education," *Scribner's Monthly* 19 (March 1880): 785–86.

7. Lewis B. Whittemore, *The Church and Secular Education* (New York: Seabury Press, 1960), chapter 2; John Rousas Rushdoony, *The Messianic Character of American Education: Studies in the History of the Philosophy of Education* (Nutley, N.J.: The Craig Press, 1963), chapter 2 and passim; Dewey, "Education as a Religion," *The New Republic* 32 (13 September 1922): 63–65. The comment by Pound is cited in Merle Curti and Vernon Carstensen, *The University of Wisconsin: A History, 1848–1925*, 2 vols. (Madison: University of Wisconsin Press, 1949), 1:33.

society, non-sectarianism in the schools could not have gained acceptance.

The religious movement known as the Second Awakening (so called to distinguish it from the great religious revivals of the mid eighteenth century) was transforming American Protestantism during the very decades that the Common School Movement was in progress. The chief instrument for promoting the Awakening was the religious revival, which Perry Miller has singled out as the "dominant theme in America from 1800 to 1860."[8] Not all religious groups embraced the "new measures" promoted by the revivalists. Although a few Lutheran, Unitarian, and Episcopal clergymen seemed interested for a time, the evangelical approach met with little response in these quarters. Revivalism, among other issues, split the Presbyterians into the Old and the New School factions in 1837–1838, the former distinctly cool toward revivalist measures. But the groups that were to become dominant in American Protestantism by 1860 embraced revivalism with fervor. Although at first disdained by some of the more staid Congregationalist clergymen, the revivalism of the Second Awakening had its origins in New England. Rev. Timothy Dwight, president of Yale, became an early champion of revivalism, and several of his students followed his example, among them the redoubtable Lyman Beecher. The more or less decorous New England revivals were far overshadowed in the public mind (and in historical accounts) by the colorful and tumultuous campaigns in the West. The first of the great western revivals was held at Cane Ridge, Kentucky, in 1801, with an estimated attendance of ten to twenty-five thousand. The meetings, which continued for six or seven days, saw both an abundance and variety of the physical manifestations that were to become customary at the western camp meetings.[9]

As the Awakening spread through the West, the dominant figure came to be Charles G. Finney, "the father of modern revivalism," a schoolteacher and lawyer who was untrained in theology. After experiencing "a mighty baptism of the Holy Ghost" he was licensed (albeit with some reluctance) by a local presbytery in 1823 and launched a revivalist career that encompassed not only the boisterous West but also the more sedate East. The revivals were models of interdenominational cooperation. This had been true of the great Cane Ridge gathering, and Finney institutionalized the practice. He mobilized all of the clergy in the vicinity of his revivals, who participated without regard to their affiliation. For several decades the great camp meet-

8. *The Life of the Mind in America from the Revolution to the Civil War* (New York: Harcourt, Brace and World, 1965), p. 7.
9. Sydney E. Ahlstrom, *A Religious History of the American People* (New Haven: Yale University Press, 1972), pp. 415, 418–22, 433.

ings of the West achieved a high degree of interdenominational support, even if the churches squabbled among themselves to garner the converts after the meetings subsided.[10]

The most striking external evidence of the strength of the Awakening was a major shift in the nation's denominational equilibrium. Methodist and Baptist growth in the trans-Allegheny regions during the prewar decades was sensational. In relative terms, the older denominations fell behind. The eminent divine and president of Yale College, Ezra Stiles, had predicted confidently in 1783 that the future of Christianity in American would lie about equally with Congregationalists, Presbyterians, and Anglicans, which had retained their prestige and dominance throughout the colonial period. But this was not to be so. By 1850, Methodists constituted the largest Protestant denomination. Baptists, Presbyterians, Congregationalists, and Lutherans followed in turn. Sixth in size were the Disciples, a group less than twenty years old. The Protestant Episcopal church had fallen to seventh place, and Joseph Smith's Mormons were eighth. Equally significant, and a source of increasing dismay in a society still predominantly Protestant, was the fact that the Roman Catholic church, which had been the tenth largest religious body at the close of the Revolution, was now the largest.[11]

Even more important were the changes wrought within Protestantism by the Awakening. The central element of Christian life, as the revivalists saw it, was the soul-wrenching experience of conversion. Theology was of peripheral importance. When asked during his licensing examination whether he subscribed to the Westminster Confession, Finney replied bluntly that he had never read it, and he steadfastly eschewed the study of theology. Evangelicalism typically had a casual attitude toward differences in doctrine, and in this sense it served as a unifying factor in Protestantism. Rev. Horace Bushnell was able to rejoice in the triumphs of the Methodists even if "sometimes their demonstrations are rude and their spirit of rivalry violent." And Charles G. Finney, although he could accuse a Universalist of having no more religion than his horse, still cautioned his converts not "to dwell upon sectarian distinctions, or to be sticklish about sectarian points."[12]

Not only did the revivalists denigrate the value of theology; they were often skeptical of the value of any education beyond the rudimentary level. The Baptists of the time, indeed, opposed the idea of

10. Miller, *Life of the Mind*, p. 45.
11. Sidney E. Mead, *The Lively Experiment: The Shaping of Christianity in America* (New York: Harper and Row, 1963), pp. 106–7.
12. Winthrop S. Hudson, *The Great Tradition of the American Churches* (New York: Harper and Brothers, 1953), p. 86.

educated, settled, and paid ministers. Peter Cartwright, most famed of the Methodist circuit riders, scorned theological education, considering it to be even a hindrance in the preaching of the Gospel. Many "illiterate Methodist preachers actually set the world on fire," he proclaimed.[13] Whatever their training and background, the revivalists sought to reduce the Christian message to the simplest possible terms.

Perry Miller's judgment on the theological and intellectual attainments of the revivalists is rather harsh: "They had few ideas and were little capable of cerebration." Henry Steele Commager's verdict is no less severe: the outcome of the forces set into motion by the Awakening was that, "during the nineteenth century and well into the twentieth, religion prospered while theology went slowly bankrupt."[14] Catholic leaders were keenly aware of the process of disintegration taking place in American Protestant theology. They found the new lack of emphasis on theology as unacceptable as the earlier systems of doctrine that were being replaced. Several of them inveighed against it. Bishop Hughes attacked it during the 1840–1842 New York school controversy. The sharp-tongued Orestes Brownson, who traversed several Protestant denominations and utopian movements before finding security in the Catholic church, referred to the non-sectarianism propounded by the revivalists as "nothingarianism."[15] Many nineteenth-century (and some twentieth-century) writers seemed to say that the doctrine of non-sectarian religious instruction in the common schools had its origin in the fertile mind of Horace Mann; nothing could be further from the truth. By the time Mann came on the educational scene, non-sectarianism was part of the conventional wisdom of evangelical Protestantism.

In yet another respect the success of the Common School Movement was dependent upon the tides of evangelical Protestantism. Voluntary societies committed to the achievement of a variety of worthy causes enjoyed a tremendous growth during the pre–Civil War period. Whereas earlier the various denominations had operated their own charitable enterprises, a distinguishing characteristic of these antebellum societies was their interdenominational sponsorship. Rev. Lyman Beecher announced as a "Great Discovery" his conclusion that many reform movements could be advanced more effectively by the myriad of voluntary agencies that flourished during

13. *Autobiography of Peter Cartwright*, ed. Charles L. Wallis (Nashville: Abingdon Press, 1956), p. 64.

14. Miller, *Life of the Mind*, p. 7; Commager, *The American Mind: An Interpretation of American Thought and Character Since the 1880's* (New Haven: Yale University Press, 1950), p. 165.

15. Orestes Brownson, *The American Republic: Its Constitution, Tendencies, and Destiny*, ed. Americo D. Lapati (New Haven: College and University Press, 1972), p. 28.

the period than by any of the denominations independently—agencies such as the American Bible Society, the American Colonization Society, the American Sunday School Union, the American Temperance Society, and many others. Beecher strongly supported such agencies, not least among them the American Education Society, organized in 1827.[16] As the westward migrations grew, the number of societies and the scope of their activities increased. Missionary societies, both home and foreign, were the first to appear. (As earlier noted, the home missionary society agents were the earliest to promote schools in the West.) Bible and tract societies soon followed. The American Sunday School Union, the American Home Missionary Society, and the American Society for the Promotion of Temperance appeared in the 1820s, and there were many others. No doubt the most numerous of the voluntary societies were those for the promotion of schools, and virtually all of these were in the forefront of the Common School Movement.

There was a close relationship between the voluntary—and for the most part interdenominational—societies and the Second Awakening. One historian, indeed, considers such societies an outgrowth of the Awakening and describes them as "a new kind of religious institution."[17] Moreover, the voluntary societies, whatever their special purposes might be, were themselves educational enterprises, some of them explicitly so. The publications of the American Tract Society and the American Sunday School Union, while serving religious purposes, were also designed as systems of reading instruction. Both organizations issued primers, and these as well as other of their publications were "graded," progressing from simpler to more difficult words and ideas. Indeed, at midcentury, more than half of the country's libraries that were designated as "public" were physically located in Sunday schools.[18]

The voluntary societies reinforced and supported each other. A contemporary observer of these events noted that all of the societies "have an interest in each other, depend upon each other, and assist each other."[19] Leaders of the Common School Movement also served as leaders in other humanitarian causes of the day.

The Common School Movement was therefore by no means an isolated phenomenon, nor is it to be understood as a merely political or civil movement. Nor was the Common School Movement merely an adumbration of the Second Awakening. But if the Awakening is

16. Hudson, *Great Tradition*, p. 72.

17. Ahlstrom, *Religious History*, p. 422.

18. Lawrence A. Cremin, *American Education: The National Experience 1783–1876* (New York: Harper and Row, 1980), pp. 68, 70.

19. William Cogswell, *The Harbinger of the Millennium* (Boston: Pierce and Parker, 1833), p. iii.

not taken into account, the school movement loses much of its meaning. The school movement was one part—albeit an important part—of a far-reaching and intertwined complex of cooperative reform efforts, all of them suffused with the spirit of evangelical Protestantism. Collectively, these efforts constituted the great Protestant *paideia* of the nineteenth century. The ensuing spiritualization of the public schools, as Professor Cremin has aptly called it, was to have profound significance for American education. Was the evangelical consensus a suitable foundation for education? Could the schools be at the same time common to all children, state-controlled, and Christian? The leaders of the Common School Movement were confident that they knew the answers to these questions. Since Protestant clergymen constituted the largest single element in the leadership of the movement, their answers to such questions might well become a self-fulfilling prophecy. We shall examine their role in the next chapter.

The Nativist Movement

The Common School Movement was from its outset deeply imbued with the conservative social and economic views of the Whig party and with the evangelical fervor of the Second Awakening. But the movement had also a dark underside, the spirit of nativism, which was at its height during the decades when the campaign for schools was most active. The school movement and nativism were not only contemporaneous; they were, as we shall see, inextricably bound up with one another.

In a broad sense, the term *nativism*, which was coined about 1840, is used to denote an anti-foreign spirit. As an element in American history, it is defined more specifically to denote the anti-foreign and anti-Catholic excitement of the 1830s and 1840s, culminating in the Know-Nothing campaigns of the 1850s. It is an "intense opposition to an internal minority on the ground of its foreign (i.e., 'un-American') connections."[20]

Hostility to foreigners may result from a fear of political radicalism or a threatened displacement of American workers. But anti-Catholicism is by far the oldest and strongest form of nativism, and it was the principal ingredient of the pre–Civil War nativist campaigns. Anti-Catholicism has been an element in Western culture since Martin Luther rallied the German princes against the Church of Rome. It was deeply ingrained in Elizabethan England, with the British engaged more or less continuously in a struggle with rival Catholic powers or their own pro-Catholic monarchs. Although the English colonists in

20. John Higham, *Strangers in the Land: Patterns of American Nativism, 1860–1925* (New Brunswick: Rutgers University Press, 1955), p. 4.

the New World were flanked by the rival Catholic empires of France and Spain, anti-Catholicism was for several generations recessive.

The middle third of the nineteenth century, however, saw a strong resurgence of anti-Catholic sentiment. In part this was because Americans regarded their newly established political liberty as their unique national attribute and supreme achievement, and as irreconcilable with the authoritarian organization of the Catholic church. This apparent threat to the American way of life was intensified by the rapidly increasing numbers of Catholic immigrants. The resulting anti-Catholic nativism called for stiff naturalization laws and the exclusion of Catholics and foreigners from public office. When sectional strife produced a general crisis in American society in the 1850s, the "no-popery" agitation became a major force in national life. As the old parties disintegrated and the Union itself neared the breaking point, the American or Know-Nothing party promised to preserve national homogeneity by unifying all native citizens against the foreigners in their midst. The party reached its climax in 1855 when it elected six governors and captured several statehouses. (The activities of several of the Know-Nothing state legislatures, and especially their school legislation, will be considered in more detail later.)[21]

The nativist movement, although eventually captured by the adventurers and ruffians of the Know-Nothing party, had its origins in Protestant pulpits and in the religious societies and publications created in large numbers by the Second Awakening. The first of these to take a stand openly against Catholicism was the American Bible Society, founded in 1816. By 1827, forty Protestant religious newspapers had been founded, all of them distinctly anti-Catholic, and the stage had been set for the nativistic drama.[22] When Horace Mann began his educational work in 1837, the nativist movement had already reached alarming proportions. Three years earlier a nativist mob, inflamed by the anti-Catholic sermons of Boston clergymen, chief among them Rev. Lyman Beecher, had burned the Ursuline Convent school on the outskirts of the town. In 1836 the greatest of all the nativistic propaganda works had appeared, Maria Monk's *Awful Disclosures of the Hotel Dieu Nunnery of Montreal*, a lurid account of alleged immorality in Catholic convents. The account was soon disclosed to be a monstrous fabrication. Maria Monk's venture was, in fact, sponsored by a

21. Ibid., pp. 5–7.

22. Ray A. Billington, *The Protestant Crusade, 1800–1860: A Study of the Origins of American Nativism* (New York: Macmillan, 1938), pp. 41–47. Although this account concentrates on the anti-Catholic component of pre–Civil War nativism and overlooks the social and economic causes of the movement, it is still the standard work on the subject.

number of Protestant ministers, one of whom wrote her book, aided by an equally unscrupulous Catholic priest. Maria Monk died in prison in 1849, but the continued popularity of her book revealed the strength of anti-Catholic xenophobia in the United States. Three hundred thousand copies of this "*Uncle Tom's Cabin* of Know Nothingism" were sold prior to the Civil War, and numerous editions appeared thereafter.[23]

Although the salacious "exposure" literature held credulous Protestants by the thousands under its spell, there were more basic issues at stake. The educational reformers and the nativist leaders (often the same persons) were in full agreement on two propositions: that the Protestant version of the Bible should be read in the public schools, and that public funds should not be used for non-public schools. Struggles over these issues were to become a major element in the Know-Nothing excitement of the 1850s and the ensuing bifurcation of American education into public and private sectors.

23. Ibid., pp. 98–108.

3

Protestant Clergy
and the Common School Movement

Contemporary Approval of Clerical Participation

When Alexis de Tocqueville visited the United States in 1831 he wrote, concerning the Protestant clergy, "Almost all education is entrusted to them." Twenty years later a Swedish visitor made the same observation, and added that the instruction in the schools was Protestant in character.[1]

The strong clerical presence in the common school crusade, largely ignored until recently by historians of the movement, was not only well known but warmly applauded at the time. Horace Mann and Henry Barnard, by general agreement the two greatest leaders of the school campaign, exhorted ministers to increase their efforts in publicizing the cause and in providing leadership for it. In his first *Report*, Mann called upon the clergy to serve as visitors in the public schools and expressed regret that some of them had failed to assume this responsibility. When critics alleged that his policy of non-sectarian religious instruction had brought the spirit of deism and rationalism into the schools, Mann countered by pointing out that the state's educational enterprise was to a large extent in the hands of clergymen. Five of the eight members of the State Board of Education, he explained, were ministers. At the local level, a large proportion of the school committees (boards) were composed entirely of ministers, and these ministers had "the entire control of the books to be used in the schools . . . and the entire control of the studies to be pursued." Barnard was equally warm in his tribute: "As a class they [the Protestant clergy] are devoting more time at greater sacrifices, than any other portion—we believe we would be safe in saying—than all the

1. De Tocqueville, *The Republic of the United States of America and Its Political Institutions, Reviewed and Examined*, trans. Henry Reeves, 2 vols. in one (New York: A. S. Barnes and Company, 1851), p. 337n; Per A. Siljestrom, *The Educational Institutions of the United States, Their Character and Organization* (London: John Chapman, 1853), pp. 27, 147–48.

31

rest of the community together . . . but we are anxious that they should do more."[2] Rev. Amory D. Mayo, also a prominent leader in the school movement, recalled later, "The old-time Congregational clergy were, to a great extent, the organizers, administrators, and teachers of the common school, and without a fair estimate of their service we shall fail to understand many things in its original constitution."[3]

Less well-known leaders also emphasized the importance of clerical participation in the movement. A Presbyterian minister, attempting to explain to Europeans the "voluntary system" of disestablished churches in this country, insisted that the separation of church and state had encouraged rather than discouraged clerical concern for education. "Primary instruction in the United States owes almost everything to Religion . . .," he said. Moreover, in the public school, "a pious and judicious teacher, if he will only confine himself to the great doctrines and precepts of the Gospel, in which all those who hold the fundamental truths of the Bible are agreed, can easily give as much religious instruction as he chooses." Even in frontier Wisconsin, only recently admitted to the Union, the message had been heard. A writer in the official journal of the state's Department of Public Instruction enjoined the clergy to be active in "their proper positions as Directors or Visitors of the Common Schools" and never to be deflected from this duty by association with non-public schools.[4]

The education of children had always been within the ambit of churchly and ministerial activity, and supporters of the Common School Movement obviously assumed that this tradition should be continued. One looks in vain for any rationale or justification for clerical participation in the movement; the propriety of such participation was regarded as self-evident. Only later, when Catholic estrangement from the Common School Movement was well underway, did it seem necessary to explain and justify the need for clerical leadership, and such an argument was published in Barnard's prestigious *Journal* in 1868. Protestant clergymen should provide leadership in the promotion of popular education, said Rev. William C. Fowler, because (among other reasons) Protestantism addresses itself

2. Mann, *The Common School Controversy: Consisting of Three Letters to the Secretary of the Board of Education . . . and Edward A. Newton . . .* (Boston, 1844), p. 9; Barnard, "Clergy and Common Schools," in *Connecticut Common School Journal* (Hartford: Published under the direction of the Board of Commissioners of Common Schools, 1840), p. 101.

3. "Education in the Northwest during the First Half Century of the Republic, 1796–1840," U.S. Commissioner of Education, *Report,* 1894–1895, 2:1523. The preceding year's *Report* (for 1893–1894) contains several "sermons" by teachers, 1:662ff.

4. Robert Baird, *Religion in America* (New York: Harper and Brothers, 1844), p. 148; "Congregational or Parochial Schools," *Wisconsin Journal of Education* 1 (September 1856): 217.

to the intellect and upholds the right of private judgment in opposition to human claims of authority in matters of faith.[5]

In the following pages, as we examine this topic further, we shall see that the entire school enterprise was suffused with the spirit of the Second Awakening. Further, we shall see frequently the intrusion of anti-Catholic sentiment into the school campaign and into the schools themselves. The latter phenomenon was uneven. A few—very few—clergymen in public education resisted the prevailing anti-Catholic attitudes; but many of them, including several state school superintendents, were among the most vitriolic anti-Romanists of their time.

Clergymen and School Societies

Various phases of the Common School Movement, although interdependent and in process of development at the same time, can be identified for examination. The publicizing of the movement by both educational and religious societies was prominent in the early stages, and was followed by the establishment of state and local administrative agencies. The founding of institutions for the training of teachers was another vital element, as was the writing of textbooks. We shall examine the role of the Protestant clergy in each of these phases of the movement, which of course came later in the frontier areas than in the older regions.

Perhaps the first of the societies to establish itself on a national scale was the American Education Society (originally the American Society for Educating Pious Youth for the Christian Ministry), incorporated in Massachusetts in 1816. (The American Bible Society was founded the same year.) Eventually, it had branches or corresponding secretaries in virtually every state. Among the clergymen associated with this group were several who were, or were to become, college presidents: Edward Beecher of Illinois College, George Gale of the Oneida Institute, Benjamin O. Peers of Transylvania University, Alva Woods of Alabama University, Francis Wayland of Brown, Heman (*sic*) Humphrey of Amherst, and Thomas H. Gallaudet, best known to posterity for his pioneer work in the education of the deaf.

Anti-Catholic fulminations were warmly received by the American Education Society. In 1841 Rev. Lyman Beecher warned members against the dangers of "Popish schools," and the society adopted several resolutions condemning Catholicism in the years that followed. The Connecticut branch of the society was told by Rev. W. W.

5. "The Clergy and Popular Education," *American Journal of Education* 17 (January 1868): 211–24.

Turner at its annual meeting in 1835 that "multitudes of foreign papists are every year pouring in upon our shores, bringing with them all the passions and prejudices of a foreign education."[6]

The Illinois branch of the society also followed the lead of the parent organization. During the 1830s it joined with the American Bible Society and other groups in exhorting Protestants to protect the West from Catholicism. In 1832 the Illinois branch was addressed by Rev. Edward Beecher, less famous than his father but equally involved in educational and nativist causes. In 1841 the elder Beecher himself addressed the society, renewing his now-familiar plea for better public educational facilities to offset the influence of "Popish schools."[7] Lyman Beecher was one of the most prominent of New England divines and an indefatigable promoter of the common schools. From his pulpit in Boston, Beecher waged an unrelenting campaign against Romanism, and his inflammatory sermons were at least partly responsible for the burning of the Ursuline Convent in 1834.[8] His son Edward later returned to a pulpit in Boston, where he kept alive the fires of anti-Catholicism kindled there by his father. In 1855 his *Papal Conspiracy* was published.

The longest-lived (1830–1918) of the early educational societies was the American Institute of Instruction, organized in 1830. Its influence also extended far beyond its New England base. Among the clergymen who served the association as officers and speakers during its early years were Lyman Beecher, William H. McGuffey, Calvin E. Stowe, Charles Brooks, Jacob Abbott, R. C. Waterson, Joshua Bates, and Heman Humphrey.[9] McGuffey was to become the author of the famous and long-lived series of *Readers*, and Stowe a state school superintendent in Ohio. It was Brooks who declared, "The Gospel is a Common School Gospel"; he explained further, "This world is our school-house, God is our Teacher and the Bible our classbook." One of many Americans who observed firsthand the famed public school system in Prussia, Brooks traveled extensively throughout New England, with Horace Mann's strong encouragement, speaking and

6. *The Quarterly Journal of the American Education Society* (title varies) 1 (January 1828): 60, also 8 (August 1835): 94; *New York Observer*, 20 May 1843, also 23 May 1846; Paul H. Mattingly, *The Classless Profession:•American Schoolmen in the Nineteenth Century* (New York: New York University Press, 1975), pp. 34–39.

7. *New York Observer*, 6 March 1830; Daniel W. Kucera, *Church-State Relationships in Education in Illinois* (Washington, D.C.: Catholic University Press, 1955), p. 46.

8. This is Charles A. Dinsmore's conclusion in his sketch of Beecher's life in the *Dictionary of American Biography*, 2:135–36. Beecher himself denied any responsibility for it. See *Autobiography, Correspondence, Etc., of Lyman Beecher, D.D.*, ed. Charles Beecher (New York: Harper and Brothers, 1864–1865), 2:335.

9. *The Massachusetts Teacher* 1 (August 1848): 240; *The American Journal of Education* 1 (March 1856): 344.

writing on the subject of public schools. At least in part as a result of his efforts, the Massachusetts State Board of Education, of which he was for some time a member, was established in 1837. Perhaps his greatest contribution was his leadership in the movement to create normal schools in his state; the importance of his work in this field has been described as "second to those of no man." During all this time (1820–1839) he served as pastor of the Third Church in Hingham.[10] Although Brooks, a Unitarian, was critical of Catholic views on education, he was much more amenable to compromise than were the majority of his clerical colleagues.

A partially successful attempt to form a national organization, the American Association for the Advancement of Education, was made in 1849. Horace Mann served as the association's first president. The next two presidents were Protestant clergymen: Eliphalet Nott of New York, president of Union College, and Alonzo Potter, an Episcopal bishop, known for his ardent support of the common school cause and for his widely used book, *The School and the Schoolmaster, A Manual for the Use of Teachers, Employers, Trustees, etc., of Common Schools*, published in Boston in 1843. Other prominent clergymen associated with this group included Samuel Lewis of Ohio and Caleb Mills of Indiana, the chief school officers in their respective states.[11] The Society for the Improvement of Common Schools, established in Hartford in 1828, was founded by clergymen, prominent among them Thomas H. Gallaudet. Rev. Thomas Robbins, who was later to become a member of the state board of education in Massachusetts, was one of Gallaudet's colleagues in this work, as were Revs. Joel Hawes, an ardent anti-Catholic, and N. S. Wheaton.[12]

Greatest of the educational associations in the West and South was the Western Literary Institute and College of Professional Teachers, with headquarters in Cincinnati. Founded in 1831 as a vehicle of religious and political orthodoxy, the Western Literary Institute had auxiliary organizations in eighteen states and two territories by 1840. Its leadership was to a very large extent provided by clergymen, among them such eminent figures as William H. McGuffey, State

10. Brooks, "Moral Education," *The American Journal of Education* 1 (March 1856): 336; John Albree, "Charles Brooks and His Work for Normal Schools," *The Medford Historical Register* 10 (January 1907): 1–27.

11. "The American Association for the Advancement of Education," *American Journal of Education* 1 (August 1855): 3–16.

12. Orwin B. Griffin, *The Evolution of the Connecticut State School System* (New York: Teacher's College, Columbia University, 1928), p. 24. For Hawes's anti-Catholic activities, see Mary Mason, *Church-State Relationships in Education in Connecticut* (Washington, D.C.: Catholic University of America Press, 1953), p. 49; and also Carroll John Noonan, *Nativism in Connecticut, 1829–1869* (Washington, D.C.: Catholic University of America Press, 1938), pp. 107ff.

School Superintendents Calvin E. Stowe and Samuel Lewis, and the rabidly anti-Catholic Alexander Campbell.[13] The McGuffey *Readers* were first published under the sponsorship of the institute. The creation of the office of superintendent of common schools in Ohio in 1837 and the basic Ohio school law of 1838 were also in large part a result of the efforts of the institute. One of the chief targets of the institute was Catholicism, but it took care also to denounce the "licentious books" of Voltaire, Volney, and Diderot.[14]

Another association, the Ohio College of Teachers, was also reminded of the sinister designs of Rome. In 1836 Rev. Alexander Campbell (mentioned above) delivered an anti-Catholic polemic to a meeting of the assembled college, and in 1837 he engaged in a public debate, which lasted seven days, with Bishop Purcell of Cincinnati. In this encounter, one of Campbell's major propositions was that the Catholic Church was "the Babylon of John, the Man of Sin of Paul, and the Empire of the Youngest Horn of Daniel's sea monster."[15]

Although the Western Literary Institute was the most prestigious and influential, many other groups were also promoting schools in the sparsely settled West. Among them were the home mission societies of the major Protestant denominations. The main purpose of these societies, which were headquartered in the East, was the winning of souls in the lawless and irreligious West, yet they were zealous also in the promoting and founding of schools. Most influential of these was probably the American Home Missionary Society, which was a joint Congregationalist-Presbyterian agency during the decades of the Common School Movement.[16] There were also Episcopal, Baptist, Dutch Reformed, and Methodist home mission societies. We shall encounter these societies and their agents again when we examine the founding of schools in the West.

13. Although the work of all these men is described, not one of them is identified as a clergyman in a standard treatment of the subject: Allen Oscar Hansen, *Early Educational Leadership in the Ohio Valley, A Study of Educational Reconstruction through the Western Literary Institute and College of Professional Teachers, 1829–1841* (Bloomington, Ill.: Public School Publishing Co., 1923).

14. William Henry Venable, *Beginnings of Literary Culture in the Ohio Valley: Historical and Biographical Sketches* (Cincinnati: R. Clark & Co., 1891), pp. 409–34; Rush Welter, *Popular Education and Democratic Thought in America* (New York: Columbia University Press, 1962), pp. 90–91; *Transactions of the Western Literary Institute* 7 (1837): 39, 50.

15. Emerson Elbridge White and Thomas W. Harney, eds., *A History of Education in the State of Ohio: A Centennial Volume* (Columbus: Gazette Printing House, 1876), pp. 360ff; Robert Richardson, *Memoirs of Alexander Campbell* (Philadelphia: J. B. Lippincott and Co., 1870), 2:425. The debates were published under the title *A Debate on the Roman Catholic Religion* (Cincinnati: J. A. James and Company, 1847). For an extended treatment of the anti-Catholic work of both Beecher and Campbell in Cincinnati, see Alfred G. Stritch, "Political Nativism in Cincinnati, 1830–1860," *Records of the American Catholic Historical Society of Philadelphia* 48 (1937): 234–40.

16. A good account of the AHMS is Colin Brummit Goodykoontz, *Home Missions on the American Frontier* (Caldwell, Idaho: Caxton Printers, 1939).

Clergymen as School Administrators

There were no significant differences in attitude among public school leaders throughout the nation concerning the non-public schools and the need for religious instruction in the public schools. Yet, wanting any better form of classification, we shall group them here into geographical regions. If only because its economic and political foundations were better established, the Northeast saw the fullest development of the Common School Movement. The greatest leaders of the movement here were Horace Mann and Henry Barnard. Both were laymen, although Mann, trained in the law, assumed ministerial duties late in life.

Although Mann strongly endorsed the participation of Protestant clergymen in public school affairs, he considered it necessary to restrict Catholic participation. To be sure, he said, it would not be proper to disqualify a teacher from the public schools "merely because he is a Catholic," but he added a condition which, in effect, would have done just that: "If I had reason to suppose the candidate to be a Catholic, I should feel perfectly authorized to inquire, and to know, whether, if approved, he would use the Bible in school in such a way as the committee should direct; whether he would use the Protestant version for a Protestant school . . . ." Mann's view that there could properly be such a thing as a Protestant public school is interesting; even more so is his implication that there could also be such a thing as a Catholic public school. He conceded that the Lowell, Massachusetts, experiment (discussed below) of using Catholic teachers in the Catholic section of the city had been inaugurated by a "very intelligent" school committee.[17]

In these utterances intended for domestic consumption, Mann's views on Catholicism were restrained. But during his tour of Europe in 1843, he was moved to concede that the sight of Catholics at worship impressed him "more and more deeply with the baneful influence of the Catholic religion upon the human mind." The "nonsense" taught to children by priests in Coblenz repelled Mann, and his impressions of France were expressed in summary form: "Frivolity, sensuality, and the Catholic religion—what will they not do for the debasement of mankind?" In Saxony, he met a Catholic priest who was "a most delightful man, full of generosity." But afterthought compelled him to add, "If such a man can grow up under the influence of Catholicism, what would he be under a nobler dispensation?" Yet, for all his misgivings about Catholicism, Mann was able to realize, with obvious reference to the United States, that in Belgian school

---

17. Mary Tyler Peabody Mann, ed., *Life and Works of Horace Mann*, 5 vols. (New York: Lee and Shepard, 1891), 1:261–64.

affairs "the Catholics are giving to the Protestants a taste of what the Protestants, in some other places, are endeavoring to force upon them."[18]

Although he had abandoned the Puritanism of his forebears, Mann's writings bear eloquent witness to his burning conviction that non-sectarian religion was an essential element of education. It is therefore wholly understandable that he should have assumed the role of a clergyman in his later years. The Unitarian Rev. Theodore Parker, when he heard that his old friend had "taken to preaching," wrote to convey his congratulations and good wishes. But he cautioned gently that Mann should preach only the "great natural religion whereof the revelations of old time are but a small part."[19]

Henry Barnard was the first state school officer in Connecticut; later he held the same position in Rhode Island. After the war, he became the first U.S. commissioner of education. An Episcopalian layman with orthodox theological views, Barnard was entirely convinced of the necessity of religious instruction in the schools, and he admonished his readers that Christ was the first great teacher. A calm and scholarly man, he did not share the anti-Catholic bias that was almost endemic in the Common School Movement. In a controversy over Bible-reading in the Hartford public schools in 1865, Barnard threw the weight of his opinion on the side of the Catholic faction, taking the then-novel position that reading in the King James version was a violation of the religious liberty of Catholic pupils. His opinion was, however, overwhelmingly rejected by the school committee.[20]

Mann's successor as secretary of the board in Massachusetts was Rev. Barnas Sears, president of the Newton Theological Institution. Like his predecessor, Sears did not join full-throated in the clamor against Rome, but he believed that much of the reported absenteeism from the public schools was the result of the efforts of "those who profess no sympathy with our system of public education," who wish "to exclude the Bible from the schools," and whose aim is "the establishment of sectarian schools under the patronage of the state."[21] The term *sectarian schools* was an important part of the public schoolmen's lexicon. It was usually intended to mean "Catholic schools," and the term was one of disparagement, even though the schoolmen were fully—even painfully—aware that some Protestant groups, defecting

18. Ibid., 1:207, 211, 217, 446.

19. Ibid., 1:459.

20. *Connecticut Common School Journal* 1 (October 1838): 19–20; *Hartford Courant*, 4 November 1865. For additional information, see Mason, *Church-State Relationships in Connecticut*, pp. 204–5.

21. *Eighteenth Annual Report of the [Massachusetts] Board of Education, Together with the Eighteenth Annual Report of the Secretary of the Board* (Boston: William White, 1855), p. 66.

from the Common School Movement, were demanding allotments from public funds for their own schools.

Massachusetts was also for a time the scene of the labors of Rev. Amory D. Mayo, who for many decades combined active pastoral work with his educational interests. Later, as a resident of Cincinnati, he served as a member of the city board of education and was an active participant in the "Bible War" of 1869–1870 (discussed below), a controversy between Protestants and Catholics concerning Bible reading in the public schools. When he returned to Massachusetts, Mayo served as a school board member in Springfield from 1872 to 1880. From 1880 to 1885 he served as associate editor of the influential *Journal of Education* (Boston), and he used this opportunity to discredit the growing tide of criticism of the common schools by Catholic authorities, on the grounds that the Catholics were under "implicit orders from an Italian Pontiff . . . to destroy the most vital institution of this Republic." During the late years of the century Mayo became one of the most influential leaders of the public school movement in the South. As a prominent member of the Christian Amendment Movement, he labored for the adoption of an amendment to the Federal Constitution to guarantee the right to teach the Bible in the public schools. In his many historical sketches of education Dr. Mayo diligently pointed out the weaknesses of the parochial schools, which, he insisted, were motivated by "sectarian bigotry disguised as zeal for Christian education."[22]

In Connecticut, one of the strongest proponents of public education was Rev. Horace Bushnell, a personal friend of Horace Mann and Henry Barnard. Bushnell firmly believed that the three greatest dangers facing America were slavery, infidelity, and "popery," a view propounded fully in his *The Crisis of the Church* (1835). Although Bushnell was critical of the "refractory un-American position taken by these Catholic strangers," he was at least consistent. He felt that the Old School Presbyterian parochial school movement was, like the Catholic schools, a threat to the public school movement. His views on the school question were expounded at some length in his 1853 sermon "Common Schools: A Discourse on the Modifications Demanded by the Roman Catholics," in which he proposed that either the Douay or the King James version of the Bible might be used in the public schools, depending upon local conditions. This was more of a

22. Harold M. Helfman, "The Cincinnati 'Bible War,' 1869–1870," *Ohio State Archaeological and Historical Quarterly* 60 (October 1951): 380; Editorial, *Journal of Education* 20 (17 July 1884): 72; A. D. Mayo, "Education in Southwestern Virginia," in U.S. Commissioner of Education, *Report*, 1890–1891, pp. 904, 912. A prolific author, Mayo's writings included *Religion in the Common Schools* (1869) and *The Bible in the Public Schools* (1870).

concession than most Protestant clergymen of the time were prepared to make, but it seemed somewhat out of place in a sermon that in its entirety consisted of a sweeping attack upon all things Catholic.[23] Bushnell was an active promoter of the Protestant League and the Christian Alliance, both strongly anti-Catholic associations. Other officials of the league included Revs. Lyman Beecher, Joel Hawes, Leonard Bacon, Nathaniel W. Taylor, and C. Goodrich, all of whom, like Bushnell, ardently supported the school movement.[24]

Only two of the nine original members of the State Board of Education in Connecticut were ministers, but at the local level a large proportion of the school officers were Protestant clergymen. When the first public normal school in the state was opened in 1850, the principalship was entrusted to Rev. T. D. P. Stone.[25] One of the great victories of the Common School Movement, and one of a purely secular nature, was achieved by Rev. Birdsley Grant Northrup during his tenure as state superintendent of schools in Connecticut. His vigorous and successful campaign to replace the "rate-bill" (a tax levied upon parents only in proportion to the number of children they had in school) with general property taxation was a necessary precondition for the establishment of free public education.[26]

In New Jersey, a statewide convention held in Trenton in 1828 provided the impetus for the common school act adopted by the state legislature the following year. The leadership of this convention was in large part provided by clergymen. Outstanding among them was the young John Maclean, whose blueprint for a state school system was adopted almost in its entirety in the following decades.[27] Although the 1829 law was repealed early in 1831, another campaign was launched in the late thirties. Again a large number of the leaders were clergymen. Among them was the Episcopal bishop, G. W. Doane, whose "Address to the People of New Jersey on the Subject of

23. George Stewart, *A History of Religious Education in Connecticut in the Middle of the Nineteenth Century* (New Haven: Yale University Press, 1924), pp. 291–92. Both Bushnell's sermon and his inflammatory "Letter to His Holiness, Pope Gregory XVI" may be found in his posthumously published *Building Eras in Religion* (New York: Scribners, 1881).

24. For the educational activities of Hawes and Bacon, see Orwin B. Griffin, *Evolution of the Connecticut State School System*, pp. 24, 138–40; and *Connecticut Common School Journal* 1 (December 1838): 46. For their anti-Catholic work, see Mason, *Church-State Relationships in Education*, pp. 149, 204–5. The names of officers are listed in *The Christian Alliance, Its Constitution, List of Officers, and Addresses* (New York, 1843), p. 11.

25. Mason, *Church-State Relationships*, pp. 106ff; *Annual Report of the [Connecticut] Superintendent of Common Schools, 1850*, p. 19.

26. In his *Annual Report of the Board of Education of the State of Connecticut, 1868*, Northrup devoted thirty-three pages to a survey of the rate-bill as it existed in various states at the time and to the successful effort to ban its use in Connecticut.

27. Nelson R. Burr, *Education in New Jersey, 1630–1871* (Princeton: Princeton University Press, 1942), p. 249.

Common Schools," prepared for a state school convention in 1838, served as a catalyst for action. The Society of Teachers and Friends, formed in 1843 to provide leadership and direction for the movement, selected a clergyman as its first president. In 1845–1846 these efforts were crowned with success and a comprehensive system of state education was established. Doane, however, later abandoned the common school cause and became a proponent of Episcopal parochial schools.[28]

In other states in the Northeast, also, clergymen provided leadership. One of the prime leaders in the movement that culminated in the Pennsylvania school law of 1834 was a Protestant clergyman. In New Hampshire the state school superintendency was held four times by clergymen between 1854 and 1867. In Rhode Island, a Protestant clergyman served as state commissioner of public schools from 1854 to 1857. Many other Protestant clergymen served as administrators at the local level, including, for example, the city of Providence.[29]

Clergymen as School Administrators in the South

Although the public school movement came later in the South than in the Northeast, Protestant clergymen were equally active in both regions. (Educational developments in Kentucky and Tennessee, both admitted to the Union before 1800, are included in this section.) By common consent, Calvin Wiley was the greatest leader of the Common School Movement in the South. Like Horace Mann, he had not been trained as a minister, but his reports and speeches reveal his deep conviction that religion is a basic and necessary element in education. Wiley was licensed as a Presbyterian minister in 1855, three years after he became state superintendent of common schools in North Carolina, and he was ordained in 1866, the year after he left the superintendency. In 1869 he began serving in the southern states as an agent of the American Bible Society.[30]

Rev. Benjamin M. Smith, one of the earliest advocates of public education in Virginia, prepared for the state legislature in 1839 a

28. John E. Trowbridge, "Presbyterian Interest in Elementary Education in New Jersey, 1816–1866" (Ph.D. diss., Rutgers—The State University, 1857), pp. 348–49; Burr, *Education in New Jersey*, pp. 249–51, 262, 265.

29. Louis G. and Matthew J. Walsh, *History and Organization of Education in New Hampshire* (Washington: Government Printing Office, 1898), p. 30; William Howe Tolman, *History of Higher Education in Rhode Island* (Washington: Government Printing Office, 1894), p. 31; Thomas B. Stockwell, *A History of Public Education in Rhode Island* (Providence: Providence Press Co., 1876), pp. 195, 317.

30. Luther W. Gobbell, *Church-State Relationships in Education in North Carolina Since 1776* (Durham, N.C.: Duke University Press, 1938), pp. 181ff. The intolerance of the antebellum southern Protestant sects for one another and their common fear of Catholicism are treated in Walter Brownlow Posey, *Religious Strife on the Southern Frontier* (Baton Rouge: Louisiana State University Press, 1965).

report on public education in Prussia. He also founded one of the first educational associations in the South.[31] Fellow Virginian Rev. Archibald Alexander, president of Hampden-Sidney College and founder of Princeton Theological Seminary, deplored the Romanists' hostility to the Bible and rejoiced that "in most parts of our country, this class of people are not found" or exist in small numbers. When necessary, however, they should be gathered into schools of their own, and not "allowed to interrupt that course of instruction which is judged to be the most efficient, in a country where four-fifths of the people are Protestants." Another antebellum educational leader in Virginia was Bishop John Early, whose greatest educational achievement was the founding of Randolph-Macon College. From 1833 to 1840 he served as agent of the college and "travelled from Virginia to Georgia preaching on education . . . ."[32]

Of the postwar school leaders in Virginia, no doubt the greatest was Rev. William H. Ruffner, elected as the first superintendent of public instruction in 1870. His plans, formulated during his eleven years in the superintendency, served as the basis for the school systems not only of Virginia but also of other southern states. He also served, later, as head of the state's first normal school. Ruffner was more detached in his views than were most of the clerics in education, seeing nothing incompatible in the existence of parallel public and denominational school systems. When he entered public service by accepting the superintendency, he obtained his demission from the ministry. Although the most effective leader in the public school movement in this state was a cleric, one of its most influential opponents was also a clergyman, Robert L. Dabney of Union Theological Seminary. "There can be no true education without . . . Christianity," he declared. In public schools, he feared, there would be a "mixture of the children of the decent and the children of the vile." The "old Virginia plan" of private and church schools should therefore be preserved.[33]

In South Carolina, at a time when the Presbyterian campaign for public support of denominational schools was at its height, the cause of public education was greatly strengthened by the leadership of

31. Edgar W. Knight, *A Documentary History of Education in the South Before 1860*, 4 vols. (Chapel Hill: University of North Carolina Press, 1950), 2:410–11; William A. Maddox, *The Free School Idea in Virginia Before the Civil War* (New York: Columbia University, 1918), p. 138.

32. "Address Before the Alumni Association of Washington College by the Reverend Archibald Alexander, D.D.," delivered 29 June 1843 (Baltimore: John Murphy and Co., 1890); "Diary of John Early, Bishop of the Methodist Episcopal Church, South," intro. Rt. Rev. Collins Denny, *Virginia Historical Magazine* 33 (April 1925): 170.

33. Sadie Bell, *The Church, the State, and Education in Virginia* (Philadelphia: Science Printing Co., 1930), p. 447; Dabney, *Universal Education in the South*, 2 vols. (Chapel Hill: University of North Carolina Press, 1936), 1:155–58.

Rev. James Henley Thornwell, president of South Carolina College in the early fifties and himself a Presbyterian. Thornwell's "Letter to Governor Manning on Public Instruction in South Carolina" (1853) has been described as "the most important contribution to education ever written by an educator in the state . . . . "[34] Thornwell was also a leader in the crusade against Rome and a strong supporter of the Know-Nothing party. "There is not a principle of the American party," he wrote in 1855, "so far as its principles are known, which does not command my most cordial approbation."[35]

In Kentucky, even before statehood, Rev. Caleb Wallace took it upon himself to persuade the parent state of Virginia to support schools in its western territory with grants of land. When he moved to Kentucky, Wallace continued to press for the establishment of public schools. Rev. James Mitchell also labored for education in Kentucky; in 1782–1783 he "preached the gospel and supported his family by teaching school."[36] After statehood, when a committee of the legislature was considering plans to establish a common school system, two clergymen were called upon for advice. One of them, Benjamin O. Peers, was lauded by Henry Barnard as "one of the most intelligent, active, and influential friends of education in the West." Revs. John H. Heywood and James Freeman Clark were active promoters of the public schools in Louisville; the latter served for a time as city superintendent of schools.[37]

Although ministers served as state school superintendents in all parts of the nation, in Kentucky this office was a virtual monopoly of the clergy for at least forty years. Of the first eleven state superintendents, during the period from 1838 to 1879, all but one were Protestant clergymen. Among them the greatest was Robert J. Breckenridge, whose monumental labors as state school superintendent during the years 1847–1852 earned for him the title of "Father of public education in Kentucky."[38] (The distinction has also been claimed, however, for Peers.)

34. Colyer Meriwether, *History of Higher Education in South Carolina, with a Sketch of the Free School System*, U.S. Bureau of Education Circular of Information, 3 November 1888, p. 198. Other efforts in behalf of public education by Thornwell, as well as by other clergymen, are mentioned in this work.

35. Benjamin M. Palmer, *The Life and Letters of James Henley Thornwell, D.D., LL.D.* (Richmond: Whittet and Shepperson, 1875), pp. 479, 299.

36. W. H. Whitsitt, *Life and Times of Caleb Wallace* (Louisville: John P. Morton & Co., 1888), pp. 99–102, 122–35; William Henry Foote, D.D., *Sketches of Virginia, Historical and Biographical*, 2 vols. (Philadelphia: J. P. Lippincott and Co., 1955), 2:136.

37. *Connecticut Common School Journal* 1 (October 1838): 23; A. D. Mayo, "Education in the Northwest during the First Half Century of the Republic, 1790–1840," in U.S. Commissioner of Education, *Report*, 1894–1895, 2:1571.

38. Alvin F. Lewis, *History of Higher Education in Kentucky*, U.S. Government Printing Office, Circular of Information, no. 3, 1899, pp. 334–38; Barksdale Hamlett, *History of Education in Kentucky*, Bulletin of the State Department of Education, no. 4, 1914, pp. 15–78.

While zeal for the common schools and opposition to Catholicism often went hand in hand, rarely were these causes joined so dramatically as in the work of Breckenridge. His rise to leadership in the nativist crusade had begun in Baltimore, where he served as pastor of the Second Presbyterian Church from 1832 to 1845. Breckenridge and his close collaborator in anti-Romanist activities, Rev. Andrew B. Cross, spurned "any intention to persecute any man on account of his religious opinions." Yet they felt compelled to deplore the "prevalent disposition [of parents] to commit the education of Protestant children to the several orders of the Romish priesthood," and they were equally dismayed that "nunneries are multiplying around us, immured within whose walls our daughters are to learn the intolerant dogmas and practice the superstitious and idolatrous ceremonies of the Church of Rome." Moreover, they insisted, the contest was manifestly unfair since "the celibacy of their clergy has given them an advantage in respect to the price of tuition which nothing but a combined effort of all the Protestant denominations can possibly counteract." Breckenridge and Cross were zealous advocates of the work of the Protestant Association of Baltimore and of its journal, *The Protestant*. But so offensive were the allegations in *The Protestant* that the city newspapers refused to publish its announcements, and some Protestant ministers refused permission for agents of the journal to go into their congregations to solicit for subscribers.[39] Such obstacles seemed only to increase the tempo of Breckenridge's anti-Catholic activities, and there were many to urge him on. In 1835 Breckenridge was commissioned by the General Presbyterian Assemblies, meeting in Philadelphia, to head a special committee to study the "Prevalence of Popery in the West." In his first report, he denounced the Pope as "Anti-Christ, a man of sin and son of Pestilence," an "apostate from God," corrupted by "profane exorcisms, idolatrous incantations, and unauthorized additions, mutilations, and ceremonies."[40]

In 1839, stirred by the preaching and publications of Breckenridge and Cross, a large mob attacked the Carmelite convent in Baltimore for three days. In 1843, Breckenridge created the militant Society of the Friends of the Reformation. He did much to lay the foundations for the period of turmoil that in the late fifties gained for Baltimore the title "mob city."[41] In 1841 Breckenridge published his major diatribe on "papism." Chapter titles reveal his perspective: "Bishops Full ver-

39. Mary St. Patrick McConnville, *Political Nativism in the State of Maryland, 1830–1860* (Washington: Catholic University of America Press, 1928), pp. 92–93, 95; *American Catholic Historical Researches* 19 (1902): 107; *The Protestant*, 27 March 1830.

40. Carlton Beals, *Brass-Knuckle Crusade; The Great Know-Nothing Conspiracy, 1820–1860* (New York: Hastings House Publishers, 1960), p. 69.

41. McConnville, *Nativism in Maryland*, pp. 88–90, 121.

sus Bishops Empty" and "Conjunction of St. Bacchus and St. Ignatius." He recommended to his readers *Six Months in a Convent* by an "escaped nun." In a section describing a visit to the Baltimore Cathedral he repeated in awesome terms the evidence—incontrovertible in his view—that deep subterranean vaults and cells existed because the church authorities needed "places of discipline, confinement and death."[42] Breckenridge had himself made an ill-fated attempt to sponsor an "escaped nun"—the most popular motif in the anti-Catholic literature of the period—but the effort had foundered when several medical doctors had declared her to be insane. Two chapters of *Papism* attempt to justify the venture. Despite the verdict of the doctors, Breckenridge insisted on the credibility of Olevia (or Isabella) Neal's testimony; similar efforts had been made earlier, he recalled, to discredit the revelations made by Maria Monk.

Such were the views and accomplishments of the man who came to the pulpit of the First Presbyterian Church in Lexington in 1847 and to the state superintendency of schools a few months later. Breckenridge was one of the most powerful orators of his day and a controversialist who gave no quarter. He had fought the liquor traffic, the Sunday mails, and the Universalists. He had been chiefly responsible for the division of his own denomination into the Old and New School factions in 1837, and after the war his activities were to figure prominently in the break between the northern and southern factions of that body. But his consuming passion was his hatred for Rome.

None will begrudge Breckenridge the credit he richly deserves for establishing within the space of a few years the principles of state responsibility for schools in Kentucky. On the other hand, he embraced the nativist cause as well, and when the Know-Nothing Movement developed, he was much in demand as a speaker for that cause, in other states as well as in Kentucky.[43] Breckenridge's successor as state superintendent of schools, Rev. John D. Matthews, also an ardent foe of Rome, was elected to office as a candidate of the Know-Nothing party, which captured the state government in 1855.[44]

In other states of the South, also, Protestant ministers were at the forefront of the school movement. One historian has concluded, "The Protestant clergy kept the public free school movement alive in pres-

42. *Papism in the XIX Century in the United States* (Baltimore: David Owen and Son, 1841), pp. 9, 64.

43. Agnes Geraldine McGann, "The Know-Nothing Movement in Kentucky," *Records of the American Catholic Society of Philadelphia* 49 (1938): 310. William H. Vaughn, in "Robert Jefferson Breckenridge as an Educational Administrator" (Ph.D. diss., George Peabody University, 1938), seems entirely oblivious to the religious and political activities of the man.

44. W. Darrell Overdyke, *The Know-Nothing Party in the South* (Baton Rouge: Louisiana State University Press, 1950), p. 106.

ent West Virginia during the two decades immediately following 1830." In Georgia, of the persons who played a leading role in public education before 1875, about half were Protestant clergymen. An early president of Emory College in that state, and an ardent publicist for the "New South," Rev. Atticus Haywood, earned national recognition for his work with the Slater Fund. In Florida, Rev. Charles Beecher, brother of Henry Ward Beecher, served as state superintendent of schools from 1871 to 1873 and was succeeded by Rev. Jonathan C. Gibbs. John Eaton was perhaps the most important leader in the school movement in Tennessee. Trained as a minister, he entered the army as a chaplain but was soon performing administrative duties, at the order of General Grant. Eaton served as the first state superintendent of schools in Tennessee during the years 1867–1869 and later as U.S. commissioner of education under President Grant.[45]

Clergymen as School Administrators in the West

In the West, Protestant clergymen were no less interested in educational work, and they were aided by educational and religious societies headquartered in the East. From the very beginning, English settlers in the New World feared the frontier. Gov. William Bradford rejoiced with the passengers of the *Mayflower* when they reached the American shore in mid-November 1620, but he had deep apprehensions about their future in this "hidious and desolate wildernes, full of wild beasts and willd men."[46] The fear persisted as the line of settlements moved westward. It was one thing to "adhere to the lessons of virtue, and the principles of piety" in the settled communities of the East, said Rev. Albert Barnes in his *Plea in Behalf of Western Colleges* (1846). But when the westward migrants left behind the familiar certainties and found themselves "thrown together without order, in interminable forests, or on boundless prairies, with commingled and unsettled views," the struggle to preserve civilized ways had to be waged anew. Means must be found to assemble these pioneers in proper Yankee towns with churches and cemeteries, common schools and perhaps a fledgling college—but surely no saloons, dancehalls, or gambling parlors. Barnes's fellow minister Robert Baird catalogued the agencies available for this great task: the Bible

45. Charles H. Ambler, *A History of Education in West Virginia, from Early Colonial Times to 1949* (Huntington: Standard Print and Publishing Co., 1951), p. 45; Dorothy Orr, *A History of Education in Georgia* (Chapel Hill: University of North Carolina Press, 1950), pp. 383–418; Harold W. Mann, *Atticus Greene Haywood, Methodist Bishop, Editor, and Educator* (Athens: University of Georgia Press, 1965), p. 147; Dabney, *Universal Education*, 1:297–300, 333.

46. Cited in Daniel Boorstin, *The Americans: The Colonial Experience* (New York: Random House, 1958), p. vii.

and Tract Societies, the American Home Missionary Society, the Home Missions of the Episcopal, Baptist, Dutch Reformed, and Methodist Churches, the American Sunday School Union, the Temperance Societies, and many others. Baird's concern for the West was shared throughout American Protestantism. Rev. Lyman Beecher spoke for many other ministers when he called for "a Bible for every family, a school for every district, and a pastor for every thousand souls."[47]

During the early stages of settlement and extending well into the period of statehood, schools in the frontier regions were in large part a product of improvisation. Tasks of more immediate need were at hand: the clearing and the breaking of land, the building of homes and roads, the establishment of an economic basis for life. In Missouri, before statehood was achieved in 1821 many schools were conducted by preachers and missionaries who advertised their wares in much the same way as did their lay colleagues. They stated their charges and omitted any reference to their denominational affiliation.[48]

School classes were often held in church buildings, or church services in school buildings. Sometimes a community would erect a building and make it available for both church and school activities. School sponsors were generally not disposed to differentiate between what later came to be called public and private schools, and the roles of various occupational groups were as yet only loosely defined. In 1834 a recent German immigrant apothecary commented on the unspecialized and unregulated character of professional practice in Missouri: "The laws of the land grant equal rights to all citizens. They permit every advocate of the law, every divine, every scientist to make his own clothes and carry on trade, and in like manner they permit every shoemaker or merchant to preach the gospel, practice medicine or law, to teach school, or do whatever his heart may desire."[49] As a class, members of the clergy were usually the best-educated people in their respective communities—and this was true even for those who were relatively unlettered. (More than half of the white people in Missouri in 1844 were illiterate, according to the state census of that year.)

The role of the agents of the home mission societies was of great importance. The contribution of the missionaries existed not only in

47. David Tyack, "The Kingdom of God and the Common School: Protestant Ministers and the Educational Awakening in the West," *Harvard Educational Review* 36 (Fall 1966): 452–53.

48. Ralph Edward Glauert, "Education and Society in Ante-Bellum Missouri" (Ph.D. diss., University of Missouri, 1973), p. 82.

49. Ibid., p. 25.

the actual teaching, much of which was done (at least in the Sunday schools) by volunteer lay people, but even more in providing the leadership in promoting and organizing schools. While the missionaries were organizing entrepreneurial and Sunday schools, they were at the same time promoting public schools, and they saw no incompatibility in these various endeavors. All would contribute to the spread of true Christianity—and the containment of Catholicism—in the West. Further, several of the missionaries who labored for schools during the territorial years became public education officers after statehood was achieved. The establishment of common school systems in the trans-Appalachian regions, with provisions for administration and partial tax support, was related to but not simultaneous with the attainment of statehood. In most cases, the beginnings of a school "system" in a given state can be traced back to its territorial period, but the process of development continued well into statehood. A review of the activities of clergymen in the founding of school systems in the states of Ohio, Michigan, Wisconsin, Illinois, Indiana, and Oregon will illustrate this point.

During the formative years of the common school system of Ohio, Protestant clergymen held a commanding place. One theme of the movement was sounded by the eminent divine Lyman Beecher of Boston. In his great campaign against Rome, Beecher became increasingly convinced that the West would be the decisive battleground. He accepted the presidency of Lane Theological Seminary in Cincinnati in 1830 so that he might more effectively carry on his campaign. His sermon "A Plea for the West" developed the thesis that education would become the major instrument for overcoming popish designs, and he solicited funds for schools to combat the feared conquest of that region by the Pope.[50]

First and in some respects greatest of the Ohio state school superintendents was Rev. Samuel Lewis, who held the office from 1837 to 1839. A worthy successor to Lewis was Rev. Samuel Galloway, who served from 1844 to 1850. In his funeral sermon for Galloway in 1895, Rev. Washington Gladden proclaimed that his late friend's life had been a great venture in "educational evangelism."[51] In 1856 Rev. Anson Smyth was elected as state superintendent of schools in Ohio, a position he held for six years. Earlier, "not doubting that he was serving his Master in this just as truly as in preaching the gospel," Smyth had led the movement that resulted in the creation of a public school system in Toledo, and for some years he served as city super-

50. *Autobiography, Correspondence . . . of Lyman Beecher*, ed. Charles Beecher, 2 vols. (New York: Harper and Bros., 1865), 2:224.

51. "Samuel Galloway," *Ohio Archaeological and Historical Publications* (title varies) 4 (1895): 255–76.

intendent. In 1866 he was elected president of the State Teachers' Association and editor ex-officio of the *Journal of Education*. After six years as state superintendent of schools, he was elected superintendent of instruction in Cleveland, and served in that capacity for five years. "During all these eighteen years, devoted to educational interests, he preached on an average one sermon every Sabbath day [and] delivered many addresses before literary and educational associations."[52]

Rev. Calvin E. Stowe of Lane Theological Seminary, an active participant in the anti-Catholic crusade, was yet another of the outstanding leaders of the Common School Movement in Ohio. In 1836 he was commissioned by the state to investigate the public school systems of Europe, especially that of Prussia. His famous *Report on Elementary Instruction in Europe*, published in 1837, was distributed to every school district in the state and reprinted by the order of several other state legislatures.[53] Also prominent in school activities in Ohio was Rev. Asa D. Lord, founder and publisher of the *Ohio School Journal*, superintendent of schools in Columbus, and leader in the establishment of the Ohio State Teachers' Association. Like Horace Mann and Calvin Wiley, Lord had not been trained for the ministry but began preaching after working many years in education. If less influential than some, Rev. B. P. Aydelott of Cincinnati was yet a staunch friend of the common schools. "The Christianity of the Bible is the salvation of our country," said Aydelott. It must therefore be taught in the schools as an antidote to pride and prejudice and—even more important—to socialism and Fourierism.[54]

In Michigan, the first superintendent of public instruction was Rev. John Pierce, a Congregationalist minister and native of New York who had gone to Michigan originally as a missionary. John Milton Gregory, an ordained minister with several years of pastoral experience, was elected president of the Michigan State Teachers' Association in 1854, was one of the founders and for a time editor of the *Michigan Journal of Education*, and was elected state superintendent of public instruction in 1858.[55]

In early Wisconsin, Rev. J. B. Pradt's educational career was typi-

52. J. Fletcher Brennan, ed., *The Biographical Cyclopedia and Portrait Gallery of the State of Ohio* (Cincinnati: Yorston & Co., 1880), 2:494.

53. See Stritch, "Political Nativism in Cincinnati, 1830–1860," p. 246, for Stowe's anti-Catholic activities.

54. Ohio Teachers' Association, *A History of Education in the State of Ohio, A Centennial Volume* (Columbus: Gazette Printing House, 1876), pp. 368–90 (the work of other clergymen is also described in this volume); Benjamin P. Aydelott, *Our Country's Evils and Their Remedies* (Cincinnati: G.L. Weed, 1843), pp. iv-vi.

55. Harry A. Kersey, "Michigan Teachers' Institutes in the Mid-Nineteenth Century: A Representative Document," *History of Education Quarterly* 5 (March 1965): 44–45.

cal. Pradt began his educational activities in a county teachers' association. Soon he became active in the work of the state teachers' association, and in 1860 became its president and also editor of the *Wisconsin Journal of Education*.[56] As the official organ of the Wisconsin State Teachers' Association and of the Wisconsin Department of Public Instruction, the *Journal* was presumably committed to the nonsectarian policy laid down in the state constitution. Yet Pradt saw no impropriety in publishing in the *Journal* an article declaring that during pre-Reformation days priests, "ignorant of the spirit of Christ, sought to procure power for themselves by . . . practicing all kinds of frauds . . . . For centuries this terrible superstition . . . wove its fatal meshes through every department of society." When taken to task by a reader, Pradt declared, "We entertained not the slightest intention of doing injury to anyone in giving place to the article, and . . . it did not occur to us that the assertions made by the writer . . . would be deemed calumnious . . . . Whether the writer of the original article misstated the facts of history is a subject which it would be unprofitable to discuss at length in the pages of the journal." But the opportunity to do so was too tempting to resist. Ignoring his own counsel, he plunged into a purely Protestant defense of the position outlined in the original article.[57]

This full-scale attack on Romanism did not seem to damage Pradt's educational career. He continued to serve as editor for several years, and in 1871 he was made assistant superintendent of public instruction, serving under a superintendent who was also a minister.[58] The heavy reliance on clerical leadership seen at the state level was also evident locally. For varying periods of time during the 1850s, Protestant clergymen served as school superintendents in Fond du Lac, Kenosha, Janesville, Racine, Beaver Dam, Brodhead, Hudson, and Madison.[59]

When Illinois became a state in 1818, Baptist missionary John Mason Peck saw vastly expanded opportunities for service. He continued to found Sunday schools, as he had done during his brief sojourn in the St. Louis area, but he now also became one of the most effective of the early common school leaders in the Prairie State. He was influential in securing the passage of the first state school law in 1825. In 1827 he helped to found the Rock Spring Seminary for the

56. *Wisconsin Journal of Education* (hereafter *WJE*) 1 (December 1856): 309; 2 (July 1857): 31; 4 (August 1859, June 1860): 56, 395.

57. G. A. Marshall, "The Philosophy of Education," *WJE* 6 (December 1861): 182–83; and the editor's defense of the article, *WJE* 6 (April 1862): 307–10.

58. *WJE*, new series, 1 (March 1871): 116.

59. *WJE* 1 (August, October 1856): 191, 252; 2 (July, September 1857; January 1858): 23, 25, 87, 220; 3 (June 1859): 378; 4 (February 1860): 253; 5 (March 1861): 278; 7 (June 1863): 379.

training of teachers and ministers. He was a leader in the educational conventions held in Vandalia in 1834 and 1835, and he used his *Pioneer and Western Baptist* to further the common school cause.[60]

When the American Home Missionary Society agent Theron Baldwin took roll in his Sunday school in Illinois in 1830, he found that only 37 of the 105 pupils present were able to read. A nearby settlement consisted of 52 families; less than half of these families contained even one literate person, child or adult. Baldwin soon organized a (Raikes-type) Sunday school "to gather in if possible young and old, and learn them to read." Repeatedly, Reverend Baldwin wrote to his sponsors in the East, urging them to send schoolteachers to the West. In many cases, he declared, "a few hundred dollars appropriated to give permanency to the labors of a devotedly pious teacher . . . would in a much higher degree promote the interests of the Redeemer's kingdom than the same amount appropriated to a preacher."[61]

Like Peck and Baldwin, the Methodist Peter Cartwright evenhandedly promoted both public and church-related schools. In a speech before the Illinois Methodist Conference in 1827, Cartwright may have been the first man to advocate the founding of a college in the Prairie State. Later he successfully urged the conference to adopt as its own the fledgling institution soon to become known as McKendree College. Cartwright served two terms in the Illinois state legislature, where he was chairman of the House Committee on Education, and introduced the first bill proposing the establishment of a state-supported college. In his church conference he urged his fellow Methodists to establish schools in their own counties and circuits, and he personally helped organize many of them. He helped Peter Akers and John F. Jaquess in establishing the Methodist college for women at Jacksonville, an institution which by 1855 had provided training for five hundred girls, most of whom became teachers in the common schools. He solicited and eventually obtained conference sponsorship for the effort, originally interdenominational, to establish the institution at Bloomington that came to be known as Illinois Wesleyan College.[62]

When the Teachers' Association was founded in Illinois in 1836, Rev. Edward Beecher (son of Lyman) was chosen as its first president, and four of its officers were Protestant ministers. In 1846

60. John W. Cook, *Educational History of Illinois* (Chicago: Henry O. Shepard Co., 1912), p. 42; John Donald Pulliam, "A History of the Struggle for a Free Common School System in Illinois from 1818 to the Civil War" (Ph.D. diss., University of Illinois, 1965), pp. 37, 107, 223.

61. Timothy Smith, "Protestant Schooling and American Nationality, 1800–1850," *Journal of American History* 53 (March 1967): 690–91.

62. Ibid., p. 693.

Beecher and another Protestant clergyman, both avowed nativists, spoke to the Ladies' Society for the Promotion of Education at the West, emphasizing the need of Protestant education to offset the influence of the Catholic church. By 1850 the society was able to announce the establishment of a fund for the education of "Protestant children recovered from Papal schools and of the children of Romanists who may be induced to attend a Protestant school . . . ."[63]

The Indiana State Teachers' Association elected as its first president in 1854 Rev. William M. Daily, who was also president of the state university. At this inaugural meeting, the association was addressed by Rev. Robert J. Breckenridge, former superintendent of public schools in Kentucky, whose ferocious attacks upon "papism" have been noted above. Caleb Mills, often regarded as the father of the public school system of Indiana, was an ordained minister who had come to the frontier in 1835 as an agent for the American Sunday School Union, and who served also as an agent of the American Home Missionary Society. He was state superintendent of public schools from 1854 to 1857, one of the founders of the state teachers' association, and a lifelong leader in educational activities.[64]

The Puritan ideal was still cherished in early Oregon, which was admitted to the Union in 1859. In 1866 the state Congregational association resolved "that the idea and practice of our fathers, that education is the handmaiden of religion, and that the school and college go hand in hand with the church, should be a living, practical idea with us in Oregon, while laying foundations here."[65] In this joint religious and educational mission, the chief architect for the Congregationalists was Rev. George Atkinson, who in 1848 became the American Home Mission Society's first emissary in Oregon. Soon after his arrival, he had called on the territorial governor to plead the cause of public education. Atkinson drafted the substance of the governor's legislative message on education early in 1849 and also the school law enacted later in the year. He visited log schoolhouses in remote corners of the territory to advise teachers about methods and textbooks, preached to the public about the need for good schools, wrote hortatory articles about school morals and discipline, helped grade the Portland schools, and was chosen president of the county teachers' association when it was formed in 1871. Atkinson also wrote a history

63. Ladies' Society for the Promotion of Education at the West, *Fourth Annual Report* (Boston: Well-Spring Press, 1850), p. 44.

64. Minutes of the First Annual Session of the Indiana State Teachers' Association, pp. 5–13, cited by Jerome Edwards Diffley, "Catholic Reaction to American Public Education, 1792–1852" (Ph.D. diss., University of Notre Dame, 1959), p. 93; *The American Biographical History of Eminent and Self-Made Men of the State of Indiana, District 8* (Cincinnati: Western Biographical Publishing Co., 1880), 2:36.

65. Cited in Tyack, "The Kingdom of God," p. 447.

of public education in Oregon for the 1876 International Centennial Exhibition in Philadelphia and communicated regularly with Rev. John Eaton, U.S. commissioner of education. All the while he waged war against the dangers of strong drink, card-playing, gambling, and dancing.

The unsettled character of frontier life weighed heavily upon Atkinson. Restlessness, always a vice of the westerner, was accentuated here by the lure of gold. Sometimes settlements seemed to be no more than temporary camping grounds. And the evil fed upon itself as unstable and uninstructed parents raised up a new generation even more susceptible to barbarism. Stable settlements, wrote Atkinson, are the "foundations of our social and moral edifice." It was also necessary, in his view, to contend against the Catholics. By the time of Atkinson's arrival there were in the province three Catholic bishops, twenty-seven priests, thirteen sisters, and two Catholic schools. And now, he complained, they were building a girls' "Papal School" right next to his own house to train "Romish Mothers"—and fickle Protestants were sending their daughters there![66] It was almost more than he could bear.

On the frontier, Sunday schools, common schools, and denominational schools open to all children were fluid, almost interchangeable, institutions. In her Sunday school class, Atkinson's wife taught precisely the same thirty-three children she taught daily in her common school. One of Atkinson's fellow missionaries, stationed in another part of the territory, explained that for his students the transition from a weekday to a Sabbath school was very easy because he taught and preached in the same room. Ministers were sought as teachers of public as well as of sectarian schools. Atkinson himself shifted easily between private and public education. Although he had written the state's public school law and was superintendent of schools in his county, he did not hesitate to establish a private female seminary when he concluded that the citizens of his town (Oregon City) would be dilatory about opening a public school to compete with the newly established Catholic girls' school. Ten years later the town purchased the seminary building, used it as a public school, and hired Atkinson and his wife as teachers. Later, while defending the Portland public high school from attacks by private schoolmen, Atkinson was at the same time founding sectarian academies in the adjoining Washington Territory.[67]

In 1888, shortly before his death, Reverend Atkinson addressed the annual convention of the National Education Association in San Fran-

66. Ibid., pp. 456–64. Although the presence of three bishops to supervise twenty-seven priests seems unlikely, this was Atkinson's tabulation.
67. Ibid., pp. 461–64.

cisco. As the influence of the family and church diminished, said Atkinson, the public school had to take over an increasing share of the task of moral indoctrination. Secular instruction is not enough. The Ten Commandments should be engraved at one end of every classroom, and the Sermon on the Mount at the other end. He concluded his oration with a call for the use of the Bible in the common schools.[68] By this time a thriving system of common schools existed in Oregon. Many others of his own and other denominations had helped, of course, but Atkinson's contribution was sufficiently important that he was included in that substantial body of Protestant clergymen honored as "fathers of public education" in their respective states.

Clearly, Protestant men of the cloth rallied to the school cause with great vigor in the West, and the results were impressive. When Horace Mann moved to Ohio in 1857 to assume the presidency of Antioch College, he perceived at once that the Great West had been conquered not only by Black Hawk but by John Calvin as well. But it was, he thought, a mixed blessing. "So far as the religious dogmas are concerned, I would rather it would be Black Hawk's again."[69] As it turned out, the battle was not yet won. It was one thing to establish Protestant-oriented public schools, but quite another to preserve them untainted from Catholic pressures. Sterner methods would be needed for that task and, as we shall see, the Protestant men of God did not shrink from their duty, as they saw it.

68. Ibid., pp. 467–68.
69. Mary P. Mann, *Life of Horace Mann* (Boston: Walker, Fuller, and Co., 1865), p. 514.

4

The Clergy, Teacher Training, and Textbooks

The Sister Professions

Nowhere was the symbiotic relationship between teaching and preaching more dramatically revealed than in the programs designed for the training of teachers. The first teacher training institution in this country was the Teachers' Seminary, established by Rev. Samuel Hall in Andover, Massachusetts, in 1823, modeled on the Andover Theological Seminary. With careful forethought, the school for intending teachers was located near the theological school, and at least two of the instructors of the small theological faculty taught also at the Teachers' Seminary. This was, to be sure, a private institution, but Hall's emphasis upon the ministerial style and evangelical power was not forgotten by the many clergymen who were called upon to establish and administer the new teacher training schools under civil sponsorship.[1]

Historically, schools had looked to religious leaders for advice and leadership. This dependence was increased by the expansion of the educational enterprise resulting from the Common School Movement and by the resulting fundamental change in the composition of the teaching corps. A petition prepared by Sarah Hale, editor of *Godey's Lady's Book*, and strongly endorsed by Horace Mann and other leaders of the Common School Movement was submitted to the United States Congress in 1853, explaining that twenty thousand additional teachers were needed to serve the needs then existing—and this was based on an estimate of one hundred pupils per classroom. "Where," asked Catherine Beecher, "are we to raise such an army of teachers as are

---

1. Paul H. Mattingly, *The Classless Profession: American Schoolmen in the Nineteenth Century* (New York: New York University Press, 1975), pp. 30–31, 40. Institutions designed exclusively for professional training were still rare. Andover Theological Seminary, founded in 1808, was the first of its kind, as was the Litchfield Law School in Connecticut, begun in 1784. Lectures in chemistry at the College of Philadelphia, starting in 1768, are regarded as the semi-systematic beginnings of professional training for physicians.

required for this great work?" For men, she said, there were in this land "many roads to wealth and honor." Few of them would turn to "the humble unhonored toil of the schoolroom and its penurious rewards." There was, Beecher concluded, only one solution: "It is *woman* who is to come at this emergency, and meet the demand— woman, whom experience and testimony have shown to be the best, as well as the cheapest guardian and teacher of childhood in the school as in the nursery."[2] By 1850, the feminization of the teaching profession at the elementary school level was well underway. By 1880 women were to constitute four-fifths of the nation's primary school teaching corps. Teaching, which had always been a transient occupation, was now largely in the hands of people who as yet lacked both legal and political status. This type of an occupational corps was not such as to encourage the emergence of leadership from within, especially since qualifications for admission to the corps were so low. The leadership came for the most part from outside the profession, and primarily from Protestant clergymen.

Hall's Teachers' Seminary, despite propitious beginnings, survived for only twelve years, and Hall sensed a need for a different approach. In 1832 he formed at Andover the School Agent's Society, two years later renamed the American School Society. Its corresponding secretaries were drawn from almost every state of the union and included such eminent clergymen as Pres. Edward Beecher of Illinois College, George Gale of the Oneida Institute, Benjamin O. Peers, who was later to become state superintendent of schools in Kentucky, and Pres. Alva Woods of Alabama University. The society saw itself as a "missionary" organization, with its major goal to provide teacher training on a massive scale. When the society moved to Boston in 1832, other godly men joined the effort: Pres. Francis Wayland of Brown, Pres. Heman Humphrey of Amherst, and the seemingly ubiquitous Thomas H. Gallaudet.[3]

The Teachers' Seminary, designed as a permanent institution with a resident faculty, may have been premature. But there was also in existence a much more modest arrangement, known as the "teachers' institute," which was soon to become the primary agency of teacher preparation in the country, yielding place to the normal school only after the Civil War. The "institutes" were classes for the training of teachers, held in such places as might be available, usually for periods of from one to three weeks. Typically, the institutes had no permanent faculties; the teaching was done by persons considered to be conversant with the "art of teaching."

The prototype for the institute may have been a program for train-

2. *Godey's Lady's Book*, January 1853, pp. 176–77; Catherine Beecher, *True Remedy* (Boston: Phillips, Sampson and Co., 1851), pp. 240–42.
3. Mattingly, *Classless Profession*, pp. 34–39.

ing teachers conceived by Henry Barnard and conducted under the supervision of the principal of the Hartford Grammar School in 1839. The program was favorably regarded, and in 1842 Barnard, with the assistance of Emma Willard, started a "permanent Normal Institute," more ambitious by far than most institutes of the period. Among the leaders in this venture were two widely known clergymen, Revs. Frederick A. Barton of the Andover Teachers' Seminary and Thomas A. Gallaudet. Barnard, a layman and an Episcopalian, caught the essence of the movement when he later described the institute as an "educational revival agency, of the most extensive, permanent, and unobjectionable character."[4] The institute was certainly not modeled upon the American college, nor was it based upon any European pedagogical institutions or theories. Conductors of institutes did indeed on occasion invoke the names of Pestalozzi, de Fellenberg, Lancaster, and even Rousseau. But they found their major inspiration in the revivalist spirit and strategies that were rapidly gaining dominance in American Protestantism.

The similarities between the institutes and revivals were many. Both were planned as series of temporary meetings located in different towns to which their organizers went as circuit riders. Like the "protracted meetings" of the revivals, institutes were advertised far in advance and timed to avoid competition with other local activities. Conductors often held their institutes during vacations when common schools were not in session, or during college commencement exercises so as to take advantage of education-oriented gatherings. Prayers and hymns held a prominent place throughout the institute proceedings, which were often held in churches. From the beginning, clergy led the institutes, which never developed a professional corps of teachers. In New England, virtually all of the leading Congregationalist clergy (and many lesser figures) served as conductors, passing with ease back and forth between the ministry and education. Among them were Charles Brooks, Noah Porter, Merrill Richardson, Horace Bushnell, Lyman Beecher, Joel Dawes, and Nathaniel Taylor.[5]

That the religious intensity of the Second Awakening should have spread into the work of the teachers' institutes was natural enough, but the process was probably hastened by the appearance of two essays during the early years of the school movement. In 1837–1838 a leading educational journal published two exhortatory articles: William A. Alcott's "Missionaries in Education" and the anonymous "District School Missionaries."[6] The articles met a warm response,

4. Ibid., pp. 63–64; Henry Barnard, ed., *Papers for the Teacher* (New York: Brownell, 1860), p. 12.
5. Mattingly, *Classless Profession*, pp. 67, 69.
6. *American Annals of Education and Instruction* 7 (April 1837): 161–62; 8 (January, February 1838): 22–23, 71–75.

and the concept of teachers as missionaries became a standard figure of speech, even to the point of being employed by Horace Mann, the Unitarian. In antebellum school rhetoric, the primary emphasis in teacher training was on the necessity of "consecration." Indeed, institute leaders preferred to say that they were engaged not so much in the training as in the "awakening" of teachers. Professionalization was thus equated much more with the awakening of the inner man than with the acquisition of any technical skills. In the absence, therefore, of any external objective standards, the competence and effectiveness of teachers tended to be measured intuitively and impressionistically. A teacher was engaged in a "holy" work; it was a career to which he was "called," not one he sought for personal status or gain.[7]

One of the most enduring elements of the educational mythology that developed as a part of the Common School Movement was the explanation of the development of educational leaders. Biographies of nineteenth-century schoolmen characteristically contained accounts of meager education, harsh farm routines, heroic mothers, and stern Calvinism. Success came as a result of fortitude in dealing with adversity. Late in the century, when he was serving as U.S. commissioner of education, Rev. A. D. Mayo wrote about Horace Mann: "He heard the call and turning his back on the brilliant opportunity of a great professional and political career" accepted the secretaryship so that the children of the Commonwealth "might be rescued from the decline into which they were falling"; Mann was thus "a man sent from heaven."[8]

To be sure, this account reflects Mayo's ministerial preconceptions in stressing a divine call, self-sacrifice, and a life of service. But this interpretation was, in fact, the same that Mann himself had employed. The facts of Mann's youth did not wholly fit the mold, but the myth was still maintained. His home had been one of the most commodious in the vicinity, and he had been able not only to enter Brown College at an early age, but also with sophomore standing. Yet he later insisted that as a youth, "I had none of those adventitious aids of wealth or powerful connections which so often . . . supply the deficiencies of merit." The day before he left the law to enter education, Mann said that momentous decisions of this type could be made only in "the spirit of self-abandonment, the spirit of martyrdom," and in his diary he pleaded, "God grant me an annihilation of selfishness."[9] Mann's first major biographer, Rev. B. A. Hinsdale, knew his subject well when he entitled his work *Horace Mann and the Common School Revival*.

7. Mattingly, *Classless Profession*, pp. 61–67.
8. *Report of the U.S. Commissioner of Education*, 1896–1897, chap. 15, p. 722.
9. Mattingly, *Classless Profession*, pp. 53, 55, 56.

Throughout the nation, laborers in the vineyard echoed the pious sentiments expressed by the leaders of the school movement. An Ohio teachers' group took note that in 1851 Lorin Andrews, chairman of the executive committee of the Ohio Teachers Association, "was induced to resign his position as principal of the Massilon Union School and become a 'Common School Missionary,' without any assurance of pecuniary reward, except the small and uncertain compensation afforded by teachers' institutes." In 1856 the Wisconsin State Teachers' Association adopted a resolution solemnly declaring that "every teacher should regard himself as an Educational Missionary."[10]

Teaching was among the humblest of callings in nineteenth-century America. Aside from the principalships, most positions paid about the same as unskilled labor received. For the vast majority of teachers it provided only temporary employment. Girls found it more attractive than domestic service, and to men it offered an opportunity to pick up a few dollars during the winter, when work on the farms was slack. Despite this lack of social and financial recognition—or possibly because of it sometimes—many of those engaged in teaching proclaimed that it was, with the possible exception of the ministry, the noblest work in which mortals could engage. In fact, explained a woman who had spent some years in the service, "in comparing it with that other sacred and divine calling, the ministry of the gospel, we are sometimes almost led to say that ours is the holier . . . ." Concluding, she warned, "Oh, teacher, beware! There is a GOD, whose ever watchful eye rests upon all thy labors . . . ." At one teachers' institute the clergyman editor of the state school journal reported with gratification, "A religious revival, in which many of the teachers found a hope in the Saviour, added greatly to the interests and benefits of the occasion." The critical importance of the teacher's work, said another, lay in the fact that he must educate for immortality: "Of all important requisites in a teacher, Christianity is certainly the foremost . . . . O, Teacher, reflect!, pause, ere you go further! . . . have you considered that you are preparing souls for eternal happiness or everlasting misery?"[11]

The theory of the teacher as missionary was not confined to the spiritual domain. Since the teacher was engaged in the great task of preparing souls for eternity, it was hardly fitting that he should tarry to quibble about material considerations. Who is fit to be a teacher?

10. Ohio Teachers Association, *A History of Education in the State of Ohio, A Centennial Volume* (Columbus: Gazette Printing House, 1876), p. 380; *Wisconsin Journal of Education* (hereafter *WJE*) 1 (September 1856): 200. The status of the frontier teacher is considered more fully in Lloyd P. Jorgenson, *The Founding of Public Education in Wisconsin* (Madison: State Historical Society of Wisconsin, 1856), chap. 9.

11. *WJE* 5 (February 1861): 243; 7 (July 1862): 27; 9 (September 1864): 78–79.

"Not they, surely, who look for their reward here. They only who look to see the clay statues their unskilled hands wrought, transformed to angels of light by the touch of the invisible hand of God." "One who teaches merely for money does not deserve the name of teacher," declared a resolution adopted by a county teachers' association. Members of another county teachers' association, after hearing an address titled "Look Up! for Heaven's Above," went home "enabled better to bear the toils and perplexities of this grand calling, and content to look away beyond the visible horizon of the earth for that reward—infinitely transcending in value any pecuniary return—which always comes to him who labors for the benefit of his fellow men, and who is a co-worker with the good and true of every age and clime, in the grand office of elevating the human race."[12]

Clearly, evangelical Protestantism was more than a theory in the common school classroom at midcentury. But there was of course a caveat attached to the schoolmen's faith in the redemptive power of education, and it was that religion must be a part of the school program. On no subject did Horace Mann lavish more attention. In his final report as secretary of the Massachusetts Board of Education, he devoted forty-six pages to the subject. He forcefully rejected any notion of "secular" or "un-Christian" or "non-Christian" schools. "I do not suppose a man can be found in Massachusetts, who would declare such a system to be his first choice." He rejoiced that, as he ended his work in Massachusetts, there was not, to his knowledge, "a single town in the state" where the Bible was not in use. He affirmed again his belief in the formula of Bible reading without comments, because this "allows it [the Bible] to do what it is allowed to do in no other system—*to speak for itself.*"[13] Bible reading was seen by the leaders of the Common School Movement as the centerpiece of the schools' instructional programs, a source of cohesiveness and strength. As we shall see in following chapters, it soon became instead the most divisive feature of the movement.

Clergymen as Textbook Writers and Editors

By the time that Horace Mann began his work, the religious content of textbooks was to a large extent "non-sectarian," in the sense that it was acceptable to most Protestants. But passages offensive to Catholics were liberally sprinkled throughout many of the most widely used schoolbooks of the period. Professor Elson, in her excellent study, makes (although she does not document) a sobering state-

---

12. *WJE* 9 (September 1864): 78–79; 3 (April 1859): 308; 3 (October 1858): 127; 4 (March 1860): 293–96.
13. *Twelfth Annual Report*, pp. 117, 121, 124. Italics in original.

ment: "No theme in these schoolbooks before 1870 is more universal than anti-Catholicism."[14] That the Roman Church supported absolutist government to the detriment of the common people, that its policy was to keep the masses in ignorance, that it forbade its members to read the Bible, that the French and Spanish explorers were motivated by avarice and cruelty while the English sought to convert and civilize those whom they found in darkness—such assertions were common in antebellum textbooks, especially in readers, histories, and geographies.[15]

Clergymen were fully as active in the writing of textbooks as in providing leadership for the Common School Movement itself. Often they carried into their writing the same anti-Catholic themes they expounded in their pulpits, but they were not alone in this. Some clerics published books that were relatively free from bias; some laymen produced works that were flagrantly offensive.[16]

Most famous of all nineteenth-century schoolbooks were the *Readers* by Rev. William Holmes McGuffey, concerning which Lyman Beecher wrote in an introduction to the *Newly Revised Fourth Reader*: "They are excellent for educational purposes—their morality the morality of the Gospel." To a greater degree than most textbook writers, McGuffey succeeded in avoiding sectarianism, although his books were suffused with the ideals of a rural, Protestant America.[17] While McGuffey permitted no overt sectarianism in his textbooks, the same was not true of his brother, Alexander McGuffey, a layman, who

14. Ruth Miller Elson, *Guardians of Tradition: American Schoolbooks of the Nineteenth Century* (Lincoln: University of Nebraska Press, 1964), p. 53. Although greatly intensified by the nativist crusade, the theme of anti-Catholicism was by no means new. An edition of the revered *New England Primer* published in Boston in 1727 contained a crude woodcut of a baleful figure captioned "The POPE, or Man of SIN."

15. Marie Leonore Fell proposed to determine the extent to which expressions of nativism in the textbooks "laid the foundations of the anti-Catholic and anti-foreign attitudes of the period" (*The Foundations of Nativism in American Textbooks, 1783–1860* [Washington, D.C.: Catholic University of America Press, 1941], p. vi). Her assumption that nativistic sentiment in textbooks was a cause rather than an effect is, of course, questionable, but her collection of sources on this subject remains valuable.

16. The titles and dates of publication cited in this section follow the information provided in the Library of Congress catalog of printed cards. A limited amount of additional information may be found in O. A. Roorback, *Catalog of American Publications, including Reprints and Original Works, from 1820–1850* (New York: Peter Smith, 1938); James Kelly, *The American Catalog of Books* (New York: Peter Smith, 1938); and Ralph R. Shaw and Richard S. Shoemaker, *American Bibliography* (New York: Scarecrow Press, 1961). Data on the publishers and places of publication are provided in the above works.

17. The best brief interpretations of the readers are Henry Steele Commager's foreword to *McGuffey's Sixth Eclectic Reader*, 1879 ed. (New York: New American Library of World Literature, 1963), and Lewis Atherton, *Main Street on the Middle Border* (Bloomington: University of Indiana Press, 1954), chap. 3. Richard D. Mosier, *Making the American Mind* (New York: King's Crown Press, 1947), contains some further insights into the social and political views expressed in the *Readers*.

prepared the *Fifth Reader*. Among the selections in this reader was one that described Franciscan friars as persons "who eat the bread of other people's, and have no plan in life but to get through it in sloth and ignorance, *for the love of God.*" And, as was common in textbooks of the time, the Spanish policies of colonization were caustically attacked. "Never in the history of the world had the 'accursed hunger for gold' exhibited itself with such fearful strength," said Alexander McGuffey in the 1844 version of his *Rhetorical Guide or Fifth Reader*. Similar charges were aired in his 1860 *New Juvenile Speaker*.

Other books of the "reader" type, widely used in their day, have been almost forgotten because they came to be overshadowed by the McGuffey works. Rev. Samuel Willard's *Franklin Primer* was published in several versions, beginning in 1803. His *General Class-Book* appeared in 1828, followed by the *Secondary Lessons, or the Improved Reader* in 1827 and *The Popular Reader* in 1834. In his *The Common Reader* (1818), Rev. Titus Strong deplored the "atrocities committed by the Spaniards" and assured his youthful readers that the English settlers "were actuated by better and more exalted motives." One of the most popular of the pre-McGuffey volumes was *The Rhetorical Reader*, first published in 1831, written by Rev. Ebenezer Porter, a professor in a Massachusetts theological seminary. The eighteenth edition was reached by 1836. The series of readers by Rev. John Pierpont appeared in 1823; the thirty-fifth edition was published in New York in 1835, and later editions were printed in Philadelphia.

William C. Fowler's *The Common School Speaker* (1844) contained several selections written by clergymen. One of them, by a "Reverend Doctor Peck," explained "The Inhumanity of Romanism." Another, by Rev. William Alger, described immigrants as a "naked mass of unkempt and priest-ridden degradation." Rev. Horace Bushnell contributed a section on "The Common School as an American Institution," which made it clear that the Catholic school was not such an institution. Fowle himself wrote for the book a selection contrasting Protestant and Catholic views on "The Bible in Our Common Schools" and a poem titled "The Priest Outwitted." Fowle also prepared textbooks on several other subjects. Rev. George B. Cheever published readers in 1829 and 1831, in addition to his numerous writings on political, literary, and religious subjects. Cheever's commencement address at Dartmouth College in 1842 was in large part devoted to an attack upon Romanism, and he developed this point of view more fully in 1859 in his volume *The Right of the Bible in the Public Schools*. The *Eclectic Reader* and the *Introduction to the Eclectic Reader* by Rev. B. B. Edwards both appeared in 1833. Calvin H. Wiley, first superintendent of common schools in North Carolina and licensed as a minister in 1855, compiled in 1851 his *North Carolina Reader*; another version appeared in 1859.

Lindley Murray, whose grammars completely dominated the field during the early decades of the century, was a recorded minister of the Society of Friends. The first American edition of his *English Grammar* (published first in England, where his works had already gained wide acceptance) appeared in 1800; there were numerous later editions. *The English Reader: or, Pieces in Prose and Poetry* was in its fourteenth edition by 1817, and there were at least seventeen reprintings thereafter. At least twelve other titles, not including his numerous religious works, appeared in this country. Even after his death in 1826, Murray's *English Grammar Revised and Simplified* had widespread use; the fifty-seventh edition was published in 1851. By 1850, Rev. Peter Bullions's grammars provided strong competition for Murray's works; in 1862 the thirty-fifth edition of his *Principles of English Grammar* was published. Nathan W. Fiske, author of the *New England Spelling-Book* (1803), was a clergyman, as was John Comly, whose spellers, readers, and grammars were many times revised or reprinted. William C. Fowler was the author of the widely used *English Grammar*, which first appeared in 1851. He was the author also of *Common School Grammar* and of *Elementary Grammar, Etymology and Syntax*.

Jedediah Morse, "father of the study of geography" in the common schools, was for more than thirty years pastor of the First Church (Congregational) in Charlestown, Massachusetts. His pioneering *Geography Made Easy* (1784) was followed by *The American Universal Geography* (1789), *Elements of Geography* (1795), *The American Gazetteer* (1797), and many other works. Several editions of each followed. These works, which brought the subject of geography into the common school curriculum, were saturated with anti-Catholicism. The conversion of the natives of Paraguay by Jesuits, said Morse, was "an exchange not much for the better." Catholicism in Spain was "of the most bigoted, superstitious and tyrannical character." In Germany, "The Protestant clergy are learned and exemplary in their deportment, the popish ignorant and libertine." In Poland, "The popish clergy are said to be in general, illiterate bigots; and the monks the most profligate of mankind." The Jesuits are guilty of falsehood and duplicity. The (British) Quebec Act of 1774 was unfortunate because it permitted the popish clergy to exact their "accustomed dues" from the faithful.[18] In 1823 Jedediah Morse and his two sons launched *The Observer*; virulently anti-Catholic, it soon became one of the leading

18. *Geography Made Easy*, 1784 ed., p. 134; 1790 ed., pp. 268, 166, 172, 106, 92–93.

Protestant journals of its day. One of the sons, Samuel F. B. Morse, later hailed by some as the inventor of the telegraph, played a major role in the development of the theory that a Catholic conquest of the United States was imminent. This thesis was developed in twelve essays, published also in book form in 1834 under the title *A Foreign Conspiracy Against the Liberties of the United States.*

Scarcely less productive than Morse as an author of geography books was Rev. William C. Woodbridge. Although he served occasionally in his capacity as a licensed minister, Woodbridge devoted most of his attention to educational activities. Beyond doubt his most significant work was his editorship during the period 1831–1838 of the most important educational journal of its time, the *American Annals of Education and Instruction*. In spite of his accomplishments as a scholar, Woodbridge shared the prevailing Protestant views about Catholicism and Catholics. The people of southern Europe, he informed his young readers, "are generally indolent, and are less virtuous and less distinguished for learning and improvements, than other nations of Europe." "In the central and northwestern countries of Europe," on the other hand, "where the Bible is best known, and Christianity most pure," justice and kindness prevail.[19] This distinction was clear enough, and was accepted by most textbook writers of the time, but sometimes it seemed rather hard to maintain. In Catholic countries, Woodbridge said, "The progress of philosophy and natural science has been checked by the prevailing superstition." But two pages later, inadvertently perhaps, he declared that France had been "distinguished, for many years, in scientific discoveries." Likewise in the case of Germany, the facts did not always seem to fit into his initial categories. "The Protestant States of Germany are distinguished from the Catholic by the superior education of the people," he averred. But in Bavaria (which Woodbridge must have known to be predominantly Catholic), "schools, academies, and colleges have been multiplied . . . and the youth of both sexes are carefully educated." Protestant missionaries had conferred lasting benefits on primitive peoples, said Woodbridge, because they had "uniformly carried the Scriptures to those whom they designed to instruct." Catholic missionaries, on the other hand, while they had built many churches, had "usually neglected or forbidden the use of the Scriptures." While Woodbridge's treatment of Catholic peoples and activities was consistently unfavorable, he was ready to attack ignorance wherever he saw it. "Mahometans," he explained, "are those who believe in the Koran, or sacred book of Mahomet, an Arabian

19. *Rudiments of Geography on a New Plan* (1828), p. 122.

imposter, who lived 600 years after Christ, and pretended to be inspired."[20]

As with the readers, many geography books, although for a time extensively used, were overshadowed by the works of Morse and Woodbridge. Rev. Nathaniel Dwight's *A Short but Comprehensive System of Geography of the World* appeared in 1795 and was followed by several later editions. Rev. John Smith's *A New Compend of Geography* appeared in 1816, and the fourth edition of Rev. Silas Blaisdale's *Primary Lessons in Geography: Consisting of Questions Adapted to Worcester's and Woodbridge's Atlases* was published in 1832. Rev. John C. Rudd's geography book apparently met with limited success, but one of Rev. Elijah Parish's three geographies went into a second printing.

Among the most prolific authors of nineteenth-century history and geography schoolbooks were two brothers, members of a prominent New England family of divines. One of them, Rev. Charles Augustus Goodrich, published in 1822 *A History of the United States of America*; by 1847, one hundred fifty editions had been printed. His *A Child's History of the United States* was also popular, and he prepared several other books. Impressive as this record was, it was surpassed, at least in volume, by the work of his brother, Samuel G. Goodrich, a layman, author (or compiler) of the famous Peter Parley books, the first of which appeared in 1827. In his *Recollections*, completed in 1856, four years before his death, Samuel Goodrich claimed authorship or editorship of about one hundred seventy volumes, with sales of about seven million copies.[21]

This almost staggering record of publication was achieved by the extensive use of compilers and the development of a method almost resembling an assembly line. It is known that Nathaniel Hawthorne compiled one of the Peter Parley books, but many of the other assistants were men of lesser stature. While the books of Charles Goodrich were in the main judicious and scholarly in tone, those of his brother were often marred by severe bias. In a section on "Rome under the Popes," Samuel Goodrich declared, "No other tyranny had ever been like theirs for they tyrannized over the souls of men." Abbeys and monasteries, he continued, were "seats of voluptuousness" where monks and nuns, "while they pretended to be engaged in religious duties, screened from the eyes of the world, often gave themselves up to luxurious pleasures."[22]

20. *A System of Modern Geography, on the Principles of Comparison and Classification* (1824), pp. 183–84, 188, 190, 192–93.

21. *Recollections of a Lifetime, or Men and Things I Have Seen . . .*, 2 vols. (New York: Miller, Orton and Co., 1857), 2:537.

22. *Peter Parley's Common School History* (1838), p. 187. See also his *A Comprehensive Geography and History, Ancient and Modern* (1853), pp. 165, 183, 185, 202.

The histories and geographies of Rev. John Blake abounded in anti-Catholic sentiment. The crusades were characterized as a "wild enterprise" initiated by "the zeal of a fanatic monk." The pope was an usurper, who pretended to pardon people who had sinned, and the Jesuits were unscrupulous, anti-Christian, and bent on personal aggrandizement. In a geography textbook, Blake explained that the cost of building St. Peter's was staggering: "It would take a person from the age of twenty-one to the age of seventy years, to count over this enormous sum, provided he counted three thousand dollars an hour, and was employed twelve hours in the day for the whole time."[23]

Rev. Fred W. Butler stated frankly in the introduction to one of his books that his "first object through the whole work" was "to contrast particularly the religion of Christ and his apostles, with the religion of the Popes and Mahomet." In another book he examined the morals and manners of the popes:

Q. What has been their [the popes'] general moral character?
A. Corrupt in the extreme; practising and tolerating all the vices, and the blackest crimes . . . .
Q. Have they generally died suddenly?
A. Yes; and very often by violence.[24]

Rev. Samuel R. Hall, principal of the first normal school and author of the famous *Lectures on School Keeping* (1827 and six later editions), was also author of *Geography and History of Vermont* and *The Child's Book of Geography* (1831). Rev. Royal Robbins was the author of *Outlines of Ancient and Modern History*, of which the eighth edition was published in 1839.

Large-scale Catholic immigration into the United States did not begin until the Common School Movement was well underway, and the appearance of Catholic textbooks on any sizable scale did not occur until the William H. Sadlier Company of New York began publication of its extensive line of *Excelsior* schoolbooks in 1875. Catholic books did not contain the frenetic assaults on differing religious beliefs so often found in Protestant texts, although they were not wholly silent on the question. The *Excelsior Geography* asserted, "There can be but one true religion . . .," although it conceded a few lines later, "Christians comprise Catholics, Greek Schismatics (siz-mat-iks), and Protestants," a concession that many Protestants of the day would have contested. In a stronger statement, the author declared, "England abandoned the Catholic faith in the 16th century, and to this

23. *The Historical Reader*, 1825 ed., pp. 122–26; 1823 ed., pp. 131, 228–29; *A Geography for Children* (1831), p. 60.

24. *Sketches of Universal History, Sacred and Profane from the Creation of the World to the Year 1818, of the Christian Era* (1821), p. iv; *The Catechitical Compound of General History Sacred and Profane* (1819), p. 118.

country belongs the ignoble distinction of having oppressed and persecuted the Irish nation with a barbarity unparalleled in the history of
man's inhumanity to man."[25]

Clergymen as Editors

A large number of educational journals, many of them short-lived,
appeared during the time of the Common School Movement, and
many (including all of those listed here) were edited by clergymen.
W. C. Woodbridge's greatest work, as noted earlier, was as editor of
the *American Annals of Education and Instruction and Journal of Literary
Institutions* (1831–1838). But he was also editor of *The School Magazine*
(1829) and of the *Reporter and Journal of Education* (1831), both published in Boston. Benjamin O. Peers was editor of the *Eclectic Institute
of Education* (1832) of Lexington, Kentucky. The *Common School Advocate* (1837) of Jacksonville, Illinois, was edited by Theron Baldwin.
John D. Pierce, as Michigan state superintendent of public instruction, served also as editor of the *Journal of Education* (1838–1840).
Samuel Lewis, who held the same position in Ohio, edited the *Ohio
Common School Director*. As president of the Ohio State Teachers' Association (1855–1861), Anson Smyth edited its organ, the *Journal of
Education*. J. B. Pradt was for a time editor of the *Wisconsin Journal of
Education*. W. H. Campbell served as editor of the *District School Journal for the State of New York*. Asa D. Lord founded the *Ohio School
Journal* in 1846 and served as its editor for four years. Merrill Richardson served as editor of the *Connecticut Common School Manual* for its
first two years of existence (1847–1848). D. R. McAnally and Thomas
MacIntire served as editors of the *Southwestern School Journal* of Tennessee (1848–1849). *The Southern School Journal* was established early
in 1853 by T. F. Scott. Later that year it was adopted as the official
organ of the Georgia State Teachers' Association, which appointed a
committee of editors, most of them ministers.

J. M. Gregory was first editor of the *Michigan Journal of Education*
(1854–1861). Robert Allyn, state school commissioner of Rhode Island, was the first editor of the *Rhode Island Schoolmaster*. Absalom
Peters served with Henry Barnard as co-editor of the first two volumes (1855–1857) of the *American Journal of Education and College Review*. The *Journal of Education* was established by N. E. Gage in 1857;
after one year the *Journal* was taken over by the New Hampshire State
Teachers' Association. S. S. Howe was editor of the *Literary Advertiser
and Public School Advocate* (1859–1860) of Iowa. Samuel Findley was

---

25. *Sadlier's Excelsior Geography Number Two . . . By a Catholic Teacher* (New York:
William H. Sadlier, 1875), pp. 12, 76. The *Excelsior Geographies* went through many
revisions, the latest, apparently, in 1924.

first editor of *The Educator* (1859), which two years later became the *Pennsylvania Teacher*.

An interesting analysis by Professor Davis reveals that 36 percent of the material published in educational journals during the time of the Common School Movement (which Davis defines as the years 1825–1855) was contributed by clergymen, and the balance by public school, normal school, and college teachers. By contrast, during the decades 1870–1900, ministers contributed only 2 percent of the articles published in such journals.[26] The decline in the proportion of articles by clergymen (in comparing the periods 1825–1855 and 1870–1900) is a reflection primarily of the professionalization of the teaching corps. But it is doubtful that the influence of clergymen in public education dropped as precipitously as the figures compiled by Davis might suggest. As a corrective, it might be noted that about one-third of the contributors to Barnard's renowned *American Journal of Education*, published during the years 1855–1882, were ministers.[27]

Horace Mann and Henry Barnard had perceived from the start the dominant role of the Protestant clergy in the Common School Movement, but they could not fully foresee the consequences. No doubt reverberations from the Second Awakening and the nativist crusade would have been felt in the schools even if they had been under entirely lay leadership. As the clergy were deeply involved in all three movements, however, the penetration of the public school enterprise by sectarian and nativist ideologies was a foregone conclusion.

26. Sheldon Emmor Davis, *Educational Periodicals During the Nineteenth Century*, U.S. Bureau of Education *Bulletin*, no. 28, 1919, p. 51. Davis recognized that his categories were not mutually exclusive; a minister might be also a college teacher, etc. My identification of clergymen editors is also from Davis, pp. 92–102.

27. Richard Thursfield, *Henry Barnard's American Journal of Education* (Baltimore: Johns Hopkins University Press, 1945), p. 87.

5

The Know-Nothings and Education

The Know-Nothing Party

Although it remained intact in most other nations in the Western world, the long tradition of voluntary/public cooperation in education came to a dramatic end in the United States in the 1850s, a casualty of the Protestant-Catholic struggles that culminated in the Know-Nothing riots. In the absence of any federal warrant for denial of public funds to non-public schools (this point will be examined in the section on the Fourteenth Amendment, below), the campaigns to disinherit the non-public schools were waged at the state level. In state after state during the fifties, with Know-Nothing leaders in the forefront of the battles, state school officers and Protestant denominational bodies were able to obtain legislation denying public funds to non-public schools and requiring Bible reading in the public schools. There was no mistaking the motivation behind these campaigns; the leaders openly and boastfully made anti-Catholicism the dominant theme of their attacks. At the best, the campaigns were brutal; at the worst they begot violence and bloodshed. But they achieved their objectives. By the end of the fifties, the principle of denying public aid to non-public schools had been firmly established in almost all states. The die was now cast. It no longer aroused much attention, during the decades after the Civil War, when the remaining states outlawed public aid to church-related schools. Much later the disinheritance of the church-related schools, a doctrine largely born of bigotry at the state level, was transmuted by the U.S. Supreme Court into high constitutional principle.

The immediate cause of the bifurcation of education into public and private (very largely church-related) sectors, which developed so dramatically during the 1850s, was the inability to reach any agreement concerning the issues commonly referred to by Catholics as the "School Question"—primarily the nature of religious instruction in the common schools and the demands for public funds for non-public schools. By about 1840 these issues became more complicated because of the rapid growth of the Catholic population. More than seven hundred thousand Catholic immigrants entered the country

during the 1840s, tripling the Catholic population during that decade.[1]

Although the Know-Nothings and their sympathizers candidly
identified immigrants and Catholics as the targets of their attacks,
they could not frame their legislative proposals in such openly dis-
criminatory terms. So they approached their goals by indirection. The
proscription of public aid to "sectarian" schools was a widely employed method. Alternatively, the legislation could prescribe that
public funds could go only to schools organized under state school
law and under the control of legally specified civil authorities. Often a
given law would incorporate both of the above provisions. Obviously, either of these formulae would at once end the eligibility of
Catholic schools for public aid. But public schools, with their Protestant religious instruction, were considered to be, and were legally
defined as, "non-sectarian" institutions, and hence were untouched
by such legislation. Protestant denominational schools would also
lose their eligibility for public aid when such legislation was adopted,
but the main bodies of Protestantism had already given up their
schools in return for the assurance that religious exercises of a type
acceptable to them would be a part of public school programs.

The most drastic method of isolating the non-public schools came
in the form of compulsory attendance laws specifying that such attendance must be in state-approved schools. Not only the financial support but the very existence of non-public schools was placed in
jeopardy by these laws. Such proposals, rejected in Massachusetts in
1855, were vigorously promoted in the late eighties, and this was the
form of the law adopted in Oregon in 1922, but voided three years
later by the U.S. Supreme Court. Although Catholic schools were
avowedly the main target of such legislation, whatever its form, other
non-public schools as well, whether or not church-related, were
caught in the net.

The Know-Nothing Movement, the culmination of antebellum
nativism, appeared first in eastern cities where Roman Catholic immigrants had settled in large numbers. Local nativist societies combined
to form the American Republican party in New York in 1843. This
party spread into neighboring states as the American party, which
became a national organization at its convention in Philadelphia in
1845. Temporarily eclipsed by the Mexican War and the debates over
slavery, the party came to the fore again after the slavery question
was temporarily stilled by the Compromise of 1850. The movement
manifested itself locally through its many secret orders, chief among

1. Gerald B. Shaughnessy, *Has the Immigrant Kept the Faith?* (New York: Macmillan,
1925), p. 34.

them the Order of United Americans and the Order of the Star Spangled Banner. Efforts to learn about the leadership of these societies were often futile, as members responded to inquiries with the reply that they knew nothing. Hence members came to be called Know-Nothings, although there was never a political organization bearing that name. At a time when traditional American values seemed to be threatened by vast waves of immigration, the party promised to reinvigorate and preserve a homogenous Protestant culture. The principal means proposed for achieving this were to restrict elective offices to native-born Americans and to establish a twenty-five-year residency requirement for citizenship. But these goals proved to be unattainable and, in practice, the Know-Nothings and their sympathizers focused their efforts primarily on the School Question.

The party showed much strength in northern and border states, and in the fall of 1854 carried Massachusetts, Delaware, and, in combination with the Whigs, Pennsylvania. About seventy-five congressmen were sent to Washington that year pledged to do battle with the Pope and his minions. The following year Rhode Island, New Hampshire, Connecticut, Maryland, and Kentucky went solidly Know-Nothing, and Tennessee remained Democratic by a narrow margin. State officers elected in New York, Pennsylvania, and California were for the most part adherents to this new party. In the South, the Know-Nothings made tremendous strides in, but did not capture, Virginia, Georgia, Alabama, and Louisiana. Less impressive gains were made in other states.[2]

At the national level the party utterly failed to achieve its antiforeign and anti-Catholic goals. At no time did the Know-Nothings control either the House or the Senate, although for a time they held the balance of power between Republicans and Democrats. As a minority group the party needed the cooperation of either major party to secure its ends, and such cooperation was not forthcoming. Both major parties recognized that an attack upon Catholicism would alienate many fair-minded persons of native birth as well as foreigners and could also raise grave constitutional questions about interference with religious freedom. A running debate on Catholicism lasted through much of the thirty-fourth session of Congress, which assembled in December 1855, but no political action resulted from this. The resumption of the slavery debate, which had been resolved only tem-

2. Ray A. Billington, *The Protestant Crusade, 1800–1860: A Study of the Origins of American Nativism* (1938; rpt. New York: Macmillan, 1964), pp. 388–89. See also W. Darrell Overdyke, *The Know-Nothing Party in the South* (Baton Rouge: Louisiana State University Press, 1950). Carleton Beals, *Brass-Knuckle Crusade, The Great Know-Nothing Conspiracy: 1820–1860* (New York: Hastings House, 1960), dwells at length on the disorderly and violent aspects of the movement.

porarily by the Compromise of 1850, split the Know-Nothing Movement as it had earlier split the Whigs. The party lost all but one of the state elections it entered in 1856, and its dramatic but brief appearance on the national political scene was ended.[3]

At the state level, however, the Know-Nothing campaigns produced a major turning point in the development of American education. These campaigns firmly established the precedent that non-public schools are ineligible to receive public financial support. Equally productive of future controversy was the widespread appearance of state laws authorizing—or requiring—the reading of the Bible in the common schools. (In a nation as yet predominantly Protestant, the term *Bible reading* in the common schools, as used by public school authorities, always meant reading the King James version.) That the common schools were Protestant institutions had been a basic assumption of the Common School Movement since its origins. By 1850, however, with a rapidly increasing proportion of Catholic children, the time had come for testing the promise made by Horace Mann and others that the common schools would be able to accommodate children of all religious persuasions. Before we examine the state-level anti-Catholic campaigns of the fifties, we should survey briefly the Protestant-Catholic relationships in education prior to that time.

Catholic and Public Education Prior to 1850

The rather small number of Catholic schools established in the United States before 1840 did not in any real sense constitute a system, nor was there yet any clearly formulated Catholic policy on the subject. True, Bishop John Carroll of Baltimore, with jurisdiction over all Catholics in the United States, had published in 1792 a pastoral letter calling for "the virtuous and Christian education of youth," but this letter contained no reference to formal schooling. A decree of the First Provincial Council of Baltimore in 1829 called for the establishment of schools "in which the young may be taught the principles of faith and morality, while being instructed in letters," but it did not fix upon anyone the responsibility for carrying this provision into effect. Nor did the two pastoral letters issued by the council clarify this.[4]

By the time of the Fourth Provincial Council of Baltimore (1840) the anti-Catholic strain in the public school movement had become increasingly clear to Catholic leaders, and the pastoral letter issued by that council strongly criticized the Protestant bias and the widespread

3. Billington, *Crusade*, pp. 408–9.
4. Peter Guilday, ed., *The National Pastorals of the American Hierarchy* (Washington: Arno Press, 1923), pp. 3, 26.

use of the Protestant Bible in public school instructional programs. Even so, the council made no explicit recommendations for the establishment of a system of Catholic schools. Parochial (i.e., parish) responsibility for schools, which was later to become a Catholic principle, was not mentioned.[5] Nor was there any legislation regarding Catholic schools or attendance of Catholic children at public schools in the decrees of the Fifth (1843), Sixth (1846), and Seventh (1849) Provincial Councils of Baltimore.

Prior to the New York City school controversy of 1840–1842 (discussed below), Bishop John Hughes of New York had not formulated definite opinions on many aspects of the church-state question in education. "I am not conversant with the matter," he had stated quite frankly in a letter to Bishop Purcell.[6] When the initial controversy over public aid to church-related schools broke out in New York in 1840, therefore, the Catholic clergy had little to guide them in the task of establishing principles for Catholic schools.

Prior to 1840, there had been no strong Catholic protest against the Common School Movement.[7] On the contrary, many Catholic leaders were at first sympathetic to the movement and indeed participants in it. The *Catholic Telegraph* of Cincinnati, the voice of Catholics in the West, in 1837 printed an address by the Ohio state superintendent of common schools (a Protestant clergyman) asking for the improvement of existing public schools and the establishment of new ones. Two years later the editor of this paper published a highly favorable article on the public schools of Cincinnati. He commended the school trustees for their "wise policy" and exhorted his fellow Catholics, "As we have one country and one government, let us, as far as we can do so, have one people also." That these views had official approval is clear because Bishop (later Archbishop) John B. Purcell himself served as an "examiner" in the Cincinnati city schools in the early forties.[8]

Perhaps an even more significant example of early Protestant-Catholic cooperation in education was the experiment carried on for some

5. Austin Flynn, "The School Controversy in New York, 1840–1842, and Its Effects on the Formulation of Catholic Elementary School Policy" (Ph.D. diss., University of Notre Dame, 1962), pp. 28–29. For the policies formulated, see Peter K. Guilday, *A History of the Councils of Baltimore, 1791–1884* (New York: Macmillan, 1932); also Guilday, *National Pastorals*, pp. 132–34.

6. John R. G. Hassard, *Life of the Most Reverend John Hughes, D.D.* (New York: D. Appleton & Company, 1866), p. 176.

7. Perhaps the most notable exception was Rev. Demetrius A. Gallitzin of Pennsylvania, who from the outset opposed public sponsorship of education. Peter H. Lemcke, *Life and Work of Prince Demetrius Augustine Gallitzin*, trans. Joseph C. Plumpe (New York: Longmans, Green, 1940), pp. 207–10.

8. *Catholic Telegraph*, 6 July 1837; 1 October 1839; John B. Shotwell, *A History of the Schools of Cincinnati* (Cincinnati: The School Life Co., 1902), p. 446.

years in Lowell, Massachusetts. In 1835 the public school committee (board) of Lowell, upon application by the Catholic authorities, incorporated into the town system two Catholic schools. The agreement specified that the teachers of these Catholic schools were to be examined and appointed by the public school committee; that the books and studies were to be those prescribed by the committee, and none other; and that the schools were to be subject to the inspection and control of the committee, in precisely the same manner as public schools. It was understood that Catholics were to be appointed as teachers in these schools, and that no books or exercises were to be used that would be offensive to Catholics. For some years the plan apparently worked very well. The school committee reported, after a few months, that the plan was "eminently successful," and in 1837 the mayor of Lowell acclaimed the schools as "public nurseries of intelligence, freedom, good order, and religion." By 1840 one secondary and five primary Catholic public schools in Lowell were conducted on this plan.[9] But events that were to spell the death knell for such cooperative ventures were fast approaching.

The New York Controversy, 1840–1842

The first major confrontation over the School Question, and a harbinger of things to come, began in New York City in 1840 and ended in the state legislature in 1842.[10] Catholics in New York City, led by their bishop, John Hughes, had been seeking public aid for their schools. They requested some portion of the state funds then received almost entirely by the voluntary New York Public School Society, whose schools constituted, to all intents and purposes, the city's "public" school system. The religious instruction in the society's schools was of the Protestant non-sectarian type widely favored by common school leaders but unacceptable to Catholics.

In 1840 Gov. W. W. Seward of New York State proposed that schools in which pupils would be taught by teachers of their own faith should receive financial aid from the state. Encouraged by this, New York City Catholics sought such aid from the city's Common Council, which was the disbursing agent for state-provided funds. After prolonged and stormy debates in which several Protestant ministers were arrayed against Bishop Hughes, the Catholic request was denied by the council. In 1841, the Catholics carried their case to the

9. Sherman M. Smith, *The Relation of the State to Religious Education in Massachusetts* (Syracuse, N.Y.: University Book Store, 1926), p. 195; Louis F. Walsh, *The Early Catholic Schools of Lowell, Massachusetts* (Lowell, Mass.: Daily News for Job Print, 1901), pp. 10ff.

10. The most comprehensive account is Vincent P. Lannie, *Public Money and Parochial Education: Bishop Hughes, Governor Seward, and the New York School Controversy* (Cleveland: Case Western Reserve University, 1968).

New York State legislature, where again anti-Catholic rhetoric was voiced. These arguments were waged in the press as well, and the legislature deferred its decision.

Finally, in 1842, the legislature enacted the Maclay Law, establishing a public New York City Board of Education to carry on the functions previously exercised by the essentially voluntary Public School Society. The Maclay Law provided that "no school . . . in which any religious sectarian doctrine or tenet shall be taught, inculcated or practiced, shall receive any portion of the school moneys to be distributed as hereinafter provided . . . ." The prohibition was continued, although the wording was changed, in an act two years later.[11]

Although the Maclay Law resulted in the removal of many overly zealous Protestant teachers from the city schools, it also had the effect of promoting secularization of the schools. It was, therefore, from the Catholic point of view, a mixed blessing. Moreover, although the law forbade sectarian instruction, it did not define the meaning of this term. There now came to be petitions against the use of the Protestant Bible in some of the wards of the New York City schools. The state superintendent of common schools expressed the view that the reading of the Bible should be made mandatory in all public schools of the state. In 1844, an amendment to the Maclay Law was passed, forbidding boards of education to exclude the reading of the Scriptures from the schools. This strengthened Hughes's growing conviction that Catholic children should attend only Catholic schools, and the decade of the 1840s witnessed the beginnings of an organized Catholic school system in the diocese of New York.[12] The Protestant majority in New York succeeded, therefore, in achieving its two major objectives—the denial of public aid to the Catholic schools and legal sanction for Bible reading in the public schools—and did so a decade before the Know-Nothing party came into existence. But the Know-Nothings, when they arrived on the scene, were shrewd enough to see that the School Question was a rich field for further political exploitation.

Although the Protestant victory in New York was decisive, one feature of the development gained scant attention at the time, and even less later as the Catholic-Protestant confrontations increased in intensity. Even during the heat of the controversy, the possibility of compromise was at least considered by both Catholics and Protestants. Under the direction of Bishop Hughes, and before the Maclay Law was passed, the Catholic interests presented to the Common

11. 65th session, chap. 150, sect. 14, act of 11 April 1842; 67th session, chap. 230, sect. 12, act of 7 May 1844.
12. Flynn, "The School Controversy," pp. 123, 167.

Council a proposal similar in many respects to the one adopted in Lowell, Massachusetts, a few years earlier. According to the Catholic petition, teachers and textbooks for the Catholic schools would be selected by the managers of these schools, but these managers in turn would be subject to the supervision of a committee of the Public School Society. Moreover, "every specified requirement of any and every law passed by the legislature of the State, or the Ordinance of the Common Council to guard against abuse in the matter of common school education, shall be rigidly enforced and exacted by the competent public authorities . . . ."[13] The trustees of the Public School Society, on their side, offered to remove from the textbooks used in the schools of their society all matters that might be regarded as offensive by Roman Catholics. Although these petitions seemed to indicate that the views of the respective groups were not far apart, a plan of cooperation was never reached. No doubt the bitterness engendered since the beginning of the controversy had destroyed the mutual understanding necessary for reaching any agreement.

The Philadelphia Bible Riots of 1844

The divergence between Protestant and Catholic viewpoints on education and the widespread and angry public rejection of the latter came into even sharper focus during the Philadelphia Bible Riots. There were few Catholic schools in the diocese of Philadelphia when the young Francis Kenrick came there in 1830 as coadjuter bishop to the aging Henry Conwell. From the beginning, Kenrick attached high priority to the establishment of such schools, but the obstacles were formidable. Immigration was rapidly swelling the number of Catholics, and the economic means of the newcomers enabled them to secure little beyond necessities. Even Kenrick's search for Catholic teachers, lay or religious, proved discouraging. Like it or not, the Catholics were dependent upon the public schools.[14]

In 1834 the Pennsylvania legislature had passed a Free School Act. School districts that elected to comply with the 1834 act were to receive allocations from the state school fund, and Philadelphia elected to do this. The 1834 Pennsylvania school law did not mention religious instruction in the schools, but most schools, the Philadelphia schools included, opened their day with the reading of a portion of

13. Oland W. Bourne, *History of the Public School Society of the City of New York* (New York: William Wood Company, 1870), pp. 320–21.
14. Vincent P. Lannie and Bernard C. Diethorn, "For the Honor and Glory of God: The Philadelphia Bible Riots of 1844," *History of Education Quarterly* 8 (Spring 1968): 45. In the original article, the date in the title was misprinted as 1840. This was corrected to 1844 in the next (Summer) issue, p. 272.

the King James version. Bishop Kenrick and his coreligionists, whatever their real views might have been, entered no formal objection to
this practice.

In 1838, however, the Pennsylvania legislature enacted a school
law stipulating that the "Old and New Testaments . . . shall be used
as a school book for Reading, without comment by the teacher, but
not as a textbook for religious discussion." Bible reading by the teacher as a part of the opening exercises was one thing; Bible reading by
the students as a required part of the instructional program was quite
another matter. No specific version of the Bible was stipulated in the
law, but Catholics and Protestants alike understood that the King
James version was intended. Now objections appeared, and the principal complainant was one (probably Bishop Kenrick himself) who
wrote letters to the *Catholic Herald* under the pseudonym "Sentinel."
Sentinel objected to the new legislation forcing Catholic children to
use the King James Bible as a textbook in reading. He warned that
efforts were underway to introduce into the public schools Sarah
Hall's *Conversations on the Bible*, a book published by the Presbyterian-
controlled Sunday School Union. If such conditions should continue,
said Sentinel, he would favor the separation of religion from education, "unnatural" though that might be. It was a view he was to
reiterate many times. Sentinel also asserted that the so-called non-
sectarianism of the public schools was in fact sectarianism and therefore a violation of the state law. "It is founded on a Protestant principle, and the books, even if free from direct invective against Catholics, which is not often the case, are all of a Protestant complexion."
He went so far as to urge Catholic parents to remove their children
from public schools that used the Bible as a textbook. Protestant
spokesmen replied with equal vigor.[15]

As the Philadelphia controversy was gathering strength, the New
York contest was moving toward its climax. Philadelphia Protestants
and Catholics alike watched the New York controversy intently and
in relative silence for several months. That restraint was in part a
result of Kenrick's admonitions on the need for patience and caution.
Not all Catholics, however, shared this view. Early in 1842, a letter to
the *Catholic Herald* urged every Catholic congregation to appoint delegates to a committee that was to approach the legislature for amendments to the existing school law, and even to organize public demonstrations to dramatize their cause. Sentinel sharply disagreed, no
doubt remembering that Hughes's effort to exert political pressure on
the New York legislature a few months earlier had only stiffened

15. Ibid., pp. 46–51.

public sentiment against Catholics. The wiser course, said Sentinel, was to insist upon evenhanded administration of the existing law against any sectarianism in the schools.

A number of events in Philadelphia in 1842 kept tension alive. In April a teacher who had served for six years was dismissed by a local ward school board for refusing to read from the King James version to her students. The City Board of Controllers refused to intervene. One child was whipped before his class for refusing to read from the Protestant Bible. Others were kept after school as punishment. Another child was reprimanded for bringing the Douay Bible (an English version of the Bible translated from the Latin Vulgate edition for the use of Roman Catholics) to class. Protestant citizens were urged to vote only for Protestant school commissioners and directors as a means of keeping the Bible in the schools.

Finally, in November 1842, Bishop Kenrick submitted to the Board of Controllers a letter detailing the complaints of Catholics, as he saw them: the required use of a Protestant version of the Bible, Protestant hymns and prayers, anti-Catholic passages in textbooks and library books, and the general Protestant orientation of the schools. He did not urge the exclusion of the King James Bible from the public schools, as nativists claimed. He asked that the Catholic Bible be used by Catholic children and the Protestant Bible by Protestant children. He reminded the board of the provision in the school law specifying that "the religious predilections of the parents shall be respected," and he noted also that Baltimore had already granted Catholic children the right to use the Catholic Bible in the public schools. The board responded in January 1843 by adopting two resolutions: that children whose parents objected would not be required to attend or unite in any Bible reading exercises, and that children might use any version of the Bible "without note or comment."[16]

Kenrick was pleased that Catholic children would not be compelled to read from the King James version but disappointed that they would not be permitted to use the Douay version because it contained "notes and comments," as required by Catholic principles. Even so, he saw the board's resolutions as an effort to compromise, tendered in good faith. Protestants, generally, saw it very differently, and a storm now broke over both Kenrick and the board. Catholics had plotted to undermine republican institutions, declared Protestant spokesmen, and the board had capitulated. Some Protestant newspapers were now pressed to the point of openly claiming the public schools as their own. Historically, said the *North American*, the public schools had been "planned by Protestants, directed by Protestants,

16. Ibid., pp. 52–57.

and almost wholly supported by Protestants." The *Presbyterian* explained, "Protestants founded these schools, and they have always been in the majority"; their views should therefore prevail. The *Baptist Record* compared Kenrick's demands for "removal of the Bible" to similar demands made earlier by the Deists. The *Episcopal Recorder* printed an address by Rev. B. Cheever, a well-known "no popery" lecturer, warning that the Christian institutions of the country would disappear forever if the demands of the Catholics were heeded. A secular journal, the *Literary Age* (Philadelphia), pronounced a plague on both religious houses.[17]

During the year following the appearance of Kenrick's letter and the board's resolutions, two anti-Catholic associations were founded in Philadelphia. The American Protestant Association's membership consisted of some eighty ministers representing every Protestant denomination in the city. The American Republican Association, anticipating the Know-Nothing platforms, urged a twenty-one-year residency requirement for all foreigners seeking citizenship and the exclusion of naturalized citizens from all public offices. The constitutions of both associations contained a catalog of Romanist sins. Both of these associations kept the Bible issue before the public by means of lectures, pulpit oratory, and the press. A widely known Congregationalist minister aided these efforts by delivering his lecture on "The Bible in Our Public Schools" in churches of several denominations. In pamphlet form, his lecture, which held up to ridicule the views of Bishop Kenrick and of the Catholic church, was presented free of charge to every public school teacher in the city.[18]

Early in 1844, a Catholic public school director (board member) in the Kensington district was accused of ordering a school principal to stop reading the Protestant Bible to her pupils. The Kensington school committee cleared the director of any wrongdoing, but reaffirmed the right of teachers and principals to include Bible reading in the daily opening exercises. At the same time, said the committee, following the Board of Controllers' directive of 23 January, children might be excused from such exercises if their parents so requested. Again the Protestant press erupted with indignation. The removal of the Bible from the schools would convert them into "infidel" institutions, said the *Presbyterian*. If this should happen, "The sooner the whole system is levelled to the dust, the better for the common weal." Several public meetings were held to "save the Bible" in the schools. Early in March 1844 a crowd of about six thousand people gathered at Independence Square in Kensington. A petition to the legislature

17. Ibid., pp. 59–60.
18. Ibid., pp. 61–64.

designed to assure Protestant control of the schools (by direct election of school officials) was adopted.

At its next monthly meeting, the Philadelphia Board of Controllers voted to reaffirm its requirement of Bible reading "without note or comment" and its authorization to excuse those who could not in conscience attend such observances. In effect, therefore, the Douay version remained under the ban, and Catholic children in public schools would receive only a secular education. Kenrick repeated his view that this was not satisfactory, but that it was better than a Protestant education.

A few days after the board meeting, three thousand members of the American Republican Association, calling themselves Native Americans, met in Independence Square, again to protest against the "removal of the Bible from the schools." Several speakers linked Kenrick's activities in Philadelphia with Hughes's agitation in New York, implying that a Catholic conspiracy was at work. They warned that they would not permit Catholics "to trample our free Protestant institutions in the dust" and called upon the board to protect the rightful place of the Bible in the schools. The board tried to explain its position in its *Annual Report* of 1844 by declaring that it had never contemplated removing the Bible from the schools, but that instead it had made determined efforts to keep sectarian practices out of the schools and to ensure religious liberty for all as guaranteed by the state constitution. Such an answer, while probably all the board could do, was less than satisfactory to Catholics and wholly unacceptable to Protestants.

Some Protestants harbored fears that went beyond their hostility to Catholicism and the Douay Bible. Would it do to let children believe that there are two Bibles? Would not reading from two versions produce confusion and disorder in Bible reading exercises? And would not the inevitable result be the exclusion of Bible reading from any version? Then the public schools would indeed be infidel institutions. Should this ever happen, warned the *Presbyterian* again, it would be better to destroy public education and return to sectarian schools.[19]

Any possibility of retreat by either side was now remote. The Philadelphia Board of Controllers had offered a compromise that made some concessions in both directions, but both protagonists viewed the concessions as capitulation. Tensions were high, and any incident could provoke violence. Kensington, adjacent to Philadelphia, was a working-class district where Catholic and Protestant laborers lived side by side. Catholics had warned nativists that there would be trouble if they tried to hold a meeting in Kensington. Armed with

19. Ibid., pp. 65–72.

clubs, Catholics dispersed such a meeting on 3 May 1844. The nativists regrouped and three days later assembled there for another meeting. Suddenly a shot was fired, and then another. The meeting ended and battle ensued between Catholics and nativists. Outnumbered, the nativists withdrew, but soon returned strengthened in numbers and arms. After an hour of bitter conflict, Catholics sought cover, but fighting continued intermittently through the night, and the first fatal casualties of the struggle ensued. A Protestant boy about eighteen years of age, George Schiffler, was shot to death and immediately became a "martyr" who had shed his blood "defending the American flag." When the nativists tried to burn a Catholic schoolhouse, shots from neighboring Catholic houses killed two men and wounded several more.

The next day, Philadelphia was a city under siege. A torn American flag inscribed "This is the flag that was trampled under foot by the Irish papists" was borne through the streets of Kensington. Kenrick distributed circulars urging Catholics to shun all public places of assemblage, but such circulars were torn down as soon as they were posted. "Another St. Bartholomew's day is begun on the streets of Philadelphia," screamed a nativist newspaper, which urged all patriots to arm. Again, the nativists invaded Kensington. Some thirty Catholic homes were burned, and hundreds of Catholic families took what belongings they could and fled the area.

On the third day of the rioting, thousands reappeared on the streets of Kensington. Entire blocks of Catholic homes were set afire. Then the mob gathered around St. Michael's Church, which, with a nearby schoolhouse, was set afire. The disorder spread to other parts of Philadelphia. Despite the presence of the mayor and police, the doors of St. Augustine's Church were battered down, and the building set afire. Then the mob moved to St. Mary's Church, but here they were met and dispersed by United States marines and sailors. Regrouping, the mob started for St. John's Cathedral. Here, too, the mob encountered military troops, and also an announcement that martial law had been imposed. Soon reinforced by several thousand militiamen ordered to the scene by the governor, the troops stood guard at all Catholic churches in the city for the next two weeks.[20]

As the rioting subsided, a chastened mood settled over the city. Several secular newspapers denounced the nativists. One editor shamed Protestant clergymen for entering into an unholy alliance with nativist brawlers. Another concluded that the Protestants had shown themselves no more desirable as rulers than the Pope. Even a nativist editor condemned the "desecration of the Christian altar."

20. Ibid., pp. 73–77.

But the contrition was short-lived. Vast funeral processions for the "martyrs" provided new occasions for professions of patriotism and hostility to "foreign papists." After a month of study, a grand jury issued its presentment that the riots had been caused by "the efforts of a portion of the community to exclude the Bible from our Public Schools." Mass meetings were held to support the grand jury and to denounce a response to it that had been drawn up by a committee of Catholic laymen.

Several citizens, including the highest-ranking military officer in the area, feared that the May riots had been quelled only temporarily. As Independence Day approached, Gen. George Cadwalader readied his troops for action if that should be needed. The sheriff secretly requested all magistrates to be ready to cope with disturbances, should they arise. An estimated seventy thousand spectators were on hand for the celebration; in the parade alone there were from five to seven thousand marchers. Nativists conspicuously displayed ribbons and signs proclaiming love for God and country. Banners depicted schoolhouses and Bibles, children reading Bibles, an American eagle grasping an open Bible in its claws. There were some minor conflicts on 4 July, but they were apparently between rival groups of nativists.

In Southwark, another district adjacent to Philadelphia, Catholics were afraid that their church, St. Philips, might be attacked. Sharing this fear, the priest had permitted the storing of muskets in the church. This became known, and crowds gathered around St. Philip's, and also around other Catholic churches, on the evening of 5 July. By agreement between the sheriff and the pastor, the arms and also some armed men were removed from the church, and the crowd withdrew for the night. But the following evening the crowd returned. A troop of militiamen, hauling a cannon, arrived to reinforce the sheriff's men. Angered by this, the crowd advanced on the militia. About twenty rioters were arrested. But the next morning the rioters were back, now reinforced by two cannon, which they placed so as to permit firing upon the church. Now the mob demanded withdrawal of the troops, and the militia commander acceded, apparently after assurance by nativist leaders that the church would be safe. But no sooner were the troops withdrawn than rioters breached a large opening in the wall of the church and for hours wandered about the interior at will. Fighting continued throughout the night. As the position of the local militia detachment had become untenable, the governor intervened, and soon five thousand troops were under arms in the city and county. Some newspapers now called for a return to sanity, but several Protestant and nativist editors instead assailed both the military and the Catholics. On 10 July a group of leading citizens joined to express support for the governor's efforts to restore peace. Slowly, law and order returned to Philadelphia.

Extant records do not permit an exact accounting of the number killed and wounded in the Philadelphia Bible Riots. Professors Lannie and Diethorn, in what is probably the most comprehensive study of these disorders, give an estimate (which they consider conservative) of one Catholic and thirteen nativists killed and over forty nativists wounded during the May riots. During the July riots an additional thirty nativists and more than fourteen soldiers were slain, and as many as a hundred others were wounded. Property damage and destruction ran to several hundred million dollars.[21]

Bishop Kenrick had spoken approvingly of the Philadelphia common schools at least as late as 1835, but the riots of 1844 convinced him that public education could never become acceptable for Catholic children. The only adequate solution would be a system of Catholic schools. It was a fateful decision, for he carried it with him into the First Plenary Council of Baltimore in 1852, which laid the groundwork for such a school system. As archbishop of Baltimore, a post which he assumed in 1851, Kenrick presided over the Plenary Council.

New Catholic School Policy Formulated

Far from resolving the School Question, the New York (1840–1842) and Philadelphia (1840–1844) school controversies served rather to intensify the conflict between Protestants and Catholics. The Know-Nothing Movement was the most explosive political development of the fifties, and the Know-Nothings, in all parts of the country, focused their efforts squarely—and aggressively—on the School Question.

Based on their experience with the School Question, the Catholic hierarchy set forth their views on education in the First Baltimore Plenary Council of 1852. (The previous Baltimore Councils had been provincial, not plenary. A Provincial Council is a convocation of the bishops of a group of dioceses that constitute a province—i.e., a regional convocation. A Plenary Council—now the National Conference of Bishops—is a convocation of all the bishops in the nation.) The decrees of this Plenary Council were both a response to existing Protestant views on education and a cause for further alarm among Protestants and Protestant-dominated governmental bodies. In this council, Bishop Hughes actively championed the cause of parochial schools. In Hughes's mind the die had been cast at the time of the New York City controversy. Concerning the reading of pro-Protes-

21. Ibid., pp. 103–4.

tant, anti-Catholic materials in the public schools of New York, Hughes later said:

> These passages were not considered as sectarian, inasmuch as they had been selected as mere reading lessons, and were not in *favor* of any particular sect, but merely *against* the Catholics. We feel it is unjust that such passages should be taught at all in schools, to the support of which we are contributors as well as others. But that such books should be put into the hands of *our own* children, and that in part at our expense, was in our opinion unjust, unnatural, and at all events to us intolerable. Accordingly, through very great additional sacrifices, we have been obliged to provide schools, under our own churches and elsewhere, in which to educate our children as our conscientious duty required.[22]

The problems to be met by the First Plenary Council of Baltimore were formidable, particularly in the field of education, and a strong statement on the subject was issued: "We exhort the bishops . . . to see that schools be established in connection with all the churches of their diocese; and, if it be necessary and circumstances permit, to provide, from the revenues of the church to which the school is attached, for the support of competent teachers."[23]

In this statement the bishops clearly endorsed the parochial school concept ("schools . . . in connection with all the churches") as contrasted with the earlier policy merely to "encourage" Catholic schools in general. (The latter had included, along with parochial schools, independent private schools conducted by nuns or by laypersons and so-called "charitable" schools controlled by groups of priests or laymen.) The method of school support is also mentioned for the first time here. There is to be support from parish funds, although only "if it be necessary and circumstances permit." Clearly, there was still some hope of securing state aid for the parochial schools, for certainly there could have been little hope that the poverty-stricken Irish immigrants could be expected to support the schools by tuition. The pastoral letter issued by this council makes it clear that the bishops saw secularism as an increasingly strong influence in the common schools and that this was as objectionable as the Protestant orientation it was gradually displacing. Parochial schools were therefore essential.[24]

Both in the council and in his publication *The Freeman's Journal*, Bishop Hughes now aggressively carried on a campaign not only for public aid to parochial schools, but also in opposition to the instruc-

22. Hassard, *Life of John Hughes*, pp. 230–31. Hassard titled chapter 14 of this work "The School Question." Clearly, the meaning of the term *School Question* was widely agreed upon by that time.

23. James A. Burns, *Growth and Development of the Catholic School System in the United States* (New York: Benziger, 1912), p. 184.

24. Guilday, *National Pastorals*, p. 191.

tional program of public schools. The *Journal* urged Catholic parents to establish Catholic parish schools and to withdraw their children from public schools, "where they are certain to learn evil, and probably very little but evil . . . ."[25] The Protestant criticisms of Catholics and Catholicism were often couched in bitter terms. But Hughes was not adverse to the use of strong language either; he once described Protestant "parsons" as "voracious mongrels of heresy who, under the plea of propagating religion, are absolutely attempting to devour everything."[26]

Hughes's paper was widely read throughout the United States, and its influence was soon felt in other places. Catholic newspapers in other cities began to agitate the question, and by 1852 (when the Plenary Council convened) Catholics in many sections were protesting the use of Protestant Bibles and biased textbooks in public schools. Many Catholic leaders who had hesitated to follow Hughes's vigorous leadership a decade earlier now felt that the time had come to demand a portion of the public funds. The Catholic school campaign ushered in by the education decree of the 1852 Plenary Council, therefore, had a twofold objective: to expand markedly the numbers of schools attached to parishes, and to renew and intensify efforts to secure public funds for these schools. This was the Catholic response to the Protestant Common School Movement.

Catholics and the Know-Nothings in the East

Catholic efforts to foster in the common schools religious exercises conformable to their own beliefs and/or to secure public aid for their own schools had been decisively rejected in New York and Philadelphia. But in the decade or so that followed, the same type of struggle was waged in most other states. The main Catholic themes were always the same: resistance to required Bible reading in the King James version and a demand for public aid for parochial schools. To obtain some notion of the scope of the opposition to Catholic ideas in education, we must consider at least some of the unique features of the anti-Catholic campaigns in the East (Massachusetts, Connecticut, and Maryland), the Middle West (Ohio, Michigan, Illinois, and Minnesota Territory), and in the Far West (California).

The state of Massachusetts was long considered a pioneer in educational matters, and the struggle over the School Question there was watched intently by people in other states. The Lowell experiment of incorporating Catholic schools into the local public school system, launched in 1835 (and described above), was certainly a unique ven-

25. Flynn, "The School Controversy," pp. 181–82.
26. Hassard, *Life of John Hughes*, p. 127.

ture. But this experiment, which had been so glowingly praised by the city officials in earlier years, foundered after the New York and Philadelphia controversies. In 1844, the Lowell school committee began to appoint non-Catholic teachers to the Catholic schools, and in 1849 the committee named the Catholic secondary school in honor of Horace Mann, the Unitarian! By this time most of the teachers in the "Irish" schools were non-Catholic. An effort by the Catholics to get the school committee to appoint members of the Sisters of Notre Dame as teachers in 1852 aroused antagonism, and the experiment perished in the passions of the Know-Nothing Movement. Within a few years the building of a system of Catholic parochial schools was underway in Lowell.[27]

Another Catholic venture in this state, also predating the rise of the Know-Nothings, came to an equally ignominious end. In 1849 the Jesuits sought a Massachusetts charter for Holy Cross College. The petition for this charter was referred to the Joint Standing Committee on Education of the state legislature (the General Court). At first, there appeared to be no serious question about the petition, except possibly about the stipulation that only Catholic students could be admitted to the college—a provision included because Catholic authorities remembered the earlier furor that had been created by the admission of Protestant pupils to the Ursuline School. Nevertheless, the committee recommendation to the General Court was that the request for a charter be denied. No reason for this decision was given. There was an immediate protest against this negative recommendation, led by the *Boston Daily Advertiser*, edited by a Catholic. The petition was again given a hearing before a legislative committee, but again the recommendation was against passage. This time an explanation was given. The majority report stated that a college was a public institution and should be open to all who sought admission. "Colleges are public bodies and it is the policy of the State to exclude from them all religious tests, if they are to enjoy the privileges that the Legislature is accustomed to grant."[28]

The minority report recommended a compromise solution whereby the college would be incorporated as a private institution, somewhat in the nature of Newton Theological Institution, Phillips Academy, and Wesleyan Academy. This was a rather equivocal position, but on another point the minority report was quite candid. Catholics were present in Massachusetts in increasing numbers, said the report, and

27. Smith, *Relation of the State*, pp. 196–97.
28. Robert H. Lord, John E. Sexton, and Edward T. Harrington, *The History of the Archdiocese of Boston in the Various States of Its Development*, 3 vols. (Boston: The Pilot Publishing Co., 1944–1945), 2:574–77. A wealth of material on anti-Catholicism is woven into this closely documented work.

they were going to stay there. There were at that time 120,000 Catholics in the state. They wanted to educate their children, and sound public policy demanded that some satisfactory means for doing this be authorized.

Although neither the majority nor the minority report mentioned it, one of the reasons for denying the charter was the fear that the Catholics might seek an appropriation of public funds for the college. Such appropriations had been made from time to time to the Protestant colleges in the state, and this indeed was one of the reasons for taking the position that institutions of higher learning were to be considered public. When the minority report proposed its substitute bill, it was very careful to specify that the college "Shall be regarded as a private corporation, for the benefit of one denomination only, and, therefore, having no claims whatever upon the Commonwealth, beyond what is herein granted."[29]

A reasonable degree of calmness had characterized the committee hearings on the bill, although the majority report pointed out that students in the Catholic college would be required to go to confession and to receive absolution from the priest not only for their acts, but for their thoughts as well. But when the question got to the floor of the House, all the old calumnies against Rome were paraded again. Rev. Erastus Hopkins, an ardent Know-Nothing who was chairman of the Committee on Education, expressed alarm that young and impressionable students should be entrusted to the care of celibates. While strongly disclaiming any prejudice, he thundered that the Church of Rome made abject slaves of men, subjecting them to a hierarchy that professed to hold the keys to heaven and earth. When the vote was taken on the bill, it was defeated by a vote of 117 to 84.[30] Catholics in Massachusetts had now suffered several decisive defeats: their Ursuline Convent had been burned in 1834; city officials in Lowell had subverted and made a mockery of the cooperative school venture launched there in 1835; and the state legislature had rejected a request for a charter for a Catholic college, although it had not only chartered but also provided funds for many Protestant colleges. By any measure these were major rebuffs, but they paled in comparison to the events that soon followed.

In 1853, the year before the Know-Nothings gained full control of the state government in Massachusetts, a convention was called for the purpose of revising the state constitution. One of the proposals made in the convention was to prohibit the appropriation of public money to sectarian schools. This proposal was made, purportedly,

29. Ibid., 2:579.
30. Ibid., 2:581–82.

because of efforts then underway in other states to obtain public funds for Catholic schools. The amendment was approved in the convention and referred to the people for approval, along with the other parts of the proposed constitution. The *Pilot*, edited by a Catholic, waged a strong campaign against the entire constitution. Its main reason for opposition was that the proposed constitution would redistrict the state so as to throw more political power into the rural districts, where the Irish vote was negligible. The *Pilot* also disapproved of the provision denying public funds to sectarian schools, arguing that the Massachusetts educational system was still in an experimental state and it would be unwise to give it permanent form by incorporating this policy into the constitution.

Those who favored the proposal for denying public funds to sectarian schools made a special effort to persuade Protestant ministers to campaign for the measure, and many of them did so. Nevertheless, the provision denying public aid to sectarian schools was narrowly defeated. Other provisions of the new constitution were turned down by much larger majorities, and this prompted supporters of the school provision to believe that if it were separated from the other parts of the proposed constitution, it might be approved.

Time was to prove them correct. The Know-Nothing forces in Massachusetts were rapidly gathering strength, and in the fall election of 1854 they captured both houses of the state legislature along with the governorship. Twenty-four members of the legislature were Protestant clergymen.[31] Nowhere was the relationship between the nativist movement and the School Question more vividly illustrated than in the work of this legislature. Two measures—both patently unconstitutional—restricted the suffrage to those with twenty-one years of residence in the country, and the right to hold office to native-born citizens. A Nunnery Investigating Committee found no evidence of sin in Catholic institutions, but the conduct of its own members was so shameless that even their fellow legislators were taken aback. The adoption of an amendment to the state constitution denying funds to sectarian schools was a foregone conclusion:

> All monies raised by taxation in the towns and cities for the support of public schools, and all monies which may be appropriated by the state for the support of common schools, shall be applied to, and expended in, no other schools than those which are conducted according to law, under the order and superintendence of the authority of the town or city in which the money is to be expended; and such monies shall never be appropri-

31. George H. Haynes, "Know-Nothing Legislature," *Annual Report of the American Historical Association for the Year 1896* (Washington, D.C.: Government Printing Office, 1897), pp. 177–87.

ated to any religious sect for the maintenance, exclusively, of its own school.[32]

Care was taken in the wording of this amendment to use the term *schools*, a term specifically not intended to include colleges and academies, most of them sponsored by Protestant denominations—and the courts upheld this interpretation. Also adopted was a bill to require daily reading in the public schools of some portion of the Bible in the "common English version." This was explicit enough, although the Senate had attempted to specify the King James version by name.[33]

Scandalous as this record was, it represented only a part of the objectives of the Know-Nothings, whose real goal was to destroy the parochial schools. Thus, the House approved a bill that would have required all teachers in non-public schools to obtain the approval of the school committee or school superintendent in the city or town where they were to teach. The fate of members of Catholic teaching orders before local school committees is not difficult to imagine. This bill did not receive Senate approval.

Another stratagem devised in an effort to destroy the parochial schools was contained in a bill ostensibly designed to control the labor of children in factories. On the face of it, the bill was to achieve the humanitarian purpose of prohibiting the employment of children in factories unless they attended schools for a specified time each year. But the bill provided further that the school had to be one authorized by a public school committee and that the teachers had to be approved by the committee. Unfortunately for the proponents of the measure, certain industrialists questioned the bill because it might limit the hours of labor performed by children. In a desperate effort to salvage the bill, its proponents were finally forced to acknowledge its true intent: "The bill had a further object, a peculiarly American object. It is true we did not wish to bring that object out fully to view. We wished to bring that object out as quietly as we could, for it is a subject that has occasioned the committee more difficulty than any that has come before them this year, and this object was, if we must say it, to break up the Catholic schools."[34] Even the Know-Nothing legislature of 1855 balked at this compulsory attendance proposal,

32. F. N. Thorpe, *Pre-Federal and State Constitutions, Colonial Charters, and Other Organic Laws* (Washington, D.C.: Government Printing Office, 1909), p. 1818.

33. Smith, *Relation of the State*, pp. 209–10; *Jenkins v. Andover*, 103 Mass., 94 (1869). One of the standard accounts of church-state separation in the United States records the passage of the 1855 measure without any reference to the fact that it was the product of a vindictive Know-Nothing legislature, openly committed to the destruction of Catholicism: R. Freeman Butts, *The American Tradition in Religion and Education* (New York: Beacon Press, 1950), p. 132.

34. *Pilot*, 19 May 1855.

and finally defeated it. No doubt much of the reason for this was that the legislature was smarting under the disclosure of the activities of its notorious Nunnery Investigating Committee.

The Know-Nothing injunction requiring Bible reading in the public schools did not, of course, solve the question. As early as 1853, the *Pilot* had urged Catholic parents to bring suit in the courts, if necessary, to protect their children from enforced participation in Protestant religious observances in the schools. If the "bigots" were not careful, said the *Pilot*, Catholics would open a vigorous campaign for their rights. "We have a constitutional right to demand that all sectarian matters shall be banished from the schools, and that the faith of Catholic children shall not be openly or covertly assailed."[35] In spite of the clear warning sounded in the *Pilot*, there was no lessening in the pressure for Bible reading in the schools, and one consequence was that many Catholic parents kept their children away from school. In 1854 the secretary of the State Board of Education, Rev. Barnas Sears, reported that there was a very large proportion of absenteeism among Catholic school-age children, and he attributed this to the opposition of Catholic parents to the use of the Protestant Bible in the schools.[36]

In 1859 the required use of the Protestant Bible in the public schools became the subject of a famous court case in Boston. In March of that year, McLaurin F. Cook, assistant principal of the Eliot School, was brought into the Boston Police Court on the charge of having assaulted Thomas J. Wall, a pupil in his school, for refusal to recite the Protestant version of the Ten Commandments. The regulations of the Boston School Committee at the time required the reading of the Bible as an opening exercise in the public schools, and recommended further the recitation of the Lord's Prayer and the Ten Commandments, and the singing of a hymn as a closing exercise. The Bible exercises were from the King James version, and the hymn generally used was the "Old Hundredth," a Reformation hymn based on Psalm 100.

There were at the time about eight hundred pupils in the Eliot School, of whom three-fourths were Catholics. On Monday, 7 March 1859, one of the teachers in the school, Miss Shepard, called upon the boys in her room to recite the Commandments individually, using as the model the Protestant version contained in their spelling book. Thomas Wall was called, and refused to say them. Called upon again, he said that his father had forbidden him to use this version. Finally, as the teacher continued to press him, he said that he did not know the Protestant version. The chairman of the Eliot School Committee

35. Ibid., 26 November 1852.
36. *18th Annual Report of the Board of Education*, 1854, p. 66.

(not the general Boston School Committee) at the time was Micah Dyer, who had been a leader in the Know-Nothing Movement. Samuel Mason, the principal of the Eliot School, consulted with Dyer and was told to expel from school any boy who did not obey the regulations.[37]

During the following weeks, Thomas Wall's father made several visits to the school. Mason read to the father from a spelling book the version of the Commandments that was purportedly used in the school. Just what this was is impossible to say; in the book that was produced at the trial, the text had been altered. In any event, when the boy returned to class, Miss Shepard informed him that his father had seen both versions and knew that they were the same. The only logical conclusion from this reasoning would have been that either version might be used. But Miss Shepard continued to insist on the Protestant text, and the boy persisted in his refusal.

On Sunday, 13 March, Father Wiget of St. Mary's Church ordered Catholic students to use only the Catholic version of the Commandments. The next morning Miss Shepard again began opening exercises by calling on each pupil to repeat the Ten Commandments. The Catholic boys refused to say the Protestant version. Each boy who refused to do so was whipped. One boy, when his turn came, fled from the room to escape punishment. Although called upon at least twice, young Wall again refused to use the Protestant version. A member of the school committee, Mr. Hazelton, was in the building and went from room to room observing the exercises. In Miss Shepard's class he ordered young Wall to recite the Commandments from the King James version. Wall again refused. Hazelton soon discovered that two-thirds of the boys in the class had the same attitude. Then, apparently deciding that Wall was the leader, Hazelton advised the teacher to turn the boy over to Mr. Cook. Wall was then taken to Cook's classroom and seated on the platform. Cook announced to the class, "Here's a boy that refuses to repeat the Ten Commandments and I will whip him till he yields if it takes the whole forenoon." The lad, still unyielding, said that he would say the Commandments if his father permitted him to do so. But this was not satisfactory, and Cook whipped the boy's hands with a rattan for half an hour, stopping at intervals to ask if Thomas would repeat the Commandments. Each time he refused. After half an hour, the boy's hands were cut and bleeding, and he yielded to Cook's demands.

Mason now again conferred with Dyer, who in turn consulted the mayor of Boston. In the afternoon Dyer went to the school and ordered all who would not recite the Commandments to leave. About

37. Lord, Sexton, and Harrington, *History of the Archdiocese*, 2:587–91.

one hundred Catholic boys were expelled. As there was now some noise and excitement, Dyer sent for a policeman to guard the building. The next morning, the principal himself opened the school day with prayer. A large number of Catholic boys refused to join, and Mason told them not to return to school. Three hundred did not come back in the afternoon, and attendance was irregular throughout the week. The following Monday a large number of Catholic boys returned, bringing with them their catechisms, prepared to recite the Catholic version of the Commandments. But they were given no opportunity to do so; Micah Dyer was on hand and expelled them. There were disturbances in some of the other schools as well, but none as serious as those in the Eliot School.[38]

These developments were serious enough, but there hovered in the background an even more ominous possibility. Under state law, children of school age who did not attend school were subject to arrest and commitment to reform school. To avert such a development, Bishop Fitzpatrick now urged Catholic parents to send their children back to school. At the same time, he prepared an exposition of the Church's position and laid it before the Boston School Committee. Conciliatory in tone, but nevertheless firm and clear, Bishop Fitzpatrick explained that Catholics could not under any circumstances accept "as a complete collection and faithful version" the Protestant translation of the Bible. Nor could they accept the recital of the Decalogue "under the form and words in which Protestants clothe it." Nor could they accept the Protestant form of public worship. Trinitarians and Unitarians, said Fitzpatrick, seemed able "to offer in brotherhood a blended and apparently harmonious worship but the Catholic cannot act in this manner . . . ." Concluding, the bishop said:

> But whenever and wherever an effort has been made by Catholics to effect such changes as they desired, the question has been distorted from its true sense, and a false issue has been set before the non-Catholic community. It has been represented that the design was to eliminate and practically annihilate the Bible. This has never been true; and yet this has always been believed, and a rallying cry, "To the rescue of the Bible!" has resounded on every side. Angry passions have been roused, violent acts have been committed, and, almost invariably, the last condition of things has been worse than the first.[39]

Meanwhile, the suit by Thomas Wall's parents against Cook, widely reported in the press, had become a *cause célèbre*. Wall's attorney contended that the issues were whether a Catholic scholar could be forced to use a version of the Scriptures forbidden by his church and

38. Ibid., 2:593–94.
39. Ibid., 2:598–99.

whether he could be punished for disobeying his teacher at his father's order. Cook's attorney ignored these points and charged that the Catholics were not seeking toleration but were trying to prevent Protestants from following their own religious beliefs. There was, he claimed, employing the old but ever-effective nativist argument, a conspiracy to drive the Bible out of the schools "in obedience to a dark and dangerous power whose hand we now see . . . ."[40]

The case was heard in the Police Court of Boston. In his decision Judge Maine, a Know-Nothing, ignored entirely the question of Wall's religious liberty or freedom of conscience. The law, said Maine, demanded that the Scriptures be read in the schools in the common English version. Pupils could be required to say the Lord's Prayer and the Ten Commandments in the version prescribed by the school authorities. Compulsory Bible reading in public school, "without sectarian explanations, is no interference with religious liberty." Therefore, no injustice had been done; Wall had been punished for insubordination.[41]

Although the School Committee took no official action on the bishop's letter, it was clear that many of them wished to find some more equitable solution to the question. This was rendered difficult by Dyer's determination to enforce compliance by Catholic pupils. Some members of the School Committee, however, became so annoyed by Dyer's activities that they requested from the city solicitor an opinion as to who had the right to expel pupils from school. The solicitor replied that only the general Boston School Committee, not the individual school committee, could do this. The city elections of 1859 saw an effort toward adjustment. Father Haskins was elected to the School Committee, the first time a Catholic had ever held this office. But the necessity of creating separate schools had been deeply impressed upon Catholics. And throughout the troubled years of the 1850s, John Bernard Fitzpatrick, third bishop of Boston, worked tirelessly in the establishment of Catholic schools and colleges. At the end of the period there were in the Boston diocese three Catholic academies, nine schools for girls, and four schools for boys, with a total enrollment of about five thousand children.[42]

In Maryland, agitation of the School Question was one of the factors that enabled the Know-Nothings to dominate politics in the middle fifties. Other factors contributed to the success of the Know-Nothings in this state, among them the popularity of Millard Fillmore, the party's presidential candidate in 1856, their ability to strad-

40. Ibid., 2:600.
41. 7 Am. L. Reg. 417, 423 (1859).
42. Lord, Sexton, and Harrington, *History of the Archdiocese*, 2:622.

dle the slavery question, and the ineffectiveness of the older parties.[43] Moreover, anti-Catholic agitation had deep roots in Maryland. Revs. Robert J. Breckenridge and Andrew Cross had earlier labored here for two decades to incite opposition to Catholicism.

The introduction of a school bill in the state legislature in the spring of 1852 served as the signal for a resumption of anti-Catholic activities. Named after the chairman of the Committee on Education of the House of Delegates, the Kerney bill sought to combine into a uniform system the several laws concerning public education in the state.[44] This objective was laudable; the state possessed at this time no general system of public education. But section 26 of Kerney's bill provided that monies from the common school fund might be appropriated for the education of children taught gratuitously in any school, in amounts no greater than that expended per pupil in the public schools. Opposition to this section, especially, developed immediately. The bill was laid on the table, and warnings were issued that any further attempts of this type would lead to serious trouble. The warnings were prophetic; within three years, Baltimore was to become known as "mob-town."

Public support for non-public schools became an issue also in the Baltimore city election in the fall of 1852, when such a proposal was supported by a number of Catholics. Newspapers at once erupted with denunciations of "popery," and the Catholic effort was repulsed. In the spring of 1853, Kerney again submitted to the House proposals substantially the same as those made earlier. Now a mass meeting was organized, ostensibly to discuss the bill but in fact to solidify opposition to it. Clergyman of several Protestant denominations served as the principal speakers. The bill was denounced as a conspiracy to destroy the public schools and to subvert all good government. One minister heaped abuse upon the Jesuits and offered to prove that no Catholic could read the Bible without permission. The meeting closed with the adoption of a number of resolutions condemning the Kerney bill.[45]

By this time organized nativist groups were in existence and made themselves known as opponents of any legislation, state or local, of the Kerney type. The United Sons of America, soon to be merged with the Know-Nothing party, was organized in Baltimore in March 1853. In May this organization carried an advertisement in the *Bal-*

43. Laurence F. Schmeckebier, *History of the Know-Nothing Party in Maryland*, Johns Hopkins Studies in History and Political Science, no. 17, April–May 1899, pp. 5–125.
44. A good account of the Kerney bill controversy is provided by Mary St. Patrick McConville, *Political Nativism in the State of Maryland, 1830–1860* (Washington, D.C.: Catholic University of America, 1928), chap. 3.
45. Ibid., p. 26.

timore Clipper declaring that the legislators who supported the Kerney bill were "servants of Pius IX, John Hughes, and all papal Rome instead of servants of their master—the American people." Concluding, the advertisement called upon all true patriots to "enlist under the red-white-and-blue banner of Native American principles and fight valiantly for those rights, for which Shifler [*sic*] and his seven compatriots fell martyrs in the blood-stained streets of Kensington."[46] The ensuing demonstration, engineered by Protestant clergyman and raucously promoted by nativists, achieved its purpose. The Kerney bill was referred to a special committee, where it died.

Meanwhile, in spite of the defeat suffered only a few months earlier, the question was again being agitated in the city of Baltimore. A petition, signed by Archbishop Kenrick and others, declared that, because of conscientious objections, Catholics were unable to participate in the advantages of the public schools for whose support they were taxed. They did not propose any changes in the existing public schools. But as they had erected at their own expense a number of schools in which from four to five thousand children were being taught, they asked the city council to grant to them a portion of the school funds, or to allow them to designate the particular school to which their school tax should be appropriated. Their petition was based, they said, on article 33 of the Declaration of Rights of the State of Maryland.

The petition was referred by the council to a committee, which in May 1853 reported that it would be unwise and dangerous to adopt the proposals of the petitioners. It was clear, said the committee, that the petition was from the heart of a foreigner, incompetent both by birth and by education to understand the genius of American institutions. This committee recommendation was approved by the city council. Although the Catholic effort to secure some division of the school funds had been repulsed at both the city and state levels, anti-Catholic agitation continued to mount. In 1854 Cardinal Bedini, the papal legate, who was visiting Baltimore, was burned in effigy in Monument Square. (Bedini was met with similar receptions in several other cities.) Late in 1854 the Know-Nothings elected their candidate for mayor of Baltimore by a large majority, and also won a majority of both branches of the city council.

In 1855 the success of the Know-Nothings in Maryland was complete. Baltimore itself and thirteen of the twenty-one counties in the state were in the Know-Nothing column, and the party gained a large majority in the lower house of the state legislature. Protestant clergymen had taken an active part in the Know-Nothing campaign, but

46. Ibid., p. 29.

they were not in a position to capitalize fully on their victory; the 1850 state constitution forbade any clergyman from holding a seat in the legislature. They continued to press for their objectives, however. Especially active was Rev. Andrew B. Cross, whose burning ambition was the suppression of convents and nunneries. In 1854 he had published his *Priests' Prisons for Women*, and this was followed in 1856 with *Young Women in Convents or Priests' Prisons to be Protected by Law*. When the state legislature convened early in 1856, Cross presented a petition asking that body to authorize the inspection of such institutions and to provide for the "protection" of persons confined therein. Other similar petitions were received; all were referred to a select committee, which, to the dismay of many, reported that the writ of habeas corpus should provide ample protection for persons unlawfully detained, and there the matter rested. In the Senate, petitions for such action were laid on the table and forgotten, as were petitions to remove the tax-exempt status of churches.

Although unsuccessful in these efforts, the Know-Nothing party survived its failures, and the fall elections in 1856 brought violence. By this time control of the movement had fallen into the hands of lawless and even criminal elements. Splinter clubs of the party, calling themselves Plug Uglies, Blood Tubs, Black Snakes, Ranters, and Rattlers, broke up meetings of the Democratic and newly organized Republican parties. The governor pleaded with the mayor for permission to send in state forces to preserve order, but the mayor haughtily refused. Four men were killed during the city election on 8 October, and more than fifty wounded. During the national election a month later the Know-Nothings bolstered their position with a small cannon. Although the Democrats were able to wrest control of this weapon from them, ten were killed and over two hundred fifty wounded in the fighting.

Know-Nothingism as a force in national political life collapsed in 1856, but in Maryland the party continued to pursue its disgraceful course through 1858. Even the *Baltimore Clipper*, which had served as the organ of the movement (and which had expected to get the state printing contracts), rejoiced when the 1858 session adjourned, giving "thanks to the Creator of all good that we have just passed from an epoch shrouded in pestilential vapors . . . spreading a pall over the future energy and justice of State Legislatures."[47]

The School Question had been settled in Maryland, at least for the time. To be sure, the Know-Nothings enacted no legislation forbidding the use of public funds for sectarian schools. But they enacted

47. Schmeckebier, *Know-Nothing Party in Maryland*, pp. 19–39; Beals, *Brass-Knuckle Crusade*, pp. 186–92.

very little legislation of any kind. As they overcame their political opponents, they turned upon one another. The treatment accorded the Kerney bill was sufficient to indicate to Catholics the futility of further efforts of this type. Protestant schools, however, continued occasionally to receive public funds.[48]

In Connecticut, where there were at the time very few Catholic schools, Bishop Bernard O'Reilly in a pastoral letter of 1851 emphasized the necessity of providing a Catholic education for children. But the increase in Catholic educational efforts, and particularly the arrival in 1852 of some members of the Sisters of Mercy to augment the teaching corps of the schools, soon provoked Protestant opposition.[49]

A leader in the criticism of Catholic educational activities was the influential Rev. Horace Bushnell, an active promoter of the Common School Movement in Connecticut and close personal friend of Horace Mann and Henry Barnard. Although certainly more moderate in his views than most Protestant clergymen of the time, Bushnell made no secret of his fear of Romanism, and he labored strenuously in the work of the Protestant League, a phrenetically anti-Catholic association, which later merged with the Christian Alliance. In a famous sermon in 1853, Bushnell launched a vigorous attack on Catholic education, which he said could prosper only to the degree that the common schools were repressed. He charged that the Catholic clergy not only in Connecticut but in other states as well were "preparing for an assault upon the common school system, hitherto in so great favor among our countrymen . . . ." Even so, Bushnell recognized that Catholics were justified in regarding the King James version as a sectarian book, a rare insight for a Protestant clergymen at the time, and he recommended that the use of the Bible in the Protestant or the Douay version be made optional.[50]

Meanwhile, the Know-Nothings were gaining strength in Connecticut, and in 1855 they carried the state elections by a decisive majority. In his inaugural address, Gov. William T. Minor declared that the rising incidence of crime and pauperism was a result of the "pernicious influence" of immigrants. And while he affirmed his intent not to "do injustice to a portion of our foreign population," he felt impelled to point out that very many of them were "blind followers of an ecclesiastical despotism." One of the first acts of the Know-Nothing legislature was to adopt a provision that any real estate used in connection with religious worship must be held in the name of a

48. McConville, *Political Nativism in Maryland*, p. 36.
49. Arthur J. Heffernan, *A History of Catholic Education in Connecticut* (Washington, D.C.: Catholic Education Press, 1937), pp. 22–26.
50. *Common Schools: A Discourse on the Modifications Demanded by the Roman Catholics* (Hartford: Press of Case, Tiffany Company, 1853), pp. 2–3, 15.

corporation—a blow at the Catholic practice of vesting ownership in bishops. A constitutional amendment limiting the right to vote to those who could demonstrate an ability to read the constitution or statutes was approved by the legislature, and by the people, but later rendered ineffective by court action.[51]

In 1855 the Connecticut State Council of the Know-Nothing party approved a platform that had been adopted earlier at the Know-Nothing national convention in Philadelphia. This included a section declaring support for common schools free from any sectarian influence and opposition to all attempts to exclude from the schools "the Holy Bible . . . the fountain of all civil and religious freedom . . . ." As a result of the excitement created, Bishop O'Reilly, while striving to increase the number of parochial schools in the diocese, made no effort to secure public funds for them.[52]

The School Question in the Middle West

On the surface, at least, it seemed for a time that Protestants and Catholics might be able to work cooperatively in building a school system in Ohio. Bishop (later Archbishop) John B. Purcell had spoken approvingly of the work of the first state school superintendent, Rev. Samuel Lewis. In addition, Purcell served for some years as a board member of the Cincinnati public school system. In Cincinnati, each of the nine Catholic parishes had its own parochial school by 1850, and there had as yet been no particular evidence of hostility toward Catholic education, although the *Cincinnati Journal* did express regret at the sight of non-Catholic children attending these schools.

But there were adverse circumstances as well. Cincinnati had a very large foreign-born population; in 1850 Germans alone comprised almost half the population. The marathon debates between Purcell and Rev. Alexander Campbell had been held there in 1836–1837. Rev. Lyman Beecher had come to Cincinnati in 1830 to wage his campaign against Rome. A nativist party had been founded in the city in 1835, and the anti-Catholic *American Protestant* magazine, edited by two local clergymen, commenced publication in 1845. The Association of Protestant Ministers of Cincinnati in 1848 appointed a committee to study "Romanism in the Nineteenth Century."[53]

The controversy over the School Question in Ohio had its beginnings in 1842. That year Bishop Purcell, while a member of the Cin-

51. Carroll John Noonan, "Nativism in Connecticut, 1829–1869" (Ph.D. diss., Catholic University of America, 1938), pp. 210, 213–16.

52. Flynn, "The School Controversy," p. 219; Noonan, "Nativism in Connecticut," p. 230.

53. Billington, *The Protestant Crusade*, pp. 131, 170, 260.

cinnati school board, proposed that the requirement of daily Bible reading in the schools in the King James version be modified so that parents might specify the version of the Bible their children were to use. The board approved this change. Objections were immediately raised in the Protestant pulpit and press, but for some time the presence of a Catholic member on the board helped to preserve a truce. In 1852, however, a movement was initiated, under the leadership of the Protestant clergy, to secure a ruling that the King James version be the only one used. The school board reaffirmed the position it had taken in 1842, but only by the small margin of 10 to 8, and the minority group issued a spirited dissenting report. Now the indignation of the anti-Catholic press mounted, and a determined effort was made to secure revocation of the board's decision.[54]

Equally threatening in the view of Catholics was a Protestant campaign at the state level to force through the legislature a measure compelling parents and guardians to send their children to a school for three months each year. This bill apparently did not specify that the attendance requirement could be met only by attendance at a public school. But the stratagem of effecting the destruction of Catholic schools under the guise of a compulsory attendance law was being tried in Massachusetts at this very time, and the *Catholic Telegraph* insisted that this was the intent of the Ohio bill. Archbishop Purcell defiantly exclaimed with reference to the three hundred orphans under his charge that he would permit his life to "be tramped out by a mob in the streets" before he would obey the bill, if enacted.[55]

The compulsory attendance bill did not pass, but legislation forbidding the use of public funds for non-public schools was enacted. The prospects for any accommodation on the School Question were, therefore, more remote than ever. The building of Catholic schools was seen as the only solution, and the provincial councils of Cincinnati between 1855 and 1866 vigorously promoted the establishment of such schools. Bishop Louis Amadeus Rappe of Cleveland considered the creation of Catholic schools as important as the building of new churches. Early in his administration, Rappe was engaged in fundraising efforts for a girls' school in Cleveland, and soon he was on his way to France looking for trained teachers. During his administration the number of schools in the Cleveland Diocese increased from a

54. Alfred G. Stritch, "Political Nativism in Cincinnati, 1830–1860," *Records of the American Catholic Society of Philadelphia* 48 (1937): 258–64.

55. James W. Taylor, *A Manual of the Ohio School System Consisting of an Historical View of its Progress and a Republication of the School Laws in Force* (Cincinnati: H. W. Derby Company, 1857), p. 218; *Catholic Telegraph*, 7 April 1858; John H. Lamott, *History of the Archdiocese of Cincinnati, 1821–1921* (New York: Frederick Pustet Company, 1921), p. 279.

mere handful to eighty-seven schools, not including academies and orphanages.[56]

In Illinois, the development of Catholic schools was in its infancy in the middle of the nineteenth century. The Diocese of Chicago had been created in 1843, and the beginnings of Catholic education were made by Bishop William J. Quarter, who arrived in his new see in 1844. These activities convinced Protestants that the Catholics constituted "a most troublesome, factious, and expensive religio-politico element." When Catholic priests requested admission to the public schools to instruct the children of Catholic parents in religion, Protestants found additional proof that these churchmen were anti-republican. They were determined to resist the "arrogant pretensions of the disciples of Rome." But Catholic activities were increased under Quarter's successor, Bishop James O. Van de Velde. Van de Velde delivered a course of controversial lectures and also organized the first Catholic newspaper in Chicago, *The Western Tablet*, in January 1852. In his newspaper, Van de Velde introduced the argument that the various Protestant denominations were losing any uniqueness, as among themselves, that they had originally had. It was because of this, he argued, that they were able in common to support the state schools. Nor did the bishop endear himself to Protestants by denouncing the public schools as "nurseries of heathenism, vice and crime."[57]

The Know-Nothing Movement in Illinois did not attain the strength it had in some other states, especially in the Northeast, but in the elections in 1854 several Know-Nothing leaders were elected to the state legislature.[58] Spurred on by the Know-Nothing agitation, Illinois in 1855 joined the list of states with legislation prohibiting public aid to sectarian institutions. Although the long-term result of this was to stimulate Catholics to increase their efforts to establish their own schools, the immediate effect was to deal a staggering blow to the non-public schools of the state. Two years after its adoption, the state superintendent of public instruction reported with obvious gratification the sweeping impact of the law: "Scarcely two years have elapsed since the Free School System went into operation in this State, and in that brief period it has nearly swept the entire field of the thousands of Private Schools which then existed." The private schools, con-

56. Michael J. Hynes, *History of the Diocese of Cleveland* (Cleveland: World Publishing Co., 1853), pp. 78, 84.

57. Mary Innocentia Montay, *The History of Catholic Secondary Education in the Archdiocese of Chicago* (Washington, D.C.: Catholic University of America Press, 1933), pp. 11–14; David W. Kucera, *Church-State Relationships in Education in Illinois* (Washington, D.C.: Catholic University of America Press, 1953), pp. 71–72.

58. John P. Senning, "The Know-Nothing Movement in Illinois from 1854–1856," *Illinois Historical Society Journal* 7 (April 1914): 7–33.

tinued the superintendent, were a holdover from the "old feudal and anti-American system" of education for "the rich alone."[59] Perhaps the superintendent's stricture on "schools for the rich alone" was true of some private schools in the rapidly developing Prairie State, but it certainly was not true of Catholic schools in the burgeoning immigrant communities.

Michigan's first state constitution, drawn up in 1835, was distinctly secular in tone. Article I, section 5 provided that "No money shall be drawn from the treasury for the benefit of religious societies or theological or religious seminaries." This prohibition was repeated (in expanded form) in Michigan's Constitution of 1850. In conformity with the Michigan constitution, and also because the Protestant and Catholic populations of the city of Detroit were at the time approximately equal, the Detroit Board of Education in 1842 excluded the use of the Bible from the schools in the city, a policy both unusual and daring for the time.[60] Protestant groups promptly charged that the board had yielded to Catholic pressures, and further that the exclusion of the Bible was in itself a sectarian act. They explained that they were not disposed to dictate which edition of the Bible was to be used, but that there was only one non-sectarian version: that authorized by King James. The Board of Education yielded early in 1845 and issued a regulation permitting the reading of either the Douay or the King James version without note or comment.[61]

The board's seemingly evenhanded directive on Bible reading did not put the controversy to rest. As a result of widespread interest in the question, State Superintendent of Public Instruction Ira Mayhew was invited to present his views before the state legislature. In a series of lectures, Mayhew supported moral and religious instruction in general terms. But as he developed his argument, he revealed that he was speaking not only for Christianity but also for Protestantism: "We, the descendants of the Puritans . . . however we may differ among ourselves in other respects, cordially unite in efforts to put the sacred treasure [of the Bible] in the hands of all the people. It is one of our cardinal principles, as Protestants, that the more they read the Scriptures the better."[62]

A public official openly espousing a Protestant point of view, with the state legislature providing an invitation and a platform for the

---

59. *Second Biennial Report of the Superintendent of Public Instruction of the State of Illinois for the Years 1857–58* (Springfield: Bailhache & Baker, Printer, 1859), p. 16.

60. Norman Drachler, "The Influence of Sectarianism, Non-Sectarism and Secularism Upon the Public Schools of Detroit and the University of Michigan, 1837–1900" (Ph.D. diss., University of Michigan, 1951), pp. 30–31.

61. Flynn, "The School Controversy," pp. 35–39.

62. *Popular Education: For the Use of Parents and Teachers and For Young Persons of Both Sexes*, 2d ed. (New York: Daniel Burgess & Company, 1852), p. 210.

expression of these views, seemed to Catholics an alarming develop-ment. A number of them now prepared a petition charging, among other things, that Mayhew had cunningly devised a system "intend-ed for the perversion of Catholic youth." The petition closed with a strong plea for the division of state funds to include parochial schools, on the grounds that Catholics could not "conscientiously send their children to the state common schools . . . ."[63]

The subsequent introduction of a bill designed to provide a share of the state educational fund for Catholic schools, and the appearance of Catholic officials in Lansing to support the bill, led to a barrage of attacks on Catholicism. Several Protestant bodies presented petitions to the legislature opposing the measure. Although it was primarily a state issue, the controversy entered the Detroit spring election in 1853, on the grounds that the election of Democrats even locally would be a blow to the cause of public education since the Democratic party supported the Catholic request. Moreover, it was alleged, the effort to divide the school funds was part of a nationwide plan, engi-neered by Jesuits, to destroy the public schools and to seize power. Voters were reminded of similar campaigns underway in Pennsyl-vania and Ohio. One Detroit newspaper, a few days prior to the election, carried a full-page attack on the Catholic clergy, and on election day warned:

WATCH YOUR SCHOOLS
LET EVERY TRUE FRIEND OF COMMON SCHOOLS BE FOUND AT THE POLLS THIS MORNING READY TO VOTE THE INDEPENDENT TICKET. FREEMEN OF DETROIT. The issue of today is between the Jesuit Priesthood and American Citi-zens.[64]

The Michigan state election on 7 March 1853 brought defeat to the Democratic party. At its annual meeting the following year, the Mich-igan State Teachers' Association adopted a stirring resolution pro-posed by a Protestant clergyman: "*Resolved* that we regard it as an arrogant assumption for those who are unfriendly to our schools to attempt to control, and for those who care least for them to claim the right to exclude their most precious treasure [the Bible] . . . ."[65] The lone dissenter, also a Protestant clergyman, was charged with having yielded to Catholic influence. For a period of at least twenty years thereafter, resolutions calling for Bible reading and daily prayers in

63. Drachler, "Influence of Sectarianism," pp. 48–49.
64. Ibid., p. 63.
65. Daniel Tutana, *A Sketch of the History of the Michigan State Teachers' Association* (Ypsilanti: Michigan State Teachers' Association, 1877), p. 69.

the schools were regularly adopted at meetings of the Michigan State Teachers' Association.[66]

In 1853, the territorial legislature of Minnesota established a committee to consider the questions connected with parochial schools, having received a number of petitions on the matter. The committee reported to the legislature that in its opinion the petitioners had just grounds for complaint, in that the school revenues were derived from all taxpayers, whereas more than one-third of the latter derived no benefit from their payments. The committee therefore submitted a bill providing that any church-related school of twenty-five or more pupils should be granted the privileges of the regular district schools, including the right to receive public monies, and might operate under the supervision of the ecclesiastical body instead of under civil school authorities.[67]

This Catholic demand for the privilege of educating their children according to the principles of their church was regarded by many as a rejection of public schools and a challenge to basic American principles. In his address to the joint session of the legislature, Governor Ramsey described the public school as the "ark of our safety." But the major responsibility for the defense of the public schools was assumed by Rev. Edward D. Neill, the territory's first superintendent of public instruction. The proposed bill, said Neill, would create serious problems in the territory. Let us assume, he said, the existence of a small community with twenty-five Presbyterian and ten Roman Catholic children. If, as would be entirely permissible under such a bill, a Presbyterian should organize a school of twenty-five children, the Catholic children would have only two choices: attendance at the Presbyterian school, where their own religious views might be derided, or no school at all. There was some substance to this argument when applied to small rural communities, although it overlooked the fact that Catholics regarded the existing public schools as Protestant institutions. Even so, the argument was to become a standard element in public school rhetoric, regardless of community size.

Neill could have let his pro-Protestant argument stand there. But as he went on, he increasingly revealed that his opposition to the parochial schools was also, and even more basically, grounded in opposition to Catholicism. Attributing authorship of the bill to the bishop of St. Paul, Neill explained that in schools under Catholic

66. Robert F. Lankton, "Attitudes toward Religion and the Schools in the Publications of the Michigan Education Association," in *Studies in the History of American Education*, ed. Claude Eggertsen (Ann Arbor: University of Michigan, 1947), p. 87.

67. *Journal of the House of Representatives during the Fourth Session* (St. Paul: Owens & Moore, Printers, 1853), pp. 130, 168.

control, "the pupils would chiefly receive oral instruction; and then civil officers would frequently be unable to read or write . . . ." Protestants should do nothing to offend Catholics, he insisted, "still they ought not for one moment give ear to the clamor of Roman Catholic Priests, who if their assertions are to be credited, never have any children, do not pay one cent into the treasury, and without exception acknowledge allegiance to a temporal power in Italy."[68] The bill was defeated by a large margin. In Minnesota, as elsewhere, if Catholics were to have schools in which their own religious views were to be respected, they would have to establish such schools themselves.

The School Question in California

Educational opportunities for the predominantly Spanish, Mexican, and Indian populations of early California were for the most part provided by agencies of the Catholic Church. The missions were centers of social and industrial activity, and "every Mission was as much a school as a church."[69] The first state superintendent of schools in California was John Marvin, elected to that office in 1850, the year that California entered the Union. As a student at Harvard Law School in the early forties, Marvin had shared the common apprehensions about the increasing numbers of immigrants, who were for the most part, he said, "at the will of insidious and artful priests who acknowledge no superior but the Vatican . . . ."[70]

By the time he assumed his educational duties as superintendent, however, Marvin apparently had changed his mind about Catholics. The first California state school law, in 1851, very probably written by Marvin, provided that any schools established by religious societies, if found to be efficiently conducted and to offer the branches of education provided in the district schools, "shall be allowed a compensation from the Public School Fund, in proportion to the number of its pupils, in the same manner as provided for District schools in the Act."[71]

The close relationship between schools and churches in California continued during the early years of statehood. Many of the public schools had their origins in the churches. The elementary school in the Baptist Church of San Francisco, founded in 1849, became the first

68. *The Nature and Importance of the American System of Public Instruction* (St. Paul: Owens & Moore, Printers, 1853), pp. 3, 7.

69. Herbert E. Bolton, "The Mission as a Frontier Institution," *The American Historical Review* 23 (October 1917): 45.

70. Howard J. Graham, "John G. Marvin and the Founding of American Legal Bibliography," *Law Library Journal* 48 (August 1955): 194–211.

71. David F. Ferris, *Judge Marvin and the Founding of the California Public School System* (Berkeley: University of California Press, 1962), p. 62.

official public school in that city in 1850. The first superintendent of schools in San Francisco, appointed in 1851, was Rev. Thomas J. Nevins, a former agent of the American Tract Society. All teachers in schools that received public funds, including those in religious orders, were certificated and licensed to teach by the county commissioners of education. One student of California school history has concluded that the work of the early ministers left a deep impression upon education in California. The pioneer ministers, he says, were not only preachers of the Gospel but frequently schoolmasters, and their influence in education persisted throughout the first fifty years of California history.[72]

Marvin's view that public assistance should be extended to all schools was not shared in all quarters, however. Perhaps the basic reason for this was that the population patterns of the state were undergoing rapid change. Beginning with the discovery of gold at Sutter's Fort, the migrants to California were predominantly Anglo-Saxon and Protestant. Despite some assimilation and intermarriage, most of the "Forty-Niners" despised the Catholic and Spanish civilization they found in the new region. Opponents of public aid to church-related schools found a stalwart leader in the person of John Swett, a champion of free public education. Swett was soon to become—and for half a century to remain—the leading educational statesman in California, as a teacher, city and state superintendent, and lobbyist. Swett was supported by many Protestant ministers and also by a Protestant magazine, the *Pacific*.

Despite Superintendent Marvin's recommendation to the contrary, the state legislature in 1852 rescinded its authorization to include church-related schools in the disbursement of public funds, and substituted in its place a provision that public monies, state or local, would be apportioned only to schools "free from any denominational and sectarian bias, control, and influences whatsoever." Nevertheless, Marvin continued to press his case. Concerned about the nonpublic and especially, because of their number, the Catholic schools in the state, he wrote to the bishop of Monterey asking for a report on Catholic educational activity. The bishop replied that about 18 percent of the total school enrollment in the state at that time was in Catholic schools, and he wrote persuasively in favor of public assistance for these schools. Convinced that the bishop's request was reasonable, Marvin asked the legislature to amend the 1852 law so that church-related schools would again be entitled to state funds on

72. Mark J. Hurley, *Church-State Relationships in Education in California* (Washington, D.C.: Catholic University of America Press, 1948), pp. 1, 4; see also William W. Ferrier, *Ninety Years of Education in California* (Berkeley: University of California Press, 1937), p. 29.

the basis of their enrollments. He recommended that the public authorities, preferably the county superintendents, visit the Catholic schools, examine the teachers, and grant regular state certificates to them if warranted, thus qualifying the schools for public money. This, he said, would "certainly be equitable to parents who paid into the accumulated school fund but were debarred from any portion of the money."[73]

But Marvin had not reckoned with the sentiment of the predominantly Protestant incoming population. The *Pacific* in San Francisco took Marvin's proposal as a signal to begin an attack on the influence of the "cowl and veil" over children, and also to launch an attack on Marvin, whom it had earlier treated favorably.[74] Others also assailed the Catholic schools. When some members of teaching orders were brought to California, the *Christian Advocate* expressed alarm at

> The large company of European priests and nuns who arrived yesterday morning . . . . we trust these ladies and gentlemen may be able to return without delay to their proper destination, particularly as the institutions of our Protestant and Republican country are known to be obnoxious to their sentiments and tastes . . . . we think it is the duty of the Attorney General of California at once to institute proceedings on behalf of this state.[75]

In spite of such controversy the legislature in 1853 followed Marvin's recommendation and again authorized a division of the school funds on a pro-rata basis to all qualified schools. John Swett complained bitterly about this, labeling it a sop to the Catholics. Protestant ministers and public school administrators in increasing numbers voiced their opposition. The *Pacific* now led a campaign to oust Marvin from office at the next election, and this effort was successful. Marvin was defeated because he favored funds for church-related schools.[76]

Curiously, the offending statute was not at once removed from the books. But the outcome was now a foregone conclusion. By this time Know-Nothingism was in the ascendancy in California, and in 1855 the party captured both houses of the legislature and the governorship. That year, with the passage of the Ashley Act, state aid for "sectarian or denominational" schools came to an end in California.[77]

73. Ferris, *Judge Marvin*, pp. 81, 92.
74. Ibid., p. 108.
75. Hurley, *Church-State Relationships in California*, p. 14.
76. Ibid., p. 23.
77. Peyton Hurt, "The Rise and Fall of the 'Know-Nothings' in California," *California Historical Society Quarterly* 9 (March-June 1930): 48. A slightly different chronology of the "sectarian" school legislation of the fifties is provided in Roy W. Cloud, *Education in California: Leaders, Organizations, and Accomplishments of the First Hundred Years* (Stanford: Stanford University Press, 1952), pp. 27ff. Yet another account is Paul Goda, "The Historical Background of California's Constitutional Provisions Prohibiting Aid to Sectarian Schools," *California Historical Society Quarterly* 46 (June 1967): 157–71.

The Protestant Denominations and the Public Schools

The struggles in several state legislatures indicate that the public school campaign was a Protestant movement and that its leaders regarded the Catholic Church as the foremost enemy of the movement. They do not tell us, however, whether the Common School Movement found support within each of the major denominations. A study by Francis X. Curran, based largely on a search of the official denominational journals of the period, enables us to learn about the discussions underway within the various Protestant church bodies.[78]

As noted earlier, several of the older Protestant denominations at first had serious misgivings about the Common School Movement. But the main body of Protestantism accepted it from the outset. This was particularly true of the most rapidly growing groups, the Methodists and Baptists. Congregationalists, although some demurred at first, soon joined the movement. And as the Catholic position on the School Question came into prominence, the leaders of these groups surged forward to defend the public school. In so doing, Protestant leaders made explicit what they had always assumed—that the public schools were Protestant institutions. The public schools were a legacy from their "Puritan ancestors," declared a committee report to the Massachusetts General Association of Congregationalist Churches in 1848. And the leading journals of the Congregationalist denomination repeatedly explained that the public school was essentially a Protestant institution.[79]

Not only was the public school regarded as a Protestant institution; it was also considered the first line of defense against the growth of Catholicism. A Methodist journal, the *Christian Advocate*, during the heat of the New York controversy published a series of articles titled "The Common Schools, the Antidote of Jesuitism."[80] The *Watchman*, a Baptist weekly, was even more outspoken: "If the children of Papists are really in danger of being corrupted in the Protestant schools of enlightened, free and happy America, it may be well for their conscientious parents and still more conscientious priests, to return them to the privileges of their ancestral homes, among the half-tamed boors of Germany . . . ."[81] Protestant journals consistently portrayed the Catholic Church as the enemy of the public schools. "The Pope hates our free schools," said the Baptist *Examiner*, and it denounced

78. *The Churches and the Schools: American Protestantism and Popular Elementary Education* (Chicago: Loyola University Press, 1954).
79. Ibid., pp. 40, 47, 49, 87–88, 101–5.
80. Ibid., p. 85.
81. Ibid., p. 101. The vehemence of the language used in denouncing Catholicism was sometimes startling. In 1874 the *Watchman* announced its discovery of a plot by the Catholic hierarchy to overcome the United States "by the porcine virtue of fertility" (ibid., p. 110).

the plot of the Man of Sin to keep the masses in ignorance. Congregationalist and Methodist journals agreed wholeheartedly.[82]

The defense of the public schools against alleged Catholic attacks thus became the leitmotif of educational discussions in these denominations, and they embraced the public school movement with militant enthusiasm. The historical claims of the church in the field of education seemed to be forgotten as their spokesmen ardently championed the rights of the state. And it was not long before they reached the only logical conclusions that could ensue from this type of reasoning: that elementary education should be a monopoly of the state, that only public schools were truly "American," that all children should be compelled to attend the state schools, that denominational schools should not be allowed to exist, and that Catholics should be permitted no voice in the management of the public schools. Such declarations began to appear in denominational journals as early as the 1840s.[83] The Baptist *Examiner* expressed this view in strong words in 1870: "When a father proposes to put his boy into the hands of masters whose alphabet of truth is that the ecclesiastical law or the church canons rule the civil law of the country, a State might be justified in interfering, and taking the boy away from father and master, placing him a system less inimical to its own safety."[84]

Although these Protestant denominations maintained virtually no elementary schools, they had long sponsored secondary and higher education. And although they all strongly affirmed the rights of the state in elementary education, they just as strongly denied the rights of the state to tax for secondary and higher education. The weakness of this position was sharply revealed by two editorials that appeared in the same issue of the *Watchman* in 1873. One asserted the right of the Baptist church to maintain its schools; the other denied the same right to Catholics. To maintain a position so equivocal as this proved to be impossible, and by the end of the century Protestant leaders had given up any claims for church priority in secondary and higher education as well.[85]

The older denominations also felt the effects of the nativist and Know-Nothing movements. The Lutheran Missouri Synod was not deflected from its course of maintaining schools, but the Episcopal and Presbyterian parochial school movements foundered and within a few years collapsed. When the Episcopal *Churchman* in 1851 editorially approved of Bishop Hughes's request for public support for

82. Ibid., pp. 39, 87–88, 102, 105.
83. Ibid., pp. 87–88.
84. Ibid., p. 106.
85. Ibid., pp. 53–55, 105, 110–17.

parochial schools, a Methodist journal shrilly denounced this coalition of "Romanist and High-Church influence." A Congregationalist clergyman admonished his erring brethren in other folds that parochial schools, whether Catholic, Episcopal, or Presbyterian, were "sectarian, divisive, narrow, clannish, anti-republican." And the *Independent*, an influential Congregationalist journal, expressed regret that Episcopalians and Presbyterians were following the bad example of Catholics in establishing separate schools. A Presbyterian editor, stung by the remark, resented this "shameless" effort to place Presbyterians "by the side of Roman Catholics."[86] Rebukes from official sources no doubt also dampened the enthusiasm of Protestant parochial school advocates. When Presbyterians pressed their demands for a share of the public school monies in the state of New York in 1850, the state superintendent replied by asking them whether Roman Catholics should also receive their share of the tax funds for their schools.[87]

As the Know-Nothing excitement of the 1850s mounted, the enthusiasm of Presbyterians and Episcopalians for their own parochial schools waned. The change was illustrated in the policy of the Episcopal *Church Review*. In 1855 this journal had sharply criticized the public schools; only a year later it reported a plot "on the part of the Romish priesthood, either to banish the Bible from our Public Schools, so as to make them absolutely atheistic in character, or else to break down the whole Common School System altogether." It was incumbent upon all Christians to support the public schools because they alone could create "true American nationality of character." By 1870 the support for Episcopalian parochial schools was all but gone. In that year the Episcopal Convention approved of parochial schools "where they are practicable," but noted that they could never take the place of public schools, which should have the support of the church not only for patriotic reasons but "for the sake of Christianity itself."[88]

The Presbyterian parochial school movement also began to decline in the fifties. It had been a difficult task from the beginning, and it was rendered more difficult by the fact that the venture was supported largely by the Old School branch of the denomination, which had broken away in 1837 on issues arising out of the Second Awakening. Although the number of Presbyterian schools reached about two hundred fifty at one time, the movement could not be sustained. The

86. Ibid., pp. 46, 87.
87. Samuel S. Randall, *History of the Common School System of the State of New York* (Troy, N.Y.: Johnson and Davis, 1871), p. 286.
88. Curran, *Churches and Schools*, pp. 28, 32.

Presbyterian Board and Assembly finally realized that the venture had failed, and it was officially discontinued in 1870.[89]

With the exception of the Lutherans, therefore, American Protestantism was now united in its support of the public elementary school. (Actually, several of the then-numerous Lutheran synods had embraced the public school long before the end of the century; the large Missouri Synod and the smaller Wisconsin Synod remained committed to the parochial school idea.) This was a major defection, but it was tempered in American minds by the fact that these groups, largely of German origin, had remained somewhat aloof, insisting upon the preservation of their own customs and language—an attitude that was later to bring them under sharp attack from native Americans.[90]

By the time of the Civil War the School Question, which had been debated so heatedly for two decades, was rapidly moving toward an answer. The decision had been foreshadowed by the position taken by the more militant Protestants in the 1840s. The basic elements of the decision were that public funds were not to be allowed for sectarian schools and that Bible reading in the King James version in the public schools was to be encouraged and, if possible, required.

The Protestant success in the campaign to bar the use of public funds for non-public schools was to become a fundamental and enduring public policy. But the policy of Bible reading in the public schools was to come under increasingly heavy attack in the closing decades of the nineteenth century.

89. Lewis J. Sherrill, *Presbyterian Parochial Schools, 1841–1870* (New Haven: Yale University Press, 1932), pp. 51–68.

90. A spirited controversy over the parochial school question occurred within the Norwegian Synod of the Lutheran Church. This was not a direct result of the Know-Nothing excitement (the synod was largely a post–Civil War development), but the conflict was one in which those who favored Old World patterns of schooling were arrayed against the champions of "Americanization." The first five presidents of the synod all possessed degrees from the National University of Norway and had served as teachers in Norway. They looked askance at the "Yankee school," which they considered to be not only irreligious but also inefficient because the instruction was largely in the hands of young and poorly educated girls. But the synod's insistence on parochial schools was challenged by many, most influential among them the young Rasmus B. Anderson, who in 1877 said provocatively, "Opposition to the American common school is treason to our country." By the late seventies, the Norwegian-American Lutherans had come to terms with the "Yankee school." There was even less enthusiasm for parochial schools in the (Swedish) Augustana Synod of the Lutheran Church. See Lawrence M. Larson, *The Changing West, and Other Essays* (Northfield, Minn.: Norwegian-American Historical Association, 1937), pp. 116–19; Theodore C. Blegen, *Norwegian Migration to America: The American Transition* (Northfield, Minn.: NAHA, 1940), chap. 8; Frank Charles Nelson, "The American School Controversy among the Norwegian Americans, 1845–1880" (Ph.D. diss., Michigan State University, 1969); Carl Emanuel Carlson, "The Adjustment of the Swedish Immigrants to the American Public School System in the Northwest" (Ph.D. diss., University of Minnesota, 1949). As a general introduction, Walter H. Beck, *Lutheran Elementary Schools in the United States* (St. Louis: Concordia Publishing House, 1939), is still useful.

6

Catholics and Protestants
Consolidate Their Positions, 1865–1885

A Brief Respite

Although always present, nativism and anti-Catholicism played a less prominent role in the political life of the United States during the Civil War and for about two decades thereafter. Everywhere during the war foreign-born Americans flocked to the colors, with five hundred thousand serving in the Union armies alone. As they did so, they gained a new standing; they were comrades in arms. Behind the lines, factories and farms clamored for immigrant labor to meet the heavy demands imposed upon them. The postwar industrial and agricultural growth only increased the need for labor. The railroads, which had started even before the war to recruit labor in Europe, now intensified these efforts. Mining enterprises throughout the country were chiefly dependent on foreign-born labor, and manufacturing only slightly less so. By 1870 one of every three employees in manufacturing and mechanical industries was an immigrant, and that proportion remained constant until after 1920.

Increasingly, the belief grew that there was nothing to be feared from the immigrant. On the contrary, he had come to be seen as a positive asset in American economic life in the Gilded Age. In these postwar years of confidence and material success—as contrasted with the prewar spirit of fear and uncertainty—it was possible for Americans to fashion an image of themselves as an inclusive nationality, diverse yet homogenous, assimilating many types of men into a unified, superior people. This concept, later to become popularized as the melting pot theory, had been advanced even before the war by Emerson, Whitman, and Melville, and was espoused after the war by Darwin, Spencer, W. T. Harris, and Frederick Jackson Turner. This optimistic and confident view prevailed until the middle 1880s; Professor Higham has described it as "The Age of Confidence."[1]

1. John Higham, *Strangers in the Land: Patterns of American Nativism 1860–1925* (New Brunswick, N.J.: Rutgers University Press, 1955), pp. 16, 21–22.

Although local disputes over the School Question arose, even during the war, it seemed for a time that compromises might be possible. In Grafton, Massachusetts, in 1862, a boy was expelled from a public school for refusing to read from the Protestant version of the Bible. There had been other such cases, and a Catholic priest submitted to the state legislature a petition asking that no student be compelled, against the wishes of his parents, to recite any particular form of prayer or to read any particular version of the Scriptures. Such a petition would have been given short shrift in the Know-Nothing legislature a few years earlier, but the debates in both the House and Senate revealed that the participation of the Irish in the military effort had put things in a new light. The legislature enacted a measure providing that "The school committee shall require the daily reading of some portion of the Bible . . . in the public schools, but they shall require no scholar to read from any particular version . . . ."[2]

This was a far cry from the compulsory reading in "the common English version" required in the 1855 law enacted by the Know-Nothings. To be sure, not all local school officials were ready to comply. In 1864 a boy and his sister were repeatedly punished by the principal of a public school in Shirley, Massachusetts, for refusing to read from the Protestant Scriptures. When their complaints brought no relief, the parents instituted legal action. Although the principal was able to escape punishment by means of later legal action, his conviction in the original trial was regarded by Catholics as an indication that some consideration of their rights might be expected.[3]

Indeed, in the more tolerant atmosphere that now existed, the charter for Holy Cross College, which had been denied in 1849, was granted. The only vestige of the old controversy was a provision that the granting of the charter should not be considered "as any pledge of the Commonwealth that pecuniary aid shall hereinafter be granted to the College."[4] Even the presence in the House of Rev. Erastus Hopkins, former Know-Nothing leader and chairman of the House Education Committee when the 1849 measure was defeated, did not now prevent its passage. But more serious problems lay ahead.

Public Aid to Church-Related Schools?

The struggle over public aid to church-related institutions resumed in a dramatic manner in 1869. That year, the proponents of public aid for parochial schools won their first major success of the postbellum

2. 1862 Mass. Acts ch. 57.
3. Katherine E. Conway and Mabel W. Cameron, *Charles Francis Donnelly, A Memoir* (New York: J. T. White & Co., 1909), p. 121; *Pilot*, 23 April 1864.
4. 1865 Mass. Acts ch. 99.

THE AMERICAN RIVER GANGES.

THE PRIESTS AND THE CHILDREN.—[See Page 911.]

As the New York City school controversy of 1869–1871 drew to a close, the country's leading political cartoonist, Thomas Nast, published in the *Harper's Weekly* of 30 September 1871 the most terrifying of his many anti-Catholic cartoons. In the background, with the flag still flying above it, is a public school building destroyed by Catholics. In the foreground, Boss Tweed and his Irish politicians prepare to sacrifice public school children to the "bishops."

period, in New York City. William M. Tweed of Tammany Hall was the architect of the 1869 plans. A Protestant himself, Tweed's plan for subsidizing parochial schools was designed to appeal to the Irish and Germans, most of them Catholic, who comprised a large part of the Ring's political strength. Public support for orphanages, hospitals, and schools conducted by voluntary associations had existed in the city long before Tweed's rise to power; it was considered more economical than the construction of public institutions. But Tweed's operations were on a much greater scale. As a member of the state Senate, he introduced a bill in 1869 to permit the city and county of New York to pay a portion of the annual expenses of parochial schools. Despite his careful management, the intent of the bill was apparent to the Republican majority, and it was defeated. Tweed then embodied substantially the same proposals in the annual tax-levy bill for the government of New York City, which was also subject to legislative approval. Imbedded in this lengthy and complex budget bill, the school provision passed. But it was not long before the Re-

publican opposition detected the ruse, and when the legislature re-
convened early in 1870, it was deluged by petitions for repeal of the
school "steal." Tweed and his lieutenants salvaged what they could
for their friends and withdrew from the fray. The next year the legislature adopted a law forbidding New York City to appropriate money
for "any institution or enterprise that is under the control of a religious denomination." It was, therefore, a fleeting success for the
proponents of public aid to church-related schools, followed by a
crushing defeat. Even so, Boss Tweed did achieve parts of a much-
needed social welfare program in an age when those in power rejected the concept of public responsibility for social welfare.[5]

Repulsed in New York, the friends of the parochial schools met
failure in other states as well during the seventies. Several states,
most of which already had statutory provisions for prohibiting such
use of public funds, now incorporated these prohibitions into their
constitutions, among them Missouri, Illinois, Pennsylvania, New
Jersey, Nebraska, Texas, Colorado, and Minnesota.[6] Clearly, the
prospects for advancement along these lines were unfavorable.

There was, however, another approach, that of incorporating a
Catholic school or schools into a public school system. Such a plan
would be worked out at the local, not the state, level, and it would
depend for its success upon a reasonable degree of local goodwill and
cooperation. Plans of this type had been tried before the war in a few
places, among them Lowell, Massachusetts, where the arrangement
had served well for several years before it was swallowed up in the
Know-Nothing excitement. In the postwar decades such plans received increased attention, especially in the East, where the Catholics
were predominantly Irish. German Catholics, more numerous west
of the Alleghenies, were less favorable to cooperative, public-parochial school ventures.

The form of public aid established in these areas was similar to that
which was to gain national attention as the "Poughkeepsie Plan." In
1890, a collection of several articles on the postwar public-parochial
school ventures, both favorable and unfavorable, was published in a
well-known journal, the *Independent*. Both the local school-board

5. John Pratt, "Boss Tweed's Public Welfare Program," *New York Historical Society
Quarterly* 45 (October 1961): 396–411. A veritable avalanche of anti-Catholic literature
was inspired by this controversy, including Samuel W. Barnum, *Romanism As It Is, An
Exposition of the Roman Catholic System* (Hartford: Connecticut Publishing Company,
1871); Dexter A. Hawkins, *Archbishop Purcell Outdone! The Roman Catholic Church in New
York City and Public Land and Public Money* (New York: Phillips and Hunt, 1887); Joseph
Hartwell, *Romanism and Politics; Tammany Hall the Stronghold of Rome* (New York: J. A.
O'Connor, 1887). The battle over the School Question played an important part in the
exposure of the Tweed Ring in 1870.

6. Alvin P. Stauffer, "Anti-Catholicism in American Politics, 1865–1900" (Ph.D. diss.,
Harvard University, 1933), pp. 54, 63–64.

president and the parish priest from Poughkeepsie, New York, reported on the widely heralded plan. Among the other contributors were U.S. Commissioner of Education W. T. Harris, Cardinal Gibbons, John Jay, and Archbishop Ireland.[7]

In 1873 the Poughkeepsie parish priest, with Archbishop McCloskey's approval, requested that the local board of education provide educational facilities for over eight hundred children attending two parochial schools that were about to be discontinued. Such closure would have created an increase of almost 50 percent in the public school enrollment of the district. The board, therefore, willingly accepted an offer made by the priest to permit the board to use the school buildings and furniture owned by the church. The agreement was that the board was to lease the school buildings from the church at the nominal rent of one dollar per year, keep them in repair, and pay for the cost of maintenance, teacher salaries, and other expenses, as for the other schools. The church was to have the privilege of using the building for its own purposes outside school hours. No religious instruction was to be given during school hours. The course of studies, textbooks, appointment of teachers, and general conduct of the school was to be entirely under the jurisdiction of the board, and its officers and agents were to be allowed free access to the building during school hours. It was further agreed that at the end of any school year either party might terminate the agreement by giving thirty days notice. "This arrangement is still in operation," concluded the school board president in 1890.[8]

Much different, however, was "The Pittsburg [sic] Failure," a title applied to his own efforts in that city by a Catholic priest. Rev. James J. McTighe accepted an appointment as principal of the public school of his ward of the city in 1887. He stated candidly that he did this because of his belief that the financial burden of maintaining the parochial school had become too heavy for his parishioners. The parochial school was closed and the pupils were transferred in a body to the public school. Arrangements were made for the teaching of religion in the parochial school building for half an hour each morning before the opening of school, but this was to be voluntary. According to his account, Father McTighe made strenuous efforts to make the school non-sectarian. He adopted the dress of a layman and required pupils to call him "Mister Principal" instead of "Father." To the priest's dismay, the plans for religious instruction during off-school

---

7. "The Education of the People: A Symposium," *The Independent* 42 (4 September 1890): 1–13.

8. The venture was, however, terminated by the public authorities in 1898 after some controversy. J. A. Burns and Bernard J. Kohlbrenner, *A History of Catholic Education in the United States* (New York: Benziger Brothers, 1937), pp. 160–62.

hours collapsed. Of the three hundred pupils who had transferred from the parochial to the public school, only some fifty were attending the religious instruction. The reason may have been, McTighe surmised, that the Catholic parents simply took it for granted, as the principal was a Catholic priest, that the spiritual welfare of their children was assured. In any event, McTighe resigned his position and reopened the parochial school, expressing profound regret about the venture: "I presided over a school that according to the American idea could not offend Protestant, Jew, Turk, infidel or agnostic, but which in fact, as I now see, must have offended the great God grievously."[9]

Several other cooperative public-parochial school ventures were reviewed in the *Independent* symposium. An agreement entered into by the board of education at Suspension Bridge, New York, was declared illegal by the State Department of Education three years later. The superintendent of the Massachusetts Board of Education wrote, "Our public schools do not allow any interference on the part of either Catholics or Protestants as such." The superintendent of public education of Savannah, Georgia, reported that a public-parochial school agreement had been in existence there for many years. He concluded, "This arrangement . . . has worked very harmoniously and to the satisfaction of all parties." Similar arrangements were in existence in Macon and in Augusta, Georgia. In Pennsylvania, for some years, the school board of the Gallitzen Borough School District employed teaching sisters as members of the public system.

There were many public-parochial school ventures less well known than those reviewed by the *Independent*. Largely through the influence of a group including Bishop Bernard J. McQuaid of Rochester, variations of the Poughkeepsie Plan were adopted in several towns in New York during the 1870s, among them Lima, Elmira, Corning, Albion, and Medina. There were also several public-parochial school ventures in Connecticut, the most widely publicized of which was the one in New Haven, started in 1868 and (although suspended during the years 1877–1879) still in existence in 1944. Daniel Coit Gilman, president of Yale, did not relish these efforts "to exhibit the power of a Roman Catholic party excited by the priests."[10]

Public-parochial school ventures were viewed less favorably by Catholic clergy in the West, although there were exceptions, notably John Ireland. During the 1840s and 1850s German Catholic immi-

9. James J. McTighe, "The Pittsburg Failure," *The Independent* 42 (4 September 1890): 7.

10. Arthur James Heffernan, *A History of Catholic Education in Connecticut* (Washington, D.C.: Catholic University of America Press, 1936), pp. 33–37, 55–73; Daniel Coit Gilman, *New Phases of the School Question in Connecticut* (New Haven: N.p., 1867), p. 7; Stauffer, "Anti-Catholicism," p. 46.

grants in large numbers had settled in the dioceses of the Province of Cincinnati, which at that time extended from the Alleghenies to the Mississippi. Most of the clergy in the province were themselves immigrants. Accustomed in their native land to parochial solidarity and the principle of elementary schools organized upon parochial lines, these clergy came to be a strong factor in the development of Catholic policy on education. Archbishop Hennessy of Dubuque, although not a German, no doubt spoke for many of them when he said concerning the public schools that it was the mission of the Church "to rescue these little ones out of the grasp of that monster," and he threatened to deny the sacraments to parents of children who attended state schools.[11]

Protestants in the West shared the distrust toward public-parochial school ventures. The collection of articles published by the *Independent* in 1890 contained comments by public school leaders in the West that were probably typical. The state commissioner of common schools of Ohio said, "I have been unable to discover any possibility of an adjustment between the [public and the] Catholic parochial schools of our State, and I do not believe such a possibility exists." The secretary of the Board of Education in Dubuque, Iowa, hotly denied a report that in his city there were "over fifty public schools which are under the complete control of Roman Catholics . . . ." Instead, he declared that the public schools there were conducted on a strictly non-sectarian basis and that the American flag flew proudly over every school.

Campaigns in the West to obtain public support for the parochial schools were mostly unsuccessful. Although the Poughkeepsie Plan was adopted for one of the two parochial schools in East St. Louis in 1875, campaigns for public support were rebuffed in Detroit, Indianapolis, and Kansas City. In St. Cloud, and in Stearns County, Minnesota, where German Catholics constituted a majority of the population, an arrangement whereby Catholic priests were permitted to enter the public schools to teach the catechism twice a week to Catholic children met with great opposition. Archbishop Ireland's plan, which became known as the Faribault-Stillwater (Minnesota) Plan, involved renting the Catholic school to the city, retaining the nuns as teachers, and conducting religious instruction outside school hours. This plan was abandoned after two years because of Protestant opposition. In Chicago, Irish and German Catholics were growing in numbers, and they supported a movement to establish church-related schools supported by the city and to strengthen Catholic representation on the school board. Although these measures were not

11. *The Independent* 63 (3 December 1891): 1786.

adopted, the reading of the Bible was abandoned in Chicago in September 1875 in spite of opposition.[12]

Given the hostility of German Catholics in the West toward public-parochial school experiments, it is understandable that a strong demand for purely church-controlled schools should come from this region. The First Provincial Council of Cincinnati, in 1855, urged the establishment of parochial schools, and the Second Council in 1858 made them obligatory in every parish unless the pastor could prove that this was economically impossible. These decrees of the Council of 1858 were approved by Pope Pius IX in 1858. When the Second Plenary Council of Baltimore met in 1866, the bishops of the Province of Cincinnati took a leading part in urging educational legislation along the lines they had already established in their own dioceses.

But the national hierarchy was not ready to proceed as far as the Cincinnati Province desired. Germans, especially those of the Cincinnati Province, resented this, and they now submitted a plea for stronger measures to the Congregation of the Propaganda, which was at the time responsible for general supervision over the Church in the United States. The Congregation, apparently yielding to these representations, in 1875 issued an "Instruction . . . concerning the Public Schools," and this was approved by the Pope. In this document the Congregation expressed their concern that for Catholic children of the United States, "evils of the gravest kind are likely to result from the so-called public schools," which are "most dangerous and very much opposed to Catholicity." Catholic parents should send their children to Catholic schools, and Catholic bishops would be regarded as "recreant to their duty if they failed to do their very utmost to provide Catholic schools . . . ."[13] Exceptions could be made only if there were no local Catholic schools, or if the available Catholic schools were not suitable to the conditions and circumstances of the pupils. But even in such cases the judgment was entrusted to the bishop, not to the local priest or parent.

With the judgment expressly delegated to the bishop, the existing tendency toward a strict interpretation among the German group increased. Bishop P. J. Baltes of Alton, Illinois, made an extended attack upon the public schools as "Seminaries of infidelity, and as such most fruitful sources of immorality." Accordingly, Baltes autho-

12. Francis E. Abbott, "The Catholic Peril," *Fortnightly Review* 25 (March 1876): 387–410; *Catholic Record* 10 (April 1887): 382; Barnum, *Romanism*, p. 778; Editorial, *Educational Review* 8 (1892): 96; Thomas McAvoy, "Americanism, Fact and Fiction," *Catholic Historical Review* 30 (April 1945): 138; Charles W. Alvord, ed., *The Centennial History of Illinois*, 5 vols. (Springfield, Ill.: Illinois Centennial Commission, 1918–1920), 4:36–38.

13. "Instruction of the Congregation of Propaganda de Fide Concerning Catholic Children Attending American Public Schools," in *Documents of American Catholic History*, ed. John Tracy Ellis (Milwaukee: Bruce Publishing Co., 1956), pp. 416–20.

rized the pastors in his diocese to exclude from the sacrament Catholic parents who did not send their children to Catholic schools. Such exclusion was exercised in other dioceses as well, and sometimes local pastors excluded errant parents from communion without authorization from their bishops.[14] A fairly widespread disposition among the Catholic clergy in the East to hope for some sort of reconciliation between the Catholics and the public school system was obviously suspect among the German clergy in the West.

In the West, as in the East, the major trial of strength came in 1869. As partisans in all parts of the country watched, the "Bible War" engulfed Cincinnati in a major episode of fear and hostility. Daily Bible reading had been practiced in the Cincinnati public school system since its establishment in 1829. The practice had been made voluntary in 1842, when Bishop (later Archbishop) John P. Purcell served as a city school examiner. In 1852 the practice was again made a requirement, although the version to be used was made optional. Meanwhile, the building of a separate system of Catholic parochial schools was underway in the city.

The possibility of consolidating the two school systems had been discussed among the Catholic and non-Catholic members of the Cincinnati Board of Education. In 1869 ten Catholic members of the forty-man board drew up a proposal for the incorporation of the church schools into the public educational system. This plan called for the purchase and consolidation of all Catholic schools by the public authorities, with the stipulation that "no religious books, papers or documents shall be permitted in them," and a further explicit statement prohibiting the reading of the Bible. But the projected removal of the Bible from the schools immediately gave rise to a vigorous no-popery crusade. Indignant pastors and newspaper editors warned against the "black brigade" of Rome. Opponents presented to the board petitions bearing the names of more than ten thousand persons, including about twenty-five hundred children from the local Sunday schools. When the plan was presented to Archbishop John P. Purcell, however, a stalemate arose. It will be recalled that Purcell had encouraged Catholics to support the Common School Movement in the late 1830s and had himself served as a school board member (examiner) in the 1840s. But that was before the Protestant coloration of the schools was fully understood by Catholics. The archbishop now declared that he could not approve of a "system of education for youth which is apart from instruction in the Catholic faith and the teachings of the Church." He countered by suggesting that the board

14. Thomas J. Jenkins, *The Judges of Faith: Christian and Godless Schools* (Baltimore: John Murphy & Co., 1886), p. 106.

consider the establishment of a plan similar to those existing in "England, France, Canada, Prussia, and other countries, where the rights of conscience in the matter of education have been fully recognized . . . ."

In the eyes of the board, the prospect of maintaining separate educational structures closed the door to further negotiations. There remained, however, the resolution proposing removal of the Bible from the schoolrooms. As the issue narrowed to this, the campaign against the Catholic Church intensified. A group calling itself the Friends of the Bible carried on a vigorous campaign. Meetings of the Board of Education became endless defenses and attacks and readings of petitions. Rev. Amory D. Mayo denounced another member of the board as a "materialist and an atheist." Finally, at midnight on 1 November 1869, the board voted 22 to 15 to exclude the Bible from the public schools of Cincinnati.

Protestants were outraged. The board was denounced for its submission to a "Scheming Priestcraft" intent upon the destruction of the American public schools—in spite of the fact that a large majority of the members of the board were Protestants. Within the month a number of citizens petitioned the Superior Court of Cincinnati for an injunction to prevent the board from carrying out its policy. Correspondence from other cities in Ohio, and from New York, Chicago, and San Francisco, indicated that the case was being closely followed by the citizens of other states. By a vote of 2 to 1, with Judge Alphonso Taft dissenting, the tribunal "saved the Bible" by upholding the injunction. But in 1873, the Supreme Court of Ohio unanimously reversed the decision of the superior court, asserting that the Cleveland school board had acted within its authority in eliminating Bible reading in its schools. It was the most stunning defeat yet suffered by the proponents of Bible reading. Several other Ohio cities followed Cincinnati's example and eliminated Bible reading from their schools.[15] So the results of the "Cincinnati Bible War" were mixed: the Catholic bid for public support of their schools was rejected, and the Protestants lost Bible reading in the public schools.

Catholic efforts to secure public funds for their parochial schools met with increasing opposition during the decades following the Civil War, and the public-parochial school ventures fared little better. In the end, they did not prove satisfactory to either Catholics or Protestants, and few survived into the new century. In many cases the public-parochial agreements were entered into at a time when neither

15. Harold M. Helfman, "The Cincinnati 'Bible War,'" *Ohio State Archaeological Historical Quarterly* 60 (October 1951): 369–86. See also Bernard Mandel, "Religion and the Public Schools of Ohio," *Ohio State Archaeological Historical Quarterly* 58 (April 1949): 185–206.

the civil nor the parish authorities could separately provide for burgeoning school enrollments. Often those schools became the casualties of community opposition. But, from the Catholic point of view also, the schools had grave defects. Religious instruction during the school day had to be given up; it was permitted only before or after school hours. But such compartmentalizing of religious instruction was not in harmony with Catholic theory, which holds that religion should permeate school activities. And the stipulation that the teachers in these schools were to be Catholic ran afoul of the growing belief that teachers should be selected without reference to their religious beliefs. In 1944, a Catholic scholar concluded his consideration of these schools by saying:

> Examination of actual practices in these schools indicates that in most cases the school board has yielded to Church authorities responsibilities (particularly over teacher selection) which cannot legally be delegated, and at the same time the abandonment of specifically Catholic practices has resulted in a school which can hardly be called either parochial or Catholic in the sense of the Baltimore Council or of the Canon Law. The fact that such arrangements are illegal under both civil and ecclesiastical law necessarily adds to their insecurity and undesirability.[16]

Clearly this was not the solution of the School Question in the United States, even though compromise plans had proved to be workable in many other nations.

The Catholic Question in State and Local Politics

Disputes concerning public aid to non-public schools and Bible reading in the public schools were waged in the political arena and were in that sense political issues. But Protestants and Catholics found themselves arrayed against each other on other political issues as well. Prime among them was the growing political power of Catholics and their increasing disposition to use that power.

To many, the conquest of the United States by Catholics, which had been predicted by Samuel F. B. Morse early in the century, seemed to be nearing reality by 1880. That year, the Irish-American William R. Grace became the first Catholic to be nominated for mayor of New York City. Republican Elihu Root warned that the election of Grace would be tantamount to delivering control over the municipal government to one sect to the exclusion of others, and a Protestant clergyman foresaw the destruction of all Protestant institutions. The *New York Times* feared that the public schools would be "romanized."

16. Francis Joseph Donohue, "The Development of American Catholic Theory, Attitudes and Practices with Regard to Public Support for Parochial Schools" (Ph.D. diss., University of Michigan, 1944), pp. 247–48.

Although Grace did not get the Protestant vote, he won the election and became the first of a long list of Catholic mayors of New York City. In 1884, Hugh O'Brien was elected the first Catholic mayor of Boston, and was subsequently re-elected. The apprehensions of native Americans were not relieved by O'Brien's boast that "this old Puritan city of Boston is, I am happy to say, the most Catholic city in the country."

Elsewhere in Massachusetts, as well, Catholics were elected as mayors in the 1880s: in Springfield, Lowell, Lawrence, and Holyoke. In Connecticut, Rhode Island, upstate New York, and New Jersey, Catholics gained a dominant position in the Democratic party. In the Midwest, many city Democratic machines were to a large extent under the control of Catholics, among them those in Chicago, Indianapolis, St. Louis, Kansas City, Omaha, St. Paul, Minneapolis, and Detroit, as well as several smaller places.[17]

Meanwhile, Republicans in many places had given their support to the movement against public aid to sectarian schools. This was understandable because the Republican party was composed almost entirely of non-Catholics. In New York the Republican platform in 1875 declared that "the free public school is the bulwark of the American Republic" and denounced any project for public support for sectarian institutions. Similar declarations were adopted by the party in Ohio, Connecticut, Missouri, Wisconsin, and California. In Indiana the Republican state convention went further, declaring that it was "incompatible with American citizenship to pay allegiance to any foreign power, civil or ecclesiastical," thereby in effect denying that Catholics had a right to citizenship. Religious and educational issues were injected into political discussions in other states also, among them Maine, Connecticut, New York, New Jersey, Pennsylvania, Maryland, Indiana, California, and Oregon. In Wisconsin, the Republicans attempted to arouse the religious prejudices of the Germans by comparing the school controversy with the struggles of Luther and Bismarck with the papacy.[18]

Although disputes over the School Question continued to arise in all parts of the country during the seventies and eighties, those in Ohio were particularly sharp. Two powerful and aggressive figures played leading roles: Rutherford B. Hayes and Bishop Gilmour. Late in 1875, the Ohio Republican Convention nominated for the governorship Rutherford B. Hayes, a strong advocate of the reading of the Bible in the public schools. Hayes had already served twice (1867–1871) in this office and was to win the presidency the following year.

17. Stauffer, "Anti-Catholicism," pp. 93–94, 102–5, 110.

18. Ibid., p. 65; Catholic Record, April 1876, p. 325; Herman J. Deutsch, "Wisconsin Politics of the Seventies," Wisconsin Magazine of History 14 (June 1931): 409–11.

In the campaign, Hayes emphasized the School Question and the alleged Democratic-Catholic alliance. In one of his addresses he declared that a "formidable part" of the Democratic party was intent upon the destruction of the public school system. In a letter he urged his fellow Republicans to keep the "Catholic question" alive and to oppose any sectarian interference with the schools. When Hayes was elected to the governorship he acknowledged the support that had been given him by the American Alliance, one of the increasing number of anti-Catholic organizations. The Geghan Law, enacted earlier in the year and regarded by Republicans as a Catholic measure, was promptly repealed. This law had provided that inmates of state institutions should be allowed to attend services conducted by clergymen of the denominations to which they belonged, prohibited compulsory attendance at religious services, and abolished salaries of all churchmen at public institutions.[19]

Bishop Gilmour was actively engaged in political activities during the course of his administration of the Cleveland diocese (1871–1891). (He was also the author of the *Gilmour Readers*, which for more than forty years were standard texts in Catholic schools throughout the country.) In his first pastoral, in 1873, Bishop Gilmour spoke forcefully on the School Question. He stated his belief that honest Americans, if they understood the situation, would see the injustice of making Catholics suffer financially because of their beliefs concerning the religious education of their children. He insisted that Catholic parents could not send their children to public schools without endangering their faith. For that reason, if at all possible financially, Catholic schools must be built, even before churches. He ordered every parish to establish and maintain such a school and all Catholic parents to send their children to them, under penalty of denial of the sacraments, except in cases where there existed a compelling reason to the contrary. Although many applauded this vigorous statement, it also aroused lively controversy. The *Cleveland Leader* and the *Cleveland Herald* mounted continuing attacks upon Gilmour and his works, to which the bishop replied, "Now that the war is over and . . . Catholic soldiers and generals are no longer needed, the Know-Nothing lodges are revived and lean cadaverous parsons begin to lecture and sharp nosed puritan tract peddlers are busy."[20]

The controversy in Cleveland had its echoes even in New York. The stridently anti-Catholic *Harper's Weekly* carried a cartoon by the

19. Charles R. Williams, *The Life of Rutherford Birchard Hayes*, 2 vols. (New York: Houghton Mifflin, 1941), 1:287, 189, 397–401, 476–78; Williams, ed., *Diary and Letters of Rutherford Birchard Hayes*, 5 vols. (Columbus, Ohio: State Archeological and Historical Society, 1922–1926), 3:284.

20. Michael J. Hynes, *History of the Diocese of Cleveland, Origin and Growth, 1847–1952* (Cleveland: World Publishing Company, 1953), p. 121.

well-known Thomas Nast portraying Bishop Gilmour on a paper throne, hurling bolts of excommunication against fearful Catholics who wished to send their children to public schools. An article accompanying the cartoon called for a rigorous system of compulsory education in the public schools and for a clause in the federal constitution prohibiting "the appropriation of public money for sectarian purposes."

In order to present the Catholic position more fully, Gilmour established in 1874 the *Catholic Universe*, which actively entered the political discussions of Ohio. That journal was very probably one of the causes for the defeat of the proposed state constitution of 1874, which would have specifically prohibited public aid to private schools, and it also played an active role in the 1875 campaign for the governorship.

Although a staunch champion of Catholic schools, Bishop Gilmour insisted that he was not opposed to state education as such. At every opportunity, however, he spoke out against purely secular education and against the establishment of a state monopoly in education. His basic argument was, of course, that religious instruction was an indispensable part of education. He publicized these views in secular journals, including the *Forum*, as well as in his own journal. On several occasions Gilmour opposed free school bills on the grounds that the revenues produced were unjustly denied to Catholic schools. Such a bill was defeated in the Ohio Assembly in 1885, in part perhaps because of his opposition. He opposed also a proposal in Cleveland in 1886 to provide free textbooks exclusively to the pupils in the public schools.

On one occasion, Gilmour offered to place the parochial schools of Cleveland under the control of the city board during school hours, when no religion would be taught, on the conditions that religious instruction would be permitted outside school hours and that the city would pay the salary of the regular teachers. He pointed out that such a system had been working with some satisfaction in other districts of the state. On another occasion, at a time when nearly half the schoolchildren of Cleveland were in Catholic schools, Gilmour challenged a comparison of the Catholic schools, grade for grade, with the public schools of the city. These proposals were not accepted by the public school board.

In 1875, a case involving the use of public money for support of a Protestant-sponsored school in Cleveland arose. To the dismay of many Protestants, there were several Catholic members on the city school board. One of them, a priest, objected to the use of public funds for the Industrial School, conducted at the time by a Protestant association. The managers of the school had allegedly criticized the religious beliefs of the Catholic boys in attendance. It was established during the inquiry that Protestant prayers and Bible reading were conducted not only in the Industrial School but in the city public schools as well. A resolution to prohibit such practices in the public schools was tabled by the board, but the board did resolve that the teaching of the Protestant religion in the Industrial School would have to be stopped if public funds were to be used to pay the teachers.[21]

The most serious controversy during Gilmour's administration concerned the taxation of church property. A local auditor ruled in 1876 that the Catholic school properties in Cleveland were delinquent in tax payments and ordered that they be put up for sale. In court, the auditor's attorney argued that even though Catholic schools were institutions of public charity they were nevertheless hostile to the public policy of the state. All the while, the *Cleveland Leader* was assailing Gilmour's position in its columns. In 1877, the common pleas court held against the county auditor, declaring that the schools were exempt from taxation. This decision was upheld by the district court, and finally, in 1883, by the Ohio Supreme Court. The tax-exempt status of Catholic schools had been established in Ohio, but only after seven years of litigation.[22]

But proposals to tax church property were less popular with Protestants than measures prohibiting state aid to church-related institutions, for the former would have subjected Protestant as well as Catholic properties to taxation. It was therefore often proposed that church buildings used solely for worship should be exempt from taxation, but that all other church property should be taxed. Thus Protestant denominations would remain virtually free from liability, while the Catholic Church would presumably be assessed for her school properties. Even in this form, such proposals were defeated in several states.

The *Catholic World* and the School Question

Although discussions of the School Question appeared in a very large range of newspapers and journals, the frequent articles on the subject in the *Catholic World* were certainly a major influence in shaping Catholic opinion. Isaac Thomas Hecker, founder of the Paulist Fathers and editor of the *Catholic World*, had come to Catholicism by a circuitous route. Born in 1819, his early education had been gained in the public schools. During early manhood he had numbered among

21. Ibid., pp. 127–29, 131.
22. Ibid., p. 130. Archbishop Purcell of Cincinnati also had been involved in legal proceedings over the taxation of Catholic school properties, but that case was resolved before it reached the state's high court. John H. Lamott, *History of the Archdiocese of Cincinnati, 1821–1921* (New York: Frederick Pustet Co., 1921), pp. 279–80.

his friends Thoreau, Emerson, Bronson Alcott, and Orestes Brownson, and he had spent some time at Brook Farm. Brownson's efforts to adapt Catholicism to American thought, although they met with little success, left a deep impression upon Hecker.[23]

Hecker's early editorials expressed the conviction that only the Catholic Church could provide the moral and spiritual guidance needed if America were to achieve its great destiny. He noted with gratification the growth in Catholic ranks, and also what he construed to be the "withering" of Protestantism.[24] Inevitably, his thoughts turned to education, and a steady succession of articles followed. His earlier articles were not unfriendly toward the public schools, although he reported that one classroom he observed resembled a Methodist Sunday school more than a schoolroom. Since Protestants appeared satisfied with the common schools, said Hecker, it did not behoove Catholics to question their choice. As for Catholics, they were following the dictates of their own religious beliefs in wanting their own schools and were logically entitled to a share of the public funds. Historically, Hecker argued, all American schools had been parochial schools and would still be so were it not for the fragmentation within Protestantism.[25]

It was not long, however, before Hecker's position on the School Question began to harden. Father Hecker was certainly one of the leaders of the liberal wing of the Catholic Church in the United States in that he felt that the Church must accommodate itself to American ideals of freedom and democracy. But many events, some of them within the Church, forced Hecker to rethink his position. The 1864 *Syllabus of Errors* had denounced as an error the theory that "popular schools open to children of every class of the people . . . should be freed from ecclesiastical authority . . . and should be fully subjected to the political and civil power . . . ." The Vatican Decree of 1870 asserting papal infallibility in matters of faith and morals created even greater difficulties, as we shall see, not only for priests but for the large majority of American prelates. This left little room for Hecker and other liberal priests to maneuver. They could reject the decree and the syllabus and face the consequences, or they could acquiesce. Hecker chose the latter course, and it was immediately apparent in the editorials and articles carried in the *Catholic World*.

The best education for American citizenship, maintained the Cath-

23. Vincent F. Holden, *The Early Years of Isaac Thomas Hecker, 1819–1844* (Washington, D.C.: Catholic University of America Press, 1939), pp. 45–46; Oscar Handlin, *Boston Immigrants* (Cambridge: Harvard University Press, 1959), pp. 149–50.

24. "Religion in New York," *Catholic World* (hereafter cited as *CW*) 3 (June 1866): 381–89; "A Few Thoughts About Protestants," *CW* 5 (October 1867): 134.

25. "In the School Room," *CW* 8 (October 1868): 135–36; "The Educational Question," *CW* 9 (April 1869): 121–35; "The School Question," *CW* 11 (April 1870): 91–106.

olic journal, "can be given only by the church or under her direction and control; and as there is for us Catholics only one church, there is and can be no proper education for us not given by or under the direction and control of the Catholic church." Hecker conceded that the state could say how much secular education it judged to be necessary in all schools. Once that was done, the church would teach the required secular curriculum along with the religious training it considered necessary. If such an accommodation could be reached, the state might even send inspectors into the parochial schools to ascertain whether or not the appropriate type of secular education was being taught.[26]

All education had to be based upon and constructed from true religious principles, said the *Catholic World*. In American society, there were such divergent religious beliefs that no common religious basis could be found for the schools, and therefore the state had no right to teach any religion in its schools. Schools operated by the state were therefore godless by simple definition and incapable of forming the character of children. Without religion in the school, even the secular aspects of education were bound to be inadequate. There was one exception to this rule, Hecker conceded: the state had a right and a duty to interfere with the education of children "where parents either through poverty, misfortune, crime, or any other cause are unable or unwilling to take proper charge of their children."[27]

However desirable and even mandatory a system of parochial schools might be, there were obvious obstacles. For one thing, such parochial schools as existed lacked any national direction or unity. For another, the quality of the parochial schools was not high. To remedy these weaknesses, Hecker insisted that each Catholic diocese must have its own school board, superintendent, and inspectors, rather than leave all control to the parish priest. From such a local organization could stem a national Catholic school system utilizing only Catholic textbooks. It was not long before the *Catholic World* was calling for the establishment of a Catholic National University to give "tone and direction" to the Catholic school system.[28]

Hecker was not alone in his criticisms. Increasingly, there were repeated and bitter attacks not only upon the public schools and their curricula but also upon the personal motives and morality of public school advocates. One such attack, by Rev. Michael Mueller, contained charges almost as reckless as those made by the more extreme anti-Romanists. In his assault, Mueller gave further currency to the

26. "Unification and Education," *CW* 13 (April 1871): 6, 11.
27. "Who Is to Educate Our Children?" *CW* 14 (January 1872): 441.
28. "Book Review," *CW* 21 (October 1874): 143; "The Next Phase of Catholicity in the United States," *CW* 23 (August 1876): 584.

story that a large proportion of the prostitutes in Boston and elsewhere had first been influenced in that direction in the public schools. Continuing, Mueller said that there had been in New York City a notorious scandal involving some of the administrators and women teachers in the common schools. Further, said Mueller, Chicago newspapers "assert openly that the Public Schools there are *assignation houses* for boys and girls above a certain age."[29] Others joined in. One priest charged that the common schools prepared their pupils chiefly for careers of vice, prostitution, dishonesty, and crime. A New York City priest asserted in a sermon in 1875: "Woe be to parents who send their children to these public schools! I would not like to be in their places on the Day of Judgement . . . ."[30]

Although less vengeful than some, Hecker's attacks on the common schools were also increasingly harsh. Wherever the public schools were the most thoroughly organized, as in Massachusetts, he said, the criminal classes increased the most. The moral results of public school education, he concluded, were exceedingly bad. A few months later he complained that bigots were in control of the public schools and that they were playing directly into the hands of "infidels, free religionists and agnostics" who were the strongest admirers of the public schools.[31]

In 1882, Hecker charged that the common schools were damaging Protestantism as well as Catholicism; he warned "Congregationalists, Baptists, Episcopalians and others" about the "visible decay of Protestantism" and alleged that one of the principal causes of this disintegration was the education given to their children in the public schools. The public school, argued Hecker, was not only dangerous to Christianity, both Catholic and Protestant, but was also un-American, for it was a departure from the fundamental principles of the republic and an abridgment of personal and parental freedom. Rather than harmonizing religious differences as its founders had envisioned, the public school had instead become the "sharpest and most poisonous thorn" in the side of religious harmony. "The public school," he charged, "more than anything else, is to blame for the widespread dishonesty, love of idleness, and impurity with which the community is infected."[32]

29. *Public School Education* (Boston: P. Donahue, 1872), pp. 107–8, 192–93. Italics in the original. The 1880 edition of Mueller's book included letters of approval from two western bishops, P. J. Baltes and John Ireland. Another scathing attack on the public schools was Thomas J. Jenkins, *The Judges of Faith: Christian and Godless Schools* (Baltimore: John Murphy & Co., 1886).

30. *Christian World*, May 1875, 129; *New York Herald*, 15 March 1875.

31. "Aspects of National Education," *CW* 31 (June 1880): 407; "Catholics and Protestants Agreeing on the School Question," *CW* 32 (February 1881): 704.

32. Hecker, "A New but False Plea for Public Schools," *CW* 36 (December 1882): 416, 421; "The School Grievance and Its Remedy," *CW* 36 (February 1883): 714–16.

As Hecker wrote this, in 1883, plans for the Baltimore Third Plenary Council of 1884 (to be discussed below) were already well underway. No doubt Hecker's long crusade against the public schools had helped to pave the way for the council's stern rejection of a public school education for Catholic children.

Catholicism vs. Americanism

Local and state governing bodies and the courts possessed the authority to settle disputes about Bible reading and public aid to non-public schools. Although their decisions would not be acceptable to everyone, at least there would be answers. But there were other issues for which there seemed to be no answers. Prime among them was the growing belief among Protestants that Catholicism was incompatible with Americanism, and hence that the parochial schools were not suitable agencies for the training of American citizens. The gravity of this charge was evident; it created deep anxiety among many Catholic churchmen.

Charges that the Catholic Church was un-American were not new. Prewar critics never tired of inveighing against the "foreign despot" in Rome. But new developments, most important among them the *Syllabus of Errors* in 1864 and the proclamation of papal infallibility in matters of faith and morals in 1870, broadened and intensified the debate. The thesis of churchly "un-Americanism" in political life was soon transferred to the sphere of education. Increasingly, non-public schools were to come under attack as "un-American" institutions. By the time of the epochal Oregon Case of 1925, to be discussed later, doubts about the Americanism of non-public schools had become as important as the religious issues of the nineteenth-century campaigns.

The *Syllabus* was a condemnation of eighty "errors" of modern thought. To many Americans, these errors seemed to include most of the basic assumptions upon which the government of the United States had been built. It was an error, said the *Syllabus*, to think that:

> 15. Every man is free to embrace and profess that religion which, guided by the light of reason, he shall consider true.
> 47. [A]ll public institutes intended for instruction and letters and philosophical sciences and for carrying on the education of youth, should be freed from all ecclesiastical authority, control and interference . . . .
> 55. The Church ought to be separated from the State and the State from the Church.
> 80. The Roman pontiff can, and ought to, reconcile himself to and come to terms with progress, liberalism, and modern civilization.[33]

33. Anson Phelps Stokes, *Church and State in the United States*, 3 vols. (New York: Harper, 1950), 2:393–94.

That the *Syllabus* should have been seized upon by critics of the Church as proof of their suspicions was to be expected. Even the president of Harvard University, Charles W. Eliot, was able to tell a group of Congregational clergymen that the principles of the Catholic Church were opposed to civil liberty.[34] Equally rash was Theodore Roosevelt's statement: "The Church is in no way suited to this country and can never have any great permanent growth except through immigration, for its thought is Latin and entirely at variance with the dominant thought of our country and institutions."[35]

In Europe as well as in the United States the *Syllabus* had repercussions. A French decree of 1 January 1865 forbade bishops to publish either the *Syllabus* or the accompanying Encyclical, both of which were alleged to contain matter opposed to the constitution of the empire. In Belgium, where freedom of worship was considered an essential part of the political order, the *Syllabus* was said to have caused "consternation."[36]

Protestant outcries against the *Syllabus* take on added meaning when it is noted that many Catholic churchmen had serious doubts about the wisdom of the pronouncement. Orestes Brownson took the line that the Pope's declaration applied only to countries where union of church and state had long existed, and consequently had no application in the United States. Father Hecker echoed Brownson's view. More important, several prelates took the same position. Archbishop Ireland explained that the propositions in the *Syllabus* were not directed against the movements of the age, but only against the "excesses and extravagancies" of those movements. The archbishop of Cincinnati and the bishops of Buffalo and Peoria took essentially the same position.[37]

Needless to say, critics of the Church both in the United States and elsewhere were not satisfied by such attempts to explain the *Syllabus*. If the Pope had meant only to condemn absolutely unqualified freedom, he was condemning something that existed nowhere in the

34. *North American Review* 158 (1894): 37. Many additional examples of criticism of the *Syllabus* may be found in Charles Louis Sewrey, "Alleged 'Un-Americanism' of the Church as a Factor in Anti-Catholicism in the United States, 1860–1914" (Ph.D. diss., University of Minnesota, 1955), pp. 81–82. Eliot could hardly be described as an enemy of the church; later, in the serious Massachusetts controversies of 1888–1889, he was to befriend the spokesmen for the Church.

35. Quoted in Charles A. and Mary R. Beard, *The Rise of American Civilization*, rev. and enl. ed., 2 vols. in 1 (New York: Macmillan, 1935), 2:400.

36. John B. Bury, *A History of the Papacy in the Nineteenth Century* (New York: Schocken, 1964), p. 42.

37. *Brownson's Quarterly Review*, last series, 3 (1875): 414–15; editorial, *CW* 10 (January 1870): 546; John Ireland, *The Church and Modern Society: Lectures and Addresses*, 2 vols. (New York: K. H. McBride and Co., 1903), 1:84; Sewery, "Un-Americanism," pp. 85–88.

world, William Gladstone pointed out; yet the Pontiff had said that he was censuring the common errors of the age.[38] The predicament of the Catholic prelates was not improved by the fact that the only statement from the Vatican to clarify the controversy was this cryptic remark: "When the Pope speaks in a solemn act, it is to be taken literally; what he has said, he intended to say."[39]

Protestant outcries against the doctrine of papal infallibility were even more vehement than those against the *Syllabus*. Here also the anguish among American Catholic churchmen ran deep. On many occasions before the issuance of the infallibility decree in 1870, Catholic officials had expressed their opposition to such a doctrine. During John England's administration as bishop of Charleston (1820–1842), the Catholic churches of North Carolina, South Carolina, and Georgia in 1822 drew up a constitution that stated: "We are not required by our faith to believe that the Pope is infallible; nor do we believe that he is impeccable." This constitution did not, however, receive papal approval.[40] In his debate with Rev. Alexander Campbell in 1837, Archbishop (then Bishop) Purcell had declared, "No enlightened Catholic holds the Pope's infallibility to be an article of faith. I do not; and none of my brethren, that I know of, do."[41]

Opposition to any declaration of papal infallibility was in fact carried into the Vatican Council of 1870. Reiterating the belief he had expressed thirty-three years earlier, Archbishop Purcell took a leading part in the preparation of a petition to the Pope in 1870, imploring him not to permit the subject of infallibility to be brought before the assembled prelates. He was joined in this petition by twenty-seven other bishops and archbishops, all but three of them American. Purcell's objection was not based merely on the belief, held by many, that the time was inopportune; it was based on objection to the doctrine itself. If Pius IX were to be declared infallible, then all his predecessors were also. And how could such a doctrine be maintained in light of the actions and statements of Honorius, Gregory II and III, Stephen II, Nicholas I, John VIII, Sergius III, Stephen VI, Romanus I, Theodore II, John IX, and Celestine III?[42] Cardinal Gibbons later wrote that the majority of the American bishops opposed the proclamation and that Archbishop Kenrick of St. Louis was "violently op-

38. *The Vatican Decrees in Their Bearing Upon Civil Allegiance* (New York: Harper and Brothers, 1875), p. 21. Originally published in London in 1874.

39. "Questions Concerning the Syllabus," *CW* 22 (October 1875): 39.

40. Peter Guilday, *The Life and Times of John England, First Bishop of Charleston, 1786–1842*, 2 vols. (New York: America Press, 1927), 1:349–51, 367. For other examples of Protestant opposition to the *Syllabus*, see Sewery, "Un-Americanism," pp. 88ff.

41. Lamott, *Archdiocese of Cincinnati*, p. 31.

42. Ibid., p. 81.

posed to the infallibility doctrine." "There were times, indeed," said Gibbons, "when the excitement rose to fever heat," and the continuance of the council seemed to be in jeopardy.[43]

For the remainder of the century, and indeed until after the First World War, the charge that a Catholic could not give full allegiance to the United States remained a vexatious issue. And many leaders of the Church were fully aware of the seriousness of the charge. "What is the great Protestant charge against the Catholic Church?" asked a writer in the *Catholic World*. "Is it not that she does not conform to the spirit of the age—that is, of the world—but is hostile to it, and anathematizes it?" Bishop Martin John Spalding reduced all the objections against the Church to two: that in religion the Church is intolerant and proscriptive; and that in politics it is the enemy of republican institutions and the friend of a foreign despotism. Cardinal Gibbons acknowledged that the charge of un-Americanism was the most deadly the Church's enemies could make against her.[44]

The prominence given in Catholic apologetical literature to questions about the relationships between Catholicism and American citizenship is ample evidence of the concern aroused over this issue. These controversies left a deep residue of distrust among many Protestants and strengthened their resolve to oppose and, if possible, to suppress the parochial schools.

Bible Reading on the Defensive

"It would be monstrous . . . to restrict religious instruction" in our schools, declared U.S. Sen. Frederick Frelinghuysen of New Jersey in 1876.[45] These words reflected a widespread and growing fear that the moral and religious foundations of public education were being eroded. It was a fear compounded of many factors. No doubt the antebellum educational leaders had promised too much when they predicted that the common school would solve the problems of poverty, crime, immorality, and social discord. Now the school systems existed, but social problems were only becoming worse. Educational leaders, as well as others, were appalled by the growing tide of labor unrest, by graft both in government and in private industry, and by the stark contrast between conspicuous wealth and grinding poverty.

43. *Retrospect of Fifty Years* (New York: John Murphy Co., 1916), pp. 31–32. Only 2 of the 601 bishops in attendance actually voted against the decree, but 150 absented themselves from the final vote. J. M. Konrad Kirch, S.J., "Vatican Council," *Catholic Encyclopedia*, 15:305–7.

44. John Harris, "The Great Commission," *CW* 12 (November 1870): 191; Robert Gorman, *Catholic Apologetical Literature in the United States, 1794–1858* (Washington, D.C.: Catholic University of America Press, 1939), pp. 1–2; Sewery, "Un-Americanism," p. xii.

45. *Congressional Record*, 44th Congress, 1st sess., 1876, p. 5562.

And now, in a time of crisis, the core of the common school philosophy—Bible reading in the schools—was increasingly under attack. Major cities had outlawed the practice, and the Supreme Court of Ohio had sustained such action in 1873.

Before the Civil War, it had been possible to portray Catholics as the sole foes of Bible reading—opposition from others was rare—but now criticisms of Bible reading were coming from sources that earlier would have been friendly. Even the widely respected U.S. commissioner of education, William T. Harris, asserted that religious instruction should be not in the public school but in "a school connected with the church." Secular instruction rests upon thinking and reason, Harris explained, and religious instruction upon faith. And there is, further, a practical aspect of the question. "So long as Protestants insist on some remnant of the Church ceremonial, such as the reading of the Scriptures or prayers, the Catholic may be expected to see in the public school an instrument for proselyting his children."[46]

In 1875, an English observer of American education noted the rising spirit of secularism, but he added that the majority of citizens were satisfied with the reading of the Bible in the public schools and that "the prevailing tone of the schools . . . is Christian and Protestant."[47] This observation was borne out by the responses to a questionnaire sent to state and local superintendents as late as 1896 by the president of a group that urged Bible reading. Overwhelmingly, with the exception of some in a few western states, the respondents reported that the Bible was read in the majority of the schools under their control. Opponents of Bible reading were called un-American despots by the author of the survey, and at her organization's display at the Chicago World's Fair in 1893 the American flag was draped over the Bible.[48]

Such reassurances could not conceal the fact that proponents of Bible reading were losing ground. The main body of postwar educators could find no response to this challenge other than to reassert with increased vigor the need for attention to moral instruction and hence, necessarily in their view, religious instruction in the public schools. This message became a rallying cry in the annual meetings of the National Education Association (founded as the National Teachers' Association in 1857) in the postwar years. A clergyman speaking at the 1869 meeting of the association insisted that every teacher should be "a person of deep religious sensibility . . . a sort of semimis-

46. "Some General Principles of Religious Instruction in the Schools," *The Independent*, 4 September 1890, pp. 1–2.

47. Francis Adams, *The Free School System of the United States* (London: Chapman and Hall, 1875), pp. 159–60.

48. Elizabeth Cook, comp., *The Nation's Book in the Nation's Schools* (Chicago: Chicago Women's Educational Union, 1898), pp. 30, 41, 43, 44, 97, 125, 172, 175.

sionary." That year the National Teachers' Association resolved that "the Bible should not only be studied, venerated, and honored as a classic for all ages, people and languages . . . but devotionally read, and its precepts inculcated in all the common schools of the land." They also took care to resolve that "the appropriation of public funds for the support of sectarian institutions is a violation of the fundamental principles of our American system of education."[49]

At the 1880 NEA meeting, the now-venerable Rev. A. D. Mayo insisted that the common school must be, "in the most pronounced and thorough sense, a school of instruction and discipline in . . . Christian morality."[50] In 1888 Rev. George Atkinson, whose prodigious educational labors in early Oregon have been recounted earlier in this work, addressed the annual meeting of the NEA. A society beset by anarchism and immorality, said Atkinson, needed instruction in the principles of rectitude contained in the Decalogue, the Proverbs, the aphorisms of Jesus in the Sermon on the Mount, and in His parables. These principles are, said Atkinson, "axioms, self-evident truths, needing only to be stated in order to be admitted . . . . If it be objected that this will infringe the rights of conscience, the answer can be made, that no right of personal conscience is so sacred as the right of self-preservation of a body politic."[51]

Catholics were often the target of NEA speakers. In 1889 John Jay accused the Roman hierarchy of a conspiracy to undermine the common school, aided in this scheme by "the foreign element, uninstructed in American civilization."[52] Archbishop John Ireland felt it necessary to assure his NEA audience in 1890 that he had never been and was not un-American or an enemy of the public school.[53]

To portray the late-nineteenth-century controversy over religious instruction in the public schools as merely a contest between proponents and opponents of Bible reading would be, however, an incomplete view. For Protestantism during that period was gradually becoming merged with Americanism, and as the lines between them became blurred a "culture religion" emerged. Despite disestablishment, many influential leaders considered the United States a Christian nation. Theology, already diluted by the prewar evangelicalism, was to some degree supplanted by middle-class Protestant mores. "As a result," Winthrop Hudson has observed, "by the end of the

49. National Teachers Association, *Proceedings* (n.p., 1869), pp. 19, 23.
50. "Object Lessons in Moral Instruction in the Common School," in *N.E.A. Proceedings* (Salem, Ohio: N.E.A., 1880), pp. 8–10.
51. "The Culture Most Valuable to Prepare Law-Abiding and Law-Respecting Citizens," in *N.E.A. Proceedings* (Topeka, Kans.: N.E.A., 1888), pp. 115–17, 120–21.
52. "Public and Parochial Schools," in *N.E.A. Proceedings* (n.p., 1889), p. 172.
53. "State Schools and Parish Schools—Is Union Between Them Possible?" in *N.E.A. Proceedings* (Topeka, Kans.: N.E.A., 1890), pp. 179–85.

century, American Protestantism had become more the creature of American culture than its creator."[54] In such a climate of opinion, it was natural for Protestants to assume that religion should be taught in the schools and that Americanism should be reinforced in the churches. The Bible thus became a symbol of a way of life as much as a source of truth and a means of salvation. Those who opposed this view were enemies of the state.

During most of the nineteenth century, few disputes about Bible reading in the schools were litigated, and when they were the state courts generally deferred to the authority of local school authorities, upholding their decisions. Beginning late in the century, however, such disputes were increasingly brought to the courts. Following Ohio's lead, the high courts of six states upheld lower-court rulings banning Bible reading in the schools: Wisconsin (1890), Nebraska (1902, modified in 1903), Illinois (1910), Louisiana (1915), Washington (1918 and 1930), and South Dakota (1929). The legal context in these cases was still that of the state constitutions. The "incorporation theory" (discussed below), holding that the Fourteenth Amendment had made the provisions of the First Amendment binding upon the states, had not yet been discovered by the U.S. Supreme Court. During the same period, however, eleven more states joined Massachusetts, which alone in 1910 already had such a law, in making Bible reading and/or prayer legally obligatory in the schools.[55]

Although the early-nineteenth-century consensus on Bible reading in the schools had been severely eroded, the practice survived in many places until past the middle of the twentieth century. A NEA survey in 1949 revealed that twelve states required Bible reading in the public schools and another twenty-five permitted it. In a nationwide survey conducted in 1962, 42 percent of the responding public school officials said that the Bible was read in their schools, and an additional 8 percent said that devotional services of some other type were present.[56]

The final blow came on 17 June 1963, when the U.S. Supreme Court, in the *Schempp* case, struck down the laws of the thirty-seven states that either permitted or required Bible reading and/or the recitation of the Lord's Prayer as devotional practices in the public schools. True, the Court's decision did not end the controversy. But officially, at least, one of the most fundamental principles of the Com-

54. *American Protestantism* (Chicago: University of Chicago Press, 1961), pp. 135–38.
55. The above history is briefly sketched in section 4 of Justice Brennan's seventy-seven-page concurring opinion in *School District of Abington Township, Pennsylvania v. Edward Lewis Schempp*, 374 U.S. 203 (1963).
56. *The Status of Religious Education in the Schools* (Washington, D.C.: Research Division, N.E.A., 1949); Richard Dierenfield, *Religion in American Public Schools* (Washingon, D.C.: Public Affairs Press, 1969), chap. 4.

mon School Movement had been destroyed. First attacked by Catholics at the very outset of the Common School Movement, and later increasingly criticized by other groups and individuals including Protestants, the opponents of "non-sectarianism" had finally prevailed. There was bitter irony in the event. The court had found the presumed "non-sectarianism" of the schools to be itself sectarian, and hence a violation of religious liberty. The very argument used by the Common School founders to justify their position was now turned against them, and they lost what they had most wanted to preserve—Bible reading in the public schools.[57]

The Fourteenth Amendment and Interpretations Thereof

A provision of the Fourteenth Amendment to the Constitution, ratified in 1868, is now widely regarded (with Supreme Court sanction) as the legal basis for denial of state funds to sectarian schools. The chain of reasoning employed to reach this conclusion has its starting point in the First Amendment statement that "Congress shall make no law respecting an establishment of religion or prohibiting the free exercise thereof . . . ." This "establishment clause" was both a denial of power to the national government and a reservation of power to the states. The former could not establish any official national religion, but neither could it touch the established churches then existing—or to be created—in the several states. This view was strengthened by the Tenth Amendment provision that "the powers not delegated to the United States are reserved to the States respectively, or to the people."

The Fourteenth Amendment to the Constitution, proposed by the Congress in 1866 and ratified by the states in 1868, contains the provision that "no state shall make or enforce any law which shall abridge the privileges or immunities of citizens of the United States . . . ." The judicial interpretation of the above clause is that it "incorporates" and makes applicable to the states the First Amendment stipulation that "Congress shall make no law respecting an establishment of religion or prohibiting the free exercise thereof." According to this so-called "incorporation theory" of the Fourteenth Amendment, as that theory was stated by Supreme Court justice Black, "one of the chief objects that the provisions of the [Fourteenth] Amendment's first section, separately, and as a whole, were to accomplish was to make the Bill of Rights applicable to the States."[58]

57. The Court outlawed only religious instruction of a "devotional" nature. However, by intent and in fact, religious instruction in the schools was and always had been devotional in nature, and Justice Brennan recognized this in his concurring opinion.
58. *Adamson v. California*, 332 U.S. 46, at 71–72 (1947).

Although this theory had been used earlier by the Court to make other provisions of the Bill of Rights applicable to the states, it was not until 1947, seventy-nine years after the ratification of the Fourteenth Amendment, that the Supreme Court, in *Everson v. Board of Education of Ewing Township*, by application of the incorporation theory found the establishment clause of the First Amendment binding on the states. In this case, the court declared, "New Jersey cannot consistently with the 'establishment of religion' clause of the First Amendment contribute tax-raised funds to the support of an institution which teaches tenets and faith of any church." Although many textbooks in school law seem to regard the incorporation theory as self-evident truth, serious doubts can be raised about the Court's interpretation.[59]

If the members of Congress in 1868 had seen in the Fourteenth Amendment the meaning ascribed to it by the Supreme Court in *Everson*, there would have been no need for any further efforts on their part to prohibit the use of state funds for sectarian schools. In fact, just the opposite happened. During the two decades following ratification of the amendment, several bills and some twenty proposed constitutional amendments that were designed to end the practice of using public funds for church-related schools appeared in Congress. This seemingly startling paradox needs further attention.

As late as 1870, neither of the major political parties had committed itself on the issue of federal participation in education. Their platforms and convention resolutions had been silent on the subject. Perhaps the first suggestion of interest in the question was contained in President Grant's remark on 30 March 1870, when (referring to newly freed blacks) he urged the Congress "to take all the means within their constitutional powers to promote and encourage popular education throughout the country."[60]

The fortunes of the Republican party had fallen sharply during the postwar years, largely because of its discredited Reconstruction policies and the scandals of the Grant administration. The party was in need of new policies that could broaden its appeal. One approach was to launch a new effort to achieve the rehabilitation of the South, and to build national unity as well, by renewed emphasis on common school education. The first of the bills proposing to bring the federal government directly into the field of education was introduced in the House of Representatives on 25 February 1870 by George F. Hoar, a

---

59. For a rather simplistic view, see Arcal A. Morris, *The Constitution and American Education*, 2d ed. (St. Paul: West Publishing Co., 1980), p. 325. For a more complete account, see, among others, C. Herman Pritchett, *The American Constitution* (New York: McGraw-Hill, 1959), pp. 530–34, 551–52.

60. *Congressional Globe*, 41st Cong., 1st sess., 1870, 49, pt. 1:1735.

Republican from Massachusetts. It was also the most drastic of such bills in that it proposed to establish a "national system of education." Hoar's bill authorized the president to ascertain whether satisfactory school systems existed in the several states. If any state was found to be delinquent, the president was empowered to appoint a federal school superintendent, under whose supervision there would be provision for the creation of inspectorships, the levying of taxes, the erection of buildings, and the production of textbooks.

Strong support for the Hoar bill was sounded by Sen. Henry Wilson in the *Atlantic Monthly* in January 1871. Wilson had entered the Senate from Massachusetts in 1854, with the backing of the Know-Nothings. Wilson added to Hoar's arguments for a national system his own warning that this country's educational system must be such as to enable it to avoid the fate of an "ignorant, priest-ridden and emasculated France."[61] In view of Wilson's long and well-known hatred for foreigners and Catholics, the *Catholic World* promptly expressed its abhorrence for any plan to effect "the social and religious unification of the American people by a system of universal and uniform compulsory education" designed to mold Americans "of European and African origin, Indians and Asiatics, Protestants and Catholics, Jews and pagans, into one homogeneous people after what may be called the New England Evangelical type."[62]

That Hoar's bill for creation of a national system of education would provoke opposition among Protestants also was a foregone conclusion. The NEA denounced it, and the Pennsylvania superintendent of common schools found it "impractical and un-American." The Republican party was in complete control of the national government at the time; Grant was midway through his first term. Hoar's bill received support only from Republicans, and from too few of them to warrant bringing it to a vote. Hoar himself said later that he allowed the bill to "disappear." The Catholic opposition was a minor element, however, in the demise of this bill; states' rights was a more important factor.[63]

In December 1875, a Republican member of the House of Representatives who was a presidential hopeful, James G. Blaine, introduced a proposed constitutional amendment:

> No State shall make any law respecting an establishment of religion, or prohibiting the free exercise thereof; and no money raised by taxation in

61. John Whitney Evans, "Catholics and the Blair Education Bill," *Catholic Historical Review* 46 (October 1960): 276.

62. Hecker, "Unification and Education," *CW* 13 (April 1871): 1–14.

63. Gordan C. Lee, *The Struggle for Federal Aid, First Phase: A History of the Attempts to Obtain Federal Aid for the Common Schools, 1870–1890* (New York: Teachers College, Columbia University, 1949), pp. 40–45, 49–52.

any State for the support of public schools, or derived from any public fund therefor, nor any public lands devoted thereto, shall ever be under the control of any religious sect; nor shall any money so raised or lands so devoted be divided between religious sects or denominations.

The measure was debated in both chambers in August 1876. The House was under Democratic control at the time, but the addition of a clause providing that the article would not enlarge or diminish the legislative power of Congress seemed to make the entire provision innocuous, and with little debate it was approved by a large majority.[64]

The members of the Judiciary Committee of the Republican-controlled Senate had little patience with the sham House version and bolstered it by adding sterner provisions. They stipulated that none of the provisions were ever to be interpreted to exclude the Bible from the public schools, they proscribed the use of all public funds—not merely school funds—for church-related schools, and for good measure they extended this prohibition to the Congress as well (for it was by no means agreed in 1876 that the First Amendment establishment clause forbade congressional aid to church-related agencies). Finally, they added an enforcement clause.[65]

The November elections were approaching as the Blaine resolution was being debated. Republicans, like the prewar Whigs, saw pluralism as a threat; Democrats championed decentralization and saw the proposed amendment as an attack upon Roman Catholics. Democratic senator Kernan, a Catholic from New York, thought that educational matters should be left to the states and communities. A Republican senator asserted that in this Protestant country there was a large and powerful group of Roman Catholics opposed to being taxed for common schools and that when they gained control they would favor their own schools.[66]

Vermont senator Edmunds, author of the Judiciary Committee version, quoted Pope Pius IX to prove that American Catholics were intent on the destruction of the common school system, instigated in this by the "universal, ubiquitous, aggressive, restless, and untiring" Holy See. Mockingly, Senator Bogy of Missouri confessed that while listening to Edmunds, he had almost imagined himself to be in the Vatican, with the Pope presiding: "I fancied that my distinguished friend from Vermont could well play the part of an infallible Pope, for if there be a member of this body who does play that part with more

64. Herman Ames, *The Proposed Amendments to the Constitution of the United States During the First Century of Its History* (Washington, D.C.: Government Printing Office, 1897), pp. 277–78.
65. *Congressional Record*, 44th Cong., 1st sess., 1876, pp. 5245–46.
66. Ibid., 2d sess., pp. 5581–83, 5585–87.

self-complacency than my friend from Vermont I really do not know him. Infallibility is a part of his nature . . . ." Religious liberty is not the issue in question, Bogy continued; it is merely the cloak for partisan maneuvers. The Republicans need a new bloody shirt, for the old one "can no longer call out the mad bull, [and] another animal has to be brought forth by these matadores to engage the attention of the people in this great arena in which we are soon all to be combatants. The Pope, the old Pope of Rome, is to be the great bull we are all to attack."[67] In one respect, at least, Bogy's analysis proved to be correct: the vote on the resolution was strictly along party lines. But as it failed to get the necessary two-thirds vote, it did not pass.[68]

The 1876 debates on the Blaine resolution are interesting for what was said, but even more revealing for what was not said. Every legislator who spoke against the resolution employed the argument that it would constitute an invasion of state rights. No senator or representative even hinted that the Fourteenth Amendment had by incorporation imposed the restrictions and guarantees of the First Amendment upon the states. They were competent judges of the meaning and intent of the Fourteenth Amendment because many of them, including Blaine, had been members of the Thirty-Ninth Congress, which had drafted the amendment, and an even larger number had been members of the state legislatures that had ratified the amendment. Blaine's view of the matter was clearly expressed in an open letter he wrote to the *New York Times* two weeks before he introduced his proposal. The First Amendment was intended to bind the Congress only, said Blaine. "At the same time, states were left free to do as they pleased in regard to 'an establishment of religion' [by virtue of] the Tenth Amendment . . . . A majority of the people in any state in this Union can, therefore, if they desire it, have an established church." It was necessary to cure this "constitutional defect," Blaine concluded, so as to prohibit state aid not only to churches, but also to church-related schools. Hence his proposed amendment was needed.[69]

Undaunted by the defeat of the Blaine resolution, the Republicans included in their fall 1876 platform a call for a constitutional amendment "forbidding the application of any public funds or property for the benefit of any school or institution under sectarian control." Senator Moynihan has made an interesting comment on this provision in the 1876 platform: "In 1876 there were those who thought that public

---

67. Ibid., 1st sess., p. 5586.
68. Ibid., 2d sess., p. 5595.
69. Quoted in F. William O'Brien, "The States and 'No Establishment': Proposed Amendments to the Constitution since 1789," *Washburn Law Journal* 4 (Spring 1965): 186–89.

aid to church schools should be made unconstitutional. But at least they were clear that the Constitution would have to be amended to do so. It is extraordinary how this so *obvious* fact got lost in the years that followed."[70]

Nothing came of the 1876 Republican call for a constitutional amendment, but in its 1880 platform the party again issued warnings about the dangers of sectarianism. By 1884, chagrined by Rev. Samuel Burchard's inept remark describing Democrats as the party of "rum, Romanism, and rebellion," Republicans were willing to abandon anti-Romanism as a party issue, especially as they had found in Mormonism a new "menace to free institutions too dangerous to be longer suffered." In 1888 both party platforms were silent on the School Question.[71] The tempo of anti-Catholicism was quickening in the late 1880s, and the Republicans were no doubt anxious to avoid any appearance of association with the newly formed nativistic groups, which styled themselves the American party.

Individual Republicans persisted in the cause, however, prime among them Sen. Henry William Blair of New Hampshire. Five times during the 1880s Blair introduced in the Senate bills, one of them a proposed constitutional amendment, "to aid in the establishment and temporary support of common schools," and five times his efforts came to naught. Introduced in late 1881, the first bill came to the floor in mid-1882 but was not acted upon.[72] The bill debated in 1884 contained several changes that were included in the remaining bills as well, among them a stipulation requiring states and territories to enact compulsory attendance laws as a condition for receiving federal aid.

Like Blaine, Blair explicitly denied that the "establishment of religion" clause had been extended to the states by the Fourteenth Amendment. Defending his proposed amendment in 1888, Blair quoted the First Amendment and pointed out, "There is no restriction whatever placed upon the power or the action of the States in this regard . . . ." This, he warned, created a serious danger. The Territory of Utah, soon to be admitted to the Union, "would come in with an establishment of religion already an accomplished fact." Once in, Utah could easily revise its constitution and "establish the Mormon religion as the religion of the State."

70. Daniel Patrick Moynihan, "Government and the Ruin of Private Education," *Educational Freedom* 13 (Fall and Winter 1979–1980): 4. Italics in original.

71. Kirk Porter and Donald Johnson, comps., *National Party Platforms, 1840–1964* (Urbana: University of Illinois Press, 1966), pp. 51–52, 82; Anson Stokes, *Church and State in the United States*, 3 vols. (New York: Harper and Bros., 1950), 2:468–69.

72. The chronology of the Blair bills, with documentation, is recorded in both Lee, *The Struggle for Federal Aid*, pp. 88–90, and in Evans, "Catholics and the Blair Bill," p. 273.

On the surface, the Blair bills breathed humanitarianism and good will. Out of a national voting population of some ten million about two million were illiterate, said Blair. The problem was especially acute in the South, with its higher ratio of children to adults, its lower per capita wealth, and its recently emancipated six million slaves. This was a dangerous situation, said Blair, for "the representative form of government cannot exist unless the people are competent to govern themselves." Blair's solution was a ten-year program of federal aid to the states and territories for the support of public education, aggregating fifteen million dollars for the first year and decreasing by one million dollars annually. (These amounts varied in the several bills.) The funds were to be distributed in accordance with the ratio that existed in each state between the total population and the population therein that was illiterate. The monies distributed under the provisions of this act were to be used only for "common schools, not sectarian in character."[73]

It might seem that the principle that sectarian schools are ineligible for public financial aid was not wholly consonant with the aim of eradicating ignorance and saving the republic through education. If children in poverty and ignorance were to be the beneficiaries of the federal aid proposed by Blair, then the church-related schools with their large numbers of such children—many of them non-English speaking—might have seemed to be logical and proper recipients for such aid. The reason for this seeming paradox became clear during the course of the debates. As soon as the first Blair bill reached the floor, charges and countercharges erupted. Catholics complained about the Protestant atmosphere, textbooks, and teachers in the common schools. The *Journal of Education* (Boston), a strong proponent of the federal aid plans, complained about the arrogant assumptions of the Catholic Church and insisted that "education has become a function of government, just as military and naval offices are governmental functions." The aging Rev. A. D. Mayo, who had belabored the parochial schools for decades, although with less vehemence than many of his colleagues, insisted that the common schools could inspire reverence for the "Invisible Law." But Bishop Bernard J. McQuaid scorned the moral instruction of the common schools as "mongrel morality, this code of compromises and concessions—a bit from Tom Paine, another from Jesus of Nazareth, some sentences from Benjamin Franklin, then Saul of Tarsus, something, too, from atheistic Frenchmen, all sifted and sorted by a school board nominated at a ward caucus and elected amid the turbulence of party strife." Bishop McQuaid had other charges: that the public school was

73. Evans, "Catholics and the Blair Bill," pp. 273–75.

wasting public funds, was presuming to take over parental rights in education, and was in principle a communistic venture. Mayo's response was that the hierarchy's opposition arose because "their religious convictions forbid them to give aid and comfort to any school which is not absolutely under their own infallible control."[74]

As his bills met with repeated failure, Senator Blair seemed to become increasingly frustrated and impatient with his opponents. In 1886, after the bill had passed the Senate for the second time only to be shunted aside in the House, Blair addressed a letter to Archbishop Michael A. Corrigan of New York predicting that help for the bill from Catholic quarters would turn "the hearts of many millions now full of prejudice and opposition . . . warmly and trustfully to your communion." But no help came, and in 1888 he felt compelled to speak out more frankly. It was the Jesuits, he avowed, who had been blocking such bills all along. Nine of them had been on the Senate floor logrolling against the Blaine Amendment twelve years earlier, and with his own eyes he had seen a letter from a Jesuit priest attacking his own bill. Not only in the halls of Congress but all over the country, this "Black Legion" was striving "to secure the control of this country by destroying the public school system . . . ." Someday, surely, these crafty deceivers would be recognized as "more the enemy of this country that the antichrist is today." He lashed out against the newspapers, charging that "upon the staff of every great paper in this country today there is a Jesuit, and the business of that man is to see that a blow is struck whenever there is an opportunity to strike at the common school system of America." He threatened to have newspaper reporters removed from the gallery if they did not provide better coverage of his bill.[75]

From this point on, it is probable that Blair did as much as his opponents to damage his bill. He reiterated his contempt for the Jesuits but insisted that he harbored no ill will for most other Catholics, and indeed said that he revered the memory of Archbishop Carroll—apparently unaware that Carroll had been a Jesuit. He also shed further light on his expressed solicitude for the South:

> . . . if the South can once be brought under the influence of free public schools—there will be an end of this struggle for the possession of the American child on the part of these outcast European Jesuits . . . . The twenty-five million people who inhabit the Southern states are naturally a more religious people than the people of the North. They are Protestants and liberal, and are free from the vast influx of immigration which has overflown and transformed the Northern states.[76]

74. Ibid., pp. 278–85.
75. Ibid., pp. 289–90.
76. *Congressional Record*, 51st Cong., 1st sess., 1890, 21:1542–45.

So by his own words Blair finally made it clear that the purpose of his bill was not only to rehabilitate the South, but also to save Protestantism. By this time his own colleagues were calling him to task for his oratorical excesses. For the last time, his proposal was voted on in the Senate in 1890, and this time it failed to pass even in his own house. Blair's long and bitter crusade against Romanism had brought him only disappointment; his term expired a year later.

The Catholic Church was not, as Blair thought, the chief foe of his proposal. The Senate rejected it on constitutional and fiscal grounds, and the House because of sectional rivalries.[77] At the same time, the Blair episode (and others like it) confirmed Catholic opposition to any expansion of the federal role in education. They had seen what the civil power could do to their schools at the state and local level, and they feared that federal intervention would only increase their problems.

Clearly the Supreme Court, in reaching the *Everson* decision by application of the "incorporation theory," found in the Fourteenth Amendment a meaning that several generations of earlier lawmakers and jurists had not perceived. It is of course true that, as Dooley reminded us long ago, "The Supreme Court follows the election returns." Yet there are those who believe that in reaching this decision the Court ignored the legislative history of the preceding seventy-five years.[78]

The Third Plenary Council of Baltimore, 1884

The Third Plenary Council of 1884 refined and consolidated Vatican policy on the School Question, urging greater moderation in some respects and increased determination in others. The Committee on Schools of the 1884 council included Archbishop Seehan of Chicago and Bishops John L. Spalding of Peoria, Kilian C. Flasch of La Crosse, and Henry Cosgrove of Davenport. Although all of these were from midwestern dioceses, only one of them (Flasch) was German-born. In consequence, the council's decrees on education were not of the laissez-faire type as the East would have preferred, nor were they as severe as the German group would have desired.

Obviously, the council was disturbed by reports that parents of Catholic children attending public schools had been denied the sacraments, and it now emphatically repudiated this practice: "We strictly

77. Evans, "Catholics and the Blair Bill," pp. 296–98.
78. A comprehensive statement of the view that the Supreme Court has usurped congressional authority, in many other instances as well as in issuing the incorporation theory of the Fourteenth Amendment, is contained in Raoul Berger, *Government by Judiciary* (Cambridge: Harvard University Press, 1977).

enjoin that no one, whether bishop or priest,—and this the Pope through the Sacred Congregation expressly forbids—should dare to repel such parents from the sacraments as unworthy, either by threat or act. And much is this to be understood concerning the children themselves."

While the council strictly ordered members of the clergy to use moderation, it also specifically ordered parish priests to establish parochial schools within two years and provided means of punishing any priest who failed to do so, or any congregation that neglected to assist its priest in this effort. The pastoral letter of the Third Plenary Council also emphasized the importance of religion in the school. However, it also introduced a new element, not previously found in the pastorals of the councils of Baltimore: Catholics do not oppose the public school. They merely consider it inadequate for the education of Catholic children because of its admittedly necessary omission of religious training.[79]

Yet the council's edicts did not still the controversies over education within the Church. Large groups continued their bitter opposition to the public schools, while other influential clergy, following Archbishop Ireland's lead, continued to seek a measure of cooperation between public and parochial schools.

Meanwhile, the increasing emphasis on the need for parochial schools aroused apprehension among the supporters of public education. A few years after the Plenary Council, the Massachusetts State Board of Education reported that enrollments in the public elementary schools in the larger cities were declining at a time when claims were being made for increases in Catholic schools. A later study, based on the annual reports of the Massachusetts State Board of Education, found that the percentage of children enrolled in private schools in that state rose from 7 percent in 1869–1870 to 10 percent in 1884–1885. It reached 16 percent by 1890 and stayed essentially at that figure for the remainder of the century.[80]

The years 1865–1885 had seen several confrontations between Catholics and Protestants over the School Question. The period had also seen scores of efforts at compromise, all at the local level. Even at the end of the period, there were those who spoke for moderation. But their voices were soon to be drowned out by a gathering storm in which no middle ground could be found.

79. J. A. Burns and Bernard Kohlbrenner, *A History of Catholic Education in the United States* (New York: Benziger Bros., 1937), pp. 143–44; Peter Guilday, ed., *National Pastorals of the American Hierarchy* (Washington, D.C.: Catholic University of America Press, 1923), pp. 243–47.

80. Massachusetts State Board of Education, *Fifty-Third Annual Report, 1888–89* (Boston: Wright and Potter Printing Company, 1890), p. 11; Vernon Lamar Mangum, *The American Normal School* (Baltimore: Warwick and York, 1928), p. 419.

7

Background of the School Controversies
of 1888–1890

Economic Problems Intensify the Spirit of Nativism

In the late 1880s, the school controversy erupted anew with an intensity not seen since the Know-Nothing turbulence of the 1850s. During two successive sessions in 1888 and 1889, the Massachusetts legislature (the General Court) was embroiled in a bitter struggle over the School Question, while outside the legislative halls a prolonged series of mass meetings, engineered for the most part by Protestant clergymen, fanned the flames of anti-Catholicism. Despite their prodigious and often raucous campaigns, the foes of church-related schools were not able to prevail in Massachusetts. But the controversies there were reported throughout the country, both in the Catholic press and in the nativist journals, which were again growing rapidly. Two state legislatures, those of Illinois and Wisconsin, did enact anti-parochial-school legislation in 1889. Public indignation against these measures, led by Catholics and Lutherans but supported also by other Protestants, was one of the causes of the defeat of the incumbent Republican governors and Republican-dominated legislatures in both states in 1889. The laws were speedily repealed by the new Democratic legislatures. Similar legislation was proposed but not enacted in other states.

On the surface, nativism and anti-Catholicism seemed to have a life and momentum of their own during the nineteenth century. In fact, however, the school controversies were an integral part of the larger social, political, and economic context. Uncertainty had always served to increase the tempo and fervor of nativism, and fears about the future were multiplying in the late years of the century. Signs of disquiet were easy to find. The wretchedness of the slums grew in the cities, and corruption infected municipal governments. Fire and rioting raged beyond control in Cincinnati for three days in 1884. The first mass movement of American workingmen—the Knights of Labor—was in the making. On the other hand, power and arrogance

146

were accumulating no less swiftly. The first of the great exposés of corporate power and aggression appeared in 1881—Henry Demarest Lloyd's study of the Standard Oil Company. The problems in the rural West and South were no less pressing: the old sense of equality and opportunity was slipping from the farmer's grasp, and declining prices and the tightening hold of the middleman were laying the foundations for the agrarian revolt that was soon to grip the region.

One effect of these crises, urban and rural, was to quicken the social conscience and to call forth a new body of middle-class reformers. A common thread ran through their analyses of the country's ills—the polarization of American society. They believed passionately in the American Dream of a homogeneous culture, yet they saw it threatened everywhere. Urbanites themselves, they for the most part found the cause of the problems in the expanding cities. Understandably, they fixed upon the immigrants as the source of current disorders. Not all of these social critics were hostile to the immigrant, but their writings gave intellectual respectability to the rising tide of anti-immigrant sentiment.

The great opening wave in this current of nationalistic sentiment came from the Congregationalist clergyman Josiah Strong. His evangelical call for reform, symptomatic of the apprehensions that had become widespread, was sounded in his *Our Country: Its Possible Future and Its Present Crisis* (1885). The enemies that strutted boldly throughout his pages were immigration, Romanism, lack of religion in the public schools, intemperance, Mormonism, socialism, corruption in municipal government. In the cities, class strife and eventually an open struggle between the selfish rich and the degraded poor threatened. A terrible upheaval in American society was imminent, said Strong in this darkly apocalyptic vision. It was the most sweeping indictment of immigrant influence since the 1850s. Yet Strong was convinced that Christianity could Americanize the immigrant and solve all social problems. No longer, however, could Christians rely on the informal moral restraints of an earlier agrarian society.

The next year, in a series of lectures, Rev. Samuel L. Loomis expressed substantially the same fears in yet more explicit form. In the cities, cried Loomis, two widely separated classes existed. Business and professional people were found on one side of the gulf; they were for the most part native-born and Protestant. On the other side was the working class, mostly foreign in background and much of it Catholic. It remained for the newspaperman Jacob Riis (himself an immigrant) to dramatize the full degradation and misery of immigrant life in the slums in his *How the Other Half Lives*. Ironically, the book aroused both sympathy for and resentment against the newcomers. In the colleges and universities, a new generation of economists, many trained in Germany, studied the effects of immigrant competition with native labor. As proponents of governmental intervention, they became the pioneer advocates of immigration restriction.[1]

For organized labor, still only in its formative stage, the questions surrounding immigrant labor posed a cruel dilemma. A large proportion of union members were themselves foreign-born, and everywhere Englishmen and Irishmen provided much of the leadership. Union leaders did oppose contract-labor schemes under which American employers paid the passage and bound the services of immigrants, but outright opposition to immigration was not possible. Unions, therefore, underwent less change of heart than did businessmen, many of whom turned full circle in the eighties.[2]

To employers, the mounting tempo of strikes and the rapid growth of the Knights of Labor portended crisis. Yet their reaction was unyielding and uncomprehending, and they could find no explanation for the unrest except the theory that foreign influence lay behind it. The strike by several thousand Hungarian coke miners in Pennsylvania in 1886 provided for industrialists dramatic confirmation of their fears. Worse yet, native-born and northern European miners joined the strike. The coke syndicate, headed by Henry Clay Frick, fulminated against the "furious Huns," threatened to evict them from their company houses in the dead of winter, and finally ordered a general lockout. By this time the anti-immigrant trend was well advanced. In 1888 the National Board of Trade, forerunner of the United States Chamber of Commerce, unequivocally called for government protection against "the scourings of foreign disease, pauperism and crime."[3]

Nationalism has been the most powerful unifying force in Western society, and as the sense of impending danger rose during the eighties the spirit of nationalism surged. Nothing did more than the Haymarket Square bombing in Chicago in 1886 to arouse nationalistic fears of immigrant radicalism. Although they were unable to ascertain the identity of the bomb thrower, Chicago authorities sentenced six immigrants and one native American to death. As a result, a torrent of racial prejudice and nationalist agitation was unleashed. The immigrant was widely portrayed as a lawless creature bent on violence and disorder. Nativist groups, styling themselves "patriotic" societies in the manner of the prewar nativist lodges, began to appear. An attempt to form a national American party failed, largely because the two-party system was by this time deeply entrenched. Moreover, the Republicans were showing interest in the immigration

1. John Higham, *Strangers in the Land: Patterns of American Nativism, 1860–1925* (New Brunswick, N.J.: Rutgers University Press, 1955), pp. 39–40.

2. Ibid., p. 50.

3. Ibid., pp. 51–52.

issue. In 1887 Republican senator Justin Morrill of Vermont introduced a bill to restrict immigration, and the Republican conventions in Pennsylvania, Ohio, and California urged such action. While the patriotic societies raged at immigrant radicalism, they played also on the oldest of nativist themes—anti-Catholicism. One zealot cried, "I believe fully that the Protestant will win, as God is on our side, and . . . I wish I could with the brave cohorts of Jesus lead on to conquer, or under his blood-stained banner die. 'Twere a death gladly to be hailed."[4]

It did not seem to matter that the Catholic hierarchy under the temperate leadership of Cardinal Gibbons was now following a less militant policy that it had in 1869 and the few years immediately thereafter. But renewed pleas by Catholics for state aid were being voiced in the late eighties, and their striking success in one special field rankled in the hearts of many native Americans. By the end of the eighties, because of successful lobbying by the Bureau of Catholic Indian Missions, Catholics were receiving a disproportionately large share of the federal appropriations for church-operated schools on Indian reservations. More important, perhaps, was the tremendous growth that was taking place in American Catholicism and in Catholic parochial schools, the latter greatly stimulated by the Third Plenary Council of 1884. The growing influence of Catholics in the Democratic party seemed even more ominous to many patriots. As mentioned earlier, many cities got their first Irish Catholic mayors in the eighties. By the late years of the decade, an anti-Catholic movement of major proportions was in the making. The culmination of this was the founding of the fanatical American Protective Association, whose members took an oath never to vote for a Catholic, never to employ one when a Protestant was available, and never to go out on a strike with Catholics.[5]

The internal tensions in late-nineteenth-century America manifested themselves also in belligerent attitudes toward foreign governments. In 1889, to the accompaniment of public excitement, the United States asserted sweeping rights over the Bering Sea, and two years later there was talk of war with Italy during a controversy of minor importance. A sailors' brawl in a Valparaiso saloon brought threats of reprisal against Chile. The Cuban Revolution aroused a fever of alarm, culminating in the Spanish-American War. Professor Higham writes concerning these developments, "It is hard to doubt that these bellicose outbursts flowed from the same domestic frustrations that generated nativism."[6]

In an atmosphere as charged as this, a reopening of the School

4. Cited in ibid., p. 59.
5. Ibid., pp. 59–62.
6. Ibid., p. 75.

Question was inevitable, especially as that question had always been at the very center of nativist concerns. This time the goal of the nativists was not to deny public funds to church-related schools, as that objective had already been mostly achieved. Now the nativists and their sympathizers had a more drastic and permanent solution in mind: they would destroy the church-related schools. The campaign to accomplish this was launched in Massachusetts early in 1888.

Contrasting Views on Education

According to Catholics, the right to educate youth belonged solely to parents or guardians. Bishop John J. Keane, in a paper read before the National Educational Association in 1889, spelled this out clearly for Americans of every belief: "The office of parents lies at the very root of character, at the very basis of civilization . . . ."[7]

The Catholic argument that the family must be the basis of the educational system was not easy to refute, for few non-Catholics could be found who would question the postulate that the family was the basic unit of society. So most Protestants were unwilling to confront the major Catholic argument of the primacy of the family. Instead, they usually approached the School Question from safer vantage points. Their arguments ran along two major channels: an attack upon the Catholic parochial schools, and the proposition that the common school was itself an effective instrument of moral and religious education.

Denunciations of the Catholic parochial schools had been from the beginning an integral part of the Common School Movement. The arguments used in the eighties to support such denunciations were the same as those that had been employed during the formative stages of the movement: the parochial school was an effort by the Catholic Church to keep its members in ignorance; since ignorance was the antithesis of the universal enlightenment necessary for the successful functioning of a democratic form of government, the parochial school was un-American. Indeed, said Secretary of the Navy Richard W. Thompson, writing about the increasing number of parochial schools in the country, the un-American flavor of these schools was calculated and deliberate. Foreign priests were selected to head the parochial schools so that they might instill into children their own views, contrary to the American way of life.[8]

John D. Philbrick, superintendent of schools in Boston, carefully avoided religious polemics, but he insisted that the growth of parochial schools would have dire consequences for the public schools.

7. "Should Americans Educate Their Children in Denominational Schools?" *Catholic World* 49 (September 1889): 809.

8. *The Papacy and the Civil Power* (New York: Harper and Brothers, 1876), pp. 23–24.

He warned that if non-public schools should increase in number, "Then the public schools will necessarily become at once poor schools, and schools for the poor."[9] Philbrick's argument was not new; it had been employed by Horace Mann and other leaders of the Common School Movement several decades earlier. Unlike the stridently anti-Catholic arguments, which very gradually were to lose their appeal to many in an increasingly secular society, the essence of Philbrick's argument was still being widely used a century later, although the facts, now as then, belie that view. Inner-city elementary schools, whether Catholic or public, are overwhelmingly schools for minority groups and the poor.[10]

Fulminations against the Catholic Church and its schools, however convincing they might seem to most Protestants, did not in any way constitute a positive rationale for the common schools. Few public school leaders even attempted to articulate a realistic basis for their dogmatic belief in the common school. Of those who attempted the task, Lester F. Ward was the most influential. This largely self-educated American sociologist developed in his *Dynamic Sociology* (1883) a theory of planned progress whereby man, through education and improvement of intellect, could direct the process of social evolution. Of necessity, the common school played an important part in this theory.

There were, said Ward, three possible motives upon which an educational system might be founded. The first of these was that of the recipients, the students. But because of their youth and because of the political and cultural customs of the country, they could not have a real voice in the matter. A second motive was the wants and desires of the parents, and this motive required careful consideration. It was, Ward recognized, upheld by the Catholic Church and formed the basis for its schools. Ward conceded that the motives of parents often did secure an adequate education for the young. But, he cautioned, the supply of education would always correspond to the demand, and no more education would ever be supplied than was demanded by the parents. Hence, those parents or guardians who did not desire education for their young would not have it; those who desired it least would have least; and each would have about the amount for which he was willing to pay. This was the nature of all private education. Moreover, the variation in the demand for education was not only quantitative but also qualitative.

The third and only realistic motive for education, argued Ward,

---

9. Massachusetts State Board of Education, *Thirty-Fifth Annual Report, 1870–1871* (Boston: Wright and Potter Printing Company, 1872), p. 244. Hereafter cited as *Annual Report*, with appropriate years given.

10. The Catholic League for Religious and Civil Rights, *Inner City Private Elementary Schools: A Study* (Milwaukee: Marquette University Press, 1982).

was to improve society by making better citizens. Since that was the case, a society would always desire most the education of those most needing to be educated. A manageable segment of society was that part which constituted the political state, and the provision of schools was therefore necessarily a responsibility of the state. In educational matters, individuals or parents were not to be trusted. A dynamic society, an expanding state, was in great need of an educational system common to all, established and maintained by the state. The state, moreover, could tolerate only a very limited number of private or parochial schools, for they constituted a genuine threat to the growth and expansion of the society and ultimately the state as well.[11]

Never in nineteenth-century America had the claims of the state in education been stated more forcefully; never had the claims of individuals, parents, and the church been more pointedly denigrated. The reasoning employed was wholly secular, devoid of any appeals to faith or authority. The impact of Ward's exaltation of the role of the state in education quickly became evident. His doctrine of state supremacy in education offered to public school leaders a positive and apparently scientific rationale for countering the Catholic insistence upon the primacy of the family. Many public schoolmen surged forward to embrace Ward's ideas, pushing aside the deeply rooted American political ideals of individualism and limited government. Even Protestant clergymen, heirs to the Reformation emphasis on the sanctity of individual conscience, now applauded the statist philosophy of Ward.

Writing in the *Forum*, Rev. J. R. Kendrick made a spirited defense of the rights of the state, and in the process disputed the Catholic claim to the sacredness of the family as the basic social unit responsible for education. Kendrick maintained that the premise upon which the common school was grounded was that "the right to exist, in individual man or nation, implies the right to employ the measures necessary for existence." Thus, in the field of education, "the state is warranted in doing whatever is essential to its own preservation and healthy activity." At a meeting of the Massachusetts State Teachers' Association held in Boston in 1886, Rev. J. R. Duryea advanced essentially the same argument.[12] It was the same argument that had been used for centuries—and would be used again—to justify absolutist rule, whether of the left or of the right.

11. *Dynamic Sociology* (New York: D. Appleton Company, 1883), pp. 584–602, 607–14.
12. Kendrick, "Romanizing the Public Schools," *Forum* 8 (September 1889): 73; Duryea, "Moral Education in the Public Schools," *Journal of Education* 24 (2 December 1886): 359.

Ward's influence on one state school official, directly or indirectly, was to become an important factor in the Massachusetts school controversies of 1888–1890. In his report of 1889, John W. Dickinson, then secretary of the Massachusetts State Board of Education, set forth in some detail his interpretation of the relationship of the state to education. After considering the nature, origin, and purpose of the state, he arrived at the conclusion that from its right to exist naturally followed its right to exercise supreme civil power. Thus, anything that was necessary for the state's well-being might rightfully be done, and especially those things necessary to train every individual citizen into harmony with the constitution of the state. There were, Dickinson wrote, three conditions necessary to the formation and continued existence of a free state: an intelligent people, a virtuous people, and a homogeneous people. It therefore followed that the existence and prevalence of intelligence and virtue and a common sympathy among the people required a wise, faithful, and universal application of the influences of a common education. Dickinson had voiced a somewhat similar statement in the preceding year and had been warmly praised for his efforts.[13]

Calling upon both tradition and precedent in support of his arguments, the secretary of education pointed out that the early colonists had been aware that popular education could be secured in no other way than by the public school, organized, controlled, and supported by the state. Dickinson was here expressing the theory that the origins of public education were to be found in the colonial schools. Father Hecker's view, cited earlier in this work, that all schools were originally parochial schools stood in stark contrast. It was clear, Dickinson continued, that the same forces that had led to the establishment of a democratic government had led also to the creation of a free common school system, and neither could exist without the other. Concluding, Dickinson defined a democratic state as a community of persons, the state and the people being one. Therefore, to affirm what the state might do was to affirm what the people might do for themselves.[14]

The following year, Dickinson warned that when any considerable portion of the people should refuse or neglect to support the common school or refuse to be subjected to its educative influences, then the state had begun to resolve itself into fragments and to decay. The nationally circulated and prestigious *Journal of Education* made the same point even more directly: "The state has almost the sole interest in the manhood of the child, hence its right to insist that the educa-

13. *Annual Report, 1887–1888*, p. 72; *Boston Evening Transcript*, 16 January 1888, p. 4.
14. *Annual Report, 1887–1888*, pp. 72–73.

tion shall be for the benefit of the state in manhood."[15] Leaders of the Common School Movement had regarded religious instruction as an essential part of the common school program. Now some public school leaders were saying that the state had "almost the sole interest" in the education of the child. It was a defensive reaction, but no less dangerous for that.

A Secular Approach to Moral Instruction

Of the dilemmas confronting public school leaders in the late decades of the nineteenth century, none was more perplexing and insistent than the question of moral instruction in the schools. To the Common School leaders of the 1830s, morality and religion were inseparable, and the centerpiece of religious instruction in the schools, as Horace Mann formulated it, was Bible reading without comment. This was not enough, as many Protestants of the time saw it, but it was all they could get. In the postbellum period, Bible reading was being abolished in many of the larger cities and in some smaller communities as well, and these actions were in many cases upheld in the courts. Yet the need for the development of moral character in children was even greater now than it had been in the rural Protestant America of the 1830s. Indeed, said the now-elderly Rev. A. D. Mayo in addressing the Massachusetts State Teachers' Association, moral training was by far the most important responsibility of the common school.[16]

There can be little doubt about the substantial decline of the religious content of the common school curriculum during the latter part of the nineteenth century. To cite one example, the *Fourth Reader* of the McGuffey Series of 1844 contained selections at least 30 percent of which were religious in nature. However, this percentage gradually decreased in the later editions until it was only 3 percent in the 1901 edition. On the other hand, the emphasis on morals increased until it reached 40 percent of the total content in the 1879 edition.[17]

Proposals to ground moral instruction in secular values were becoming increasingly frequent and insistent. Some of this demand came from avowed, and often vocal, secularists. In 1867 a group of them, including Ralph Waldo Emerson, founded the Free Religious Association, which called for "an end of the intolerance of American Christianity toward new ideas—toward Darwinism and historical criticism of the Scriptures." Frances E. Abbott, first editor of the asso-

15. *Annual Report, 1888–1889*, p. 219; "The Parent and the State," *Journal of Education* 28 (8 November 1888): 304.

16. *Boston Evening Transcript*, 30 December 1875, p. 6.

17. John A. Nietz, "Why the Longevity of the McGuffey Readers?" *History of Education Quarterly* 4 (June 1964): 123.

ciation's journal, the *Index*, insisted that the reading of the King James version of the Bible in the schools was "just as much a symbol of the Protestant faith as saying Mass or making the sign of the cross is a symbol of the Catholic faith," and should therefore be abolished.[18] Other liberal journals, including the *Nation*, agreed that the effort to maintain the Bible in the schools was in reality an effort on the part of Protestants to retain control of the schools. In 1876, the Free Religious Association at a meeting in Boston evenhandedly rejected both the Catholic and the Protestant faiths as suitable foundations for moral instruction, the former because it owed allegiance to a foreign power and put religion above morals, and the latter because it was more interested in otherworldliness. Hence, it was the duty of the state to provide a moral education on a secular basis to all its future citizens.[19]

The secular trends of the last quarter of the century created apprehension and uncertainty within the Protestant fold. It was, said Arthur Schlesinger, "a critical period in American religion."[20] Prominent among those who urged a secular approach to education was William Torrey Harris, superintendent of the St. Louis public school system (1868–1880), later (1889–1906) U.S. commissioner of education, and in his day perhaps the leading American exponent of Hegelianism. Although not a secularist himself, Harris defined the common school in purely secular terms. He made a sharp distinction between the roles of the church and the school in moral instruction. The state, said Harris, defined what was negative to justice as crime, while the church defined what was negative to its ideal state of holiness as sin. Harris thus argued that the union of church and state in the operation of the schools would confuse these standards, which would prevent either religion or the state from being elevated. Separation of the churches from the schools was therefore absolutely necessary. It naturally followed, believed Harris, that the secular schools were not necessarily godless institutions; rather, the school was essentially auxiliary to the church. The secular school saved the church the endless labor that would be necessary to prepare the minds of the illiterate to receive spiritual doctrine and to prevent such minds from lapsing into idolatry and superstition.[21]

In Harris's scheme, the five most important institutions of society were the family, the civil community, the political state, the school,

18. Ralph Henry Gabriel, *The Course of American Democratic Thought* (New York: The Ronald Press Company, 1940), p. 176; *The Index*, 30 July 1870.

19. Sherman Merritt Smith, *The Relation of the State to Religious Education in Massachusetts* (Syracuse: Syracuse University Book Store, 1926), pp. 262–63.

20. See his article using that phrase as title in *Proceedings of the Massachusetts Historical Society* 64 (June 1983): 523–47.

21. "Religious Instruction in the Public Schools," *The Andover Review* 11 (June 1889): 591.

and the church. All institutions in society were responsible for character education, said Harris, but each in its own way. The school, however, was the most effective agent for moral training through its atmosphere of discipline. The discipline—the development of moral habits in the school—could, and indeed did, lay the groundwork for religious education in the church. But only the church, he cautioned, because of its authoritarian methods and its sacred surroundings, could teach religious truth. The teaching of the virtues of faith, hope, and charity was, however, a part of the school's moral task since those virtues all possessed a secular base. In applying his theory of moral instruction, Harris's prescription was simple and straightforward: "Moral education, therefore, must begin in merely mechanical obedience and develop gradually out of this stage towards that of individual responsibility." Yet, he cautioned, "Strictness, which is indispensable, must be tempered by such devices as cause the pupil to love, to obey the law for the law's sake."[22] Harris therefore parted company with Mann on the subject of Bible reading in the public schools. There could be no non-sectarian approach to religion in the common school, said Harris, since that simply constituted the establishment of one more sect.

Although Protestant-oriented religious instruction was still included in most common school programs in the 1880s, Harris's views commanded widespread attention and respect. The influential Edwin D. Mead of Boston maintained that the common school was the greatest moral instrument in the community. The school's moral power lay in the teaching of the habits of punctuality, obedience, cleanliness, order, decorum, industry, concentration, love of country, justice, equality, and respect for pure and simple merit. Always, wrote Mead, the teaching of morals had to be indirect. Another observer expressed the same view more succinctly: "The whole apparatus of education, from top to bottom, fails," wrote F. D. Huntington, "unless it chastens and molds the mind to orderly method."[23]

Yet Protestants who claimed that morality could be taught apart from religion faced a dilemma. The Protestant church had always taught that goodness was possible without religion; at the same time, almost every orthodox Protestant had been told since childhood that while goodness might be sufficient for the present life, it was not good enough to secure his soul's salvation. But this dualism in Protestant thought should not be carried over into the common schools,

22. "Moral Education in the Common Schools," in *American Institute of Instruction, Lectures, Discussions, and Proceedings* (Boston: Willard Small, 1884), pp. 35, 46.
23. "Can Morality Be Taught Without Sectarianism?" (a symposium), *Journal of Education* 29 (14 February 1889): 99. Huntington, "Education and Lawlessness," *Forum* 4 (October 1887): 139.

said one observer: "While conduct in this world is vital to the welfare of the state, it is none of the state's business to establish an insurance bureau for the safety of souls after they have passed beyond the limit of the state's jurisdiction."[24]

There was, of course, a purely pragmatic argument for separating moral instruction in the schools from religious sanctions. Solomon Schindler, a Jewish rabbi and a member of the Boston School Committee, asked the question that had remained unanswered since Horace Mann had launched his "non-sectarian" doctrine half a century earlier. How could all the young of the state be enticed to enter the public schools if information offensive to certain groups was included?[25]

Another approach to moral instruction enjoyed wider currency than Harris's secular scheme: the doctrine that the example of the teacher was the most important element in moral instruction. The two approaches were not incompatible, but the doctrine of the teacher as moral exemplar skirted the secular/religious issue, and as generally propounded had rather scanty philosophical underpinning. Few would have quarreled with William Elliot Griffis when he wrote, "The purer and more earnest the teacher, the nobler the exemplar, the better will morals be taught and enforced." Yet, even Griffis hedged his argument somewhat, believing that morals could be taught, "not the best morals, but sufficient for the making of good citizens." Edwin T. Home, headmaster of the Prescott School of Boston, believed that moral teaching depended upon the influence of the teacher who stood before the children each day, "a patient and courageous example, with high moral purpose, encouraging every honest effort, discountenancing shame and meanness." Kate Gannett Wells, a member of the Massachusetts State Board of Education, insisted that not only *could* morality be taught, but it *was* taught at all times through the power of the teacher's example and through her attitude of mental reverence toward all truth.[26]

In the normal schools, which had become the standard institutions for the training of common school teachers by the latter part of the century, a tremendous amount of attention was devoted to the subject of moral instruction. Emerson E. White's widely used textbook on classroom management provides an interesting example. In this book, 198 out of the total of 303 pages of text were devoted to moral instruction in the public schools. In White's book and in many similar texts, teachers-in-training were told that moral instruction involved

24. M. J. Savage, "What Shall the Public School Teach?" *Forum* 4 (December 1887): 466, 469.

25. "The Study of History in the Public Schools," *Arena* 1 (December 1889): 53.

26. "Can Morality Be Taught Without Sectarianism?" pp. 99–101. Italics added.

two distinct elements: training and instruction. The essential purpose of training was to influence the child's will to act habitually from right motives. The means for achieving these motives were called training incentives, and they were of two kinds—natural and artificial. The natural incentives (there were nine of them, usually referred to as the "royal nine") ranged from a desire on the part of the individual for good standing to a sense of duty. The artificial incentives, more concrete and definite, consisted of the awarding of prizes, privileges, and immunities from required tasks.[27]

The instruction element was, however, equally important and consisted primarily of stories, poems, and fables that expressed a moral or praised a virtue. Alice Cary was apparently a favorite of the normal school instructors, and as a consequence thousands of children in the common schools were expected to memorize her verses. On the virtue of kindness, Cary wrote:

> Kind hearts are the gardens
> Kind thoughts are the roots
> Kind words are the flowers
> Kind deeds are the fruits.[28]

By the late part of the last century, an imposing argument for state monopoly in education had been constructed. Lester F. Ward was the high priest of this school of thought, which was eagerly embraced by many public school leaders. True, Ward's scheme completely ignored religious principles as a foundation for moral instruction. But a parallel theory of moral instruction based on secular values was also being developed. Although this secular theory was never to be accepted by all Protestants, it did reassure many of them that they could continue to send their children to the common schools, secure in the belief that they were not remiss in their duties as parents. As for Catholics—and many Lutherans as well—statism and secularism in education were both flatly unacceptable. During the bitter school controversies of 1888–1890, they would vigorously reassert their historic beliefs that the family and the church were the basic agencies for education and that the only proper role of the state was to assist them.

---

27. *School Management* (New York: American Book Co., 1894), pp. 112–89. White has a rather elaborate outline of his moral training scheme on the latter page.
28. Ibid., p. 244. For children in the higher grades, more complex poems were included.

8

The School Question in Massachusetts, 1888–1889

Deterioration of the Common Schools

The social problems that perplexed and divided the larger society afflicted the common schools as well. In 1876, the Massachusetts State Board of Education sadly reported, "The Puritan element is fast dying out, and a people with different tastes and different tendencies is gradually taking possession of the land." Each year an "avalanche of ignorance and illiteracy" landed upon the shores of the Bay State, said the board. Never had the importance of education been more apparent.[1]

The great debate over the School Question in Massachusetts came at a time when public support for the common schools, throughout the non-Catholic community, was at a low ebb. The almost naive faith of the antebellum years had waned. As early as the mid-seventies, an official of the Massachusetts Board of Education had enumerated the weaknesses of the state's common schools, among them irregularity of attendance, paucity of instructional equipment, lack of trained teachers, and frequent change of teachers by local school districts.[2] Year after year, officials of the board continued to submit similar disheartening appraisals of the schools.

State and local officials agreed that the most frustrating problem they encountered was that of irregular attendance at school, or "truancy." Historically, it had been the duty of the local clergy to encourage school attendance. An 1835 Massachusetts law reaffirmed this principle, requiring ministers along with the selectmen and school committees to see that the youth of their towns attended school. The

1. Massachusetts State Board of Education, *Thirty-Ninth Annual Report, 1874–1875* (Boston: Wright and Potter Printing Co., 1876), p. 17. Hereafter cited as *Annual Report*, with appropriate year numbers given. In this chapter, I have drawn rather heavily, with the author's permission, on a Ph.D. dissertation completed under my supervision: James M. Benjamin, "The School Question in Massachusetts, 1870–1900: Its Background and Influence on Public Education" (University of Missouri, 1968).

2. *Annual Report, 1874–1875*, pp. 110–14.

same provision was made in the General Statutes of 1859 and in the Public Statutes of 1882.[3] But it had long been apparent that exhortatory efforts by local officials were of little avail. In 1852 Massachusetts had become the first state to enact a compulsory school attendance law, but for several decades this too proved to be ineffective. Compulsion as a means of securing school attendance was widely regarded as an invasion of personal freedom. Worse yet, the truancy problem was greatest in the factory towns, where the families of the newly arrived immigrants were concentrated and where the need for Americanization was most acute. In Fall River in 1870–1871, average daily attendance was barely 50 percent of the pupils enrolled in the common schools.[4]

The truancy problem afflicted the parochial as well as the common schools. And as parochial schools were not required by law to report absenteeism from their schools to the public truancy officers, it was difficult to assess the true proportions of the problem. Too often, says Professor Handlin, an insistence upon a parochial school education by church officials and parents became a shield for truancy and a contributing factor to child vagrancy.[5] One must not forget, however, that the children of the immigrants and of the poor were regarded by their parents—and often necessarily so—as an economic asset to the family. The meager wages they earned in the mills and factories were needed to sustain their families. One should remember also that the development of effective school attendance laws was inextricably bound up with the development of effective child labor laws. By and large, the public school interests in this country lobbied aggressively for the former but were seemingly oblivious to the need for the latter.[6]

Another criticism was that the narrowly academic curriculum of the schools did little to prepare the children of the immigrants and the poor for the type of life they were likely to enter, and thus there were many demands for industrial education (commonly called "manual training") in the schools. Another, and a more obvious, weakness was overcrowding in the schools. In the elementary grades in Boston, long regarded as one of the better systems in the country, the pupil-teacher ratio was 46:1. In some other large cities, one-teacher classrooms with eighty to one hundred children were not unknown. Conditions in the elementary schools seemed so universally poor to the

---

3. Samuel Windsor Brown, *The Secularization of American Education* (New York: Columbia University Press, 1912), p. 41.
4. *Annual Report, 1870–1871*, p. 34.
5. *Annual Report, 1885–1886*, p. 172; Oscar Handlin, *Boston Immigrants* (Cambridge: Harvard University Press, 1959), p. 159.
6. Lloyd P. Jorgenson, "The Social and Economic Orientation of the National Education Association," *Progressive Education* 34 (July 1957): 98–101.

editors of the widely read *Scribner's Monthly* that they felt compelled
to suggest methods by which parents might teach their children at
home, since they were merely "recited" at school and must be "studied" and "explained to" at home.[7] It came to be almost fashionable to
ridicule the institution that had once been the pride of the Commonwealth. To speak about the "superiority" of the Massachusetts
schools, said a leading newspaper, was now sheer "buncombe." Not
even educators arose to contradict the charge. One of the bleakest
pictures of the rural school to be found in educational literature was
painted by an agent of the board: "They stand on the bleakest hill-
top, black and shapeless without . . . not a curtain within, not a tree
for shade without . . . ."[8]

Two decades of criticism of public education coalesced, in a sense,
in 1892 in the writings of J. W. Rice, a young physician, who was
commissioned to write a series of articles for the *Forum*. He spent
more than five months visiting classrooms throughout the eastern
and midwestern states. He observed more than twelve hundred
teachers at work, and found much to condemn and little to praise. He
pictured the common schools as examples of mechanical drudgery,
compartmentalized and isolated subject matter, and rote memoriza-
tion. Professor Cremin has credited Rice with awakening the citizens
not only of Massachusetts but of the country as a whole to the need
for improvement of the public schools, an effort which, drawing from
other sources as well, developed into the Progressive Education
Movement.[9]

At a time when the public schools seemed to be deteriorating,
Protestants in Massachusetts were much exercised by what they saw
as the alarming rate of growth of Catholic parochial schools. In fact,
however, as late as 1889, the parochial schools could accommodate
little more than 10 percent of the school-age population in Massachusetts, while slightly more than 50 percent of the school-age
children in the state were from Catholic families. The establishment
of parochial schools was indeed a settled policy of the Catholic
Church, forcefully reaffirmed by the Third Plenary Council. But the
Irish Catholics in New England, and their leaders, showed less zeal in
carrying out this policy than did the German Catholics in the Midwest.[10]

7. Gail Hamilton, *Our Common School System* (Boston: Estes and Lauriat, 1880), p. 37;
"Two Ways of Teaching at Home," *Scribner's Monthly* 15 (February 1876): 583.
8. *Boston Evening Transcript* (hereafter cited as *BET*), 9 April 1875, p. 4; *Annual Report,
1875–1876*, pp. 55–56.
9. Rice's articles were later published in book form as *The Public School System of the
United States* (New York: The Century Publishing Co., 1893); Lawrence A. Cremin, *The
Transformation of the School* (New York: Vintage Books, 1961), p. 8.
10. John Gilmary Shea, "Bostonian Ignorance of Catholic Doctrine," *American Catholic*

The School Controversy Arises in Boston, 1888

In his message to the Massachusetts state legislature (the General Court) in January 1888, newly reelected Gov. Oliver Ames noted that the number of children enrolled in private schools was increasing. Expressing alarm, he called for an effort on the part of the state to take the steps necessary to defend the public schools. This statement was in harmony with the platform of the state Republican party, which had nominated Ames.[11] Opponents of the parochial schools construed Ames's message as a call to arms, and within the month the city of Boston, as well as the General Court, was embroiled in a bitter two-year struggle over the School Question.

Many citizens and officials of the state were ready to wave the banner of anti-Catholicism, and they were joined by agitators from elsewhere. On 23 January 1888, Rev. Justin D. Fulton, D.D., a Baptist minister, spoke to almost four thousand people at Mechanics Hall in Boston on the topic "Popery vs. Prosperity, Which?" In his lecture, Fulton detailed his knowledge of Catholic plans to take over the United States. In the cities, he said, "the Pope controls the ballots of the men, and the priests of the women . . . ." He charged also that Catholics already had control of the military establishment. On the following evening, Fulton spoke on the subject "Priests and Our Homes." He insisted that the United States Congress was wasting its time in an investigation of Mormonism, and he demanded that the confessional be probed instead.[12] Fulton presented to everyone who had purchased tickets for both of his lectures a copy of his book *Why Priests Should Wed*.

A native of New York, Fulton had filled pulpits for some thirty years in Ohio, New York, Massachusetts, and as far west as St. Louis. Everywhere he went he made sensational pronouncements on various subjects, but his favorite target was "popery." Early in 1887, Fulton had resigned his pulpit in Brooklyn, New York, apparently to the relief of his congregation, and began to devote all his time to his favorite topic. Soon he organized his Pauline Propaganda, a society with dues-paying members pledged to combat the legions of Rome. Later in 1887, he transferred his scene of operations to Boston, and in August of that year he began to hold weekly meetings on Sunday afternoons, first at the (Baptist) Tremont Temple and then at Music Hall. A secular newspaper reported one of his appearances in scath-

---

Quarterly Review 14 (October 1889): 99; Robert H. Lord, John E. Sexton, and Edward T. Harringon, *The History of the Archdiocese of Boston*, 3 vols. (Boston: The Pilot Publishing Company, 1945), 3:80.

11. *BET*, 5 January 1888, p. 6.

12. Ibid., 24 January 1888, p. 6; 25 January 1888, p. 1.

ing terms: "We condemn the performance in Music Hall as slanderous and indecent. No self-respecting newspaper would condescend to print, even for the purpose of censuring, the filth that was uttered by one who, we believe, misrepresents the Protestant clergy as grossly as he does the general Christian sentiment of Boston."[13]

The book that Fulton presented to those who attended his performances had been published in the latter part of 1887, although it had been turned down by the house that originally planned to publish it as "obscene and indecent" and "unfit for any establishment in America to print." A Catholic historian describes this work as "perhaps the most indecent to which any clergyman in America has ever set his signature."[14] Consequently, some of the worst passages were blocked out before publication. Enough of the text remained, however, to reveal the nature of Fulton's diatribe against the Church of Rome, "the mother of harlots and abominations." There is a colorful and rather long section on the "Blessed Creatures" or "consecrated prostitutes." The Blessed Creature (or BC) "must be subservient to the will of her masters at all times," said Fulton, and he felt impelled to elaborate on this point: "At first the female may be a little timid, and somewhat surprised to learn that the priest or bishop requires the unusual, apparently wrong, mysteriously right, service from her; and she may object . . . . But the priest, representing God's angel in this office, gently soothes the mind and quiets the fears of his future spouse . . . ."[15] Fulton's chapter on the School Question was titled "No Surrender to Rome." In an appendix he reprinted the "Statement of Principles" of the ferociously anti-Catholic American Protective Association.

Others of equally colorful background also appeared on the scene. Early in 1887, a Mrs. Margaret L. Shepherd had arrived in Boston and in August received baptism at Trinity Baptist Church. A short time later she published a small book titled *The Little Mother*, which purported to be an account of her life as a nun until her conversion one day when she "accidentally" came upon a copy of the Bible. A number of Protestant publications recommended the book to their readers. The *Baptist Watchman* hailed it as an "uncommonly thrilling" story and recommended its inclusion in Sunday school libraries. By early 1888, Mrs. Shepherd had established herself as a figure of influence in Boston, with two lectures weekly in Tremont Temple, one for "ladies only."[16]

13. *Boston Advertiser*, 12 December 1887, p. 2.
14. Lord et al., *Archdiocese*, 3:106.
15. *Why Priests Should Wed* (New York: The Paulist Propaganda, 1894), pp. 100, 103. The original edition was published in 1887.
16. Lord et al., *Archdiocese*, 3:108.

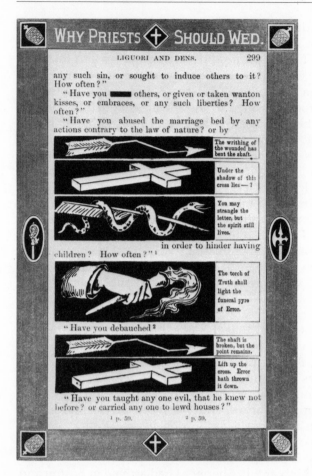

This page from Fulton's *Why Priests Should Wed* shows the heavy blocking done by the publisher to censor some of the more salacious passages.

Several Protestant clergymen were in the forefront of the anti-Catholic movement in Massachusetts. Most prominent was Rev. Alonzo Ames Miner, a Universalist and an influential member of the State Board of Education. Miner was a respected minister with almost fifty years in the pulpit in and around Boston. A former president of Tufts College, he was perhaps the foremost clergyman of his denomination. Despite these impressive credentials, Miner was obsessed with hatred for the Catholic Church. He was quoted in an anti-Catholic journal in 1887 as stating that the Catholic Church was "as sly as a serpent, and a great deal more venomous. There are things going on in Boston today in that church, which, if known to the public and understood, would make them horror-stricken. What is the meaning

"Assaulting the Organist," from Fulton's *Why Priests Should Wed*. Fulton presented priests as diabolic, scheming, lustful creatures with nearly hypnotic power over Catholic women.

of the cells under our own Cathedral here in Boston?"[17] (He was later to repeat this charge in a legislative hearing.) Miner's presence in the crusade was unusual because Unitarians and Universalists had rarely shown zeal for the anti-Catholic cause. Meanwhile, another member of the State Board of Education, E. C. Carrigan, argued at a meeting of the Boston Congregational Club that it was the duty of the state to insure that local school committees knew what was being taught in all private schools as well as the way in which it was taught.[18] Throughout 1888, despite concern about the tariff question, the temperance

17. Cited in ibid., 3:106–7.
18. "Boston Letter," *Journal of Education* 26 (3 November 1887): 261.

issue, and the forthcoming presidential campaign, anti-Catholic tirades were daily features in many Massachusetts newspapers.

Early in January 1888, a special joint committee of the General Court submitted a report on the employment and schooling of minors. There were already in effect several state statutes bearing on the schooling required of minors employed in factories. Legislation enacted in 1873 empowered local school committees to grant their approval to private schools. An 1878 act required that employed children between the ages of ten and fourteen must attend a school providing instruction in English at least twenty weeks out of the year. The school could be either public or private, but if the latter it had to be approved by the local school committee. These stipulations were clear enough, but another provision of the law introduced a deep ambiguity. This provision, which had originally appeared in the state's first compulsory attendance law in 1852, read, in part, ". . . or that such child has been otherwise furnished with the means of education for a like period of time."[19] Catholic authorities held that this provision exempted them from the necessity of seeking approval for their schools. Moreover, the law contained no provision for enforcement. They feared that the atmosphere prevailing in many communities in Massachusetts—and elsewhere—made approval of a Catholic school unlikely, whatever its program might be.

Members of the State Board of Education and their secretary, John Dickinson, strongly rejected the Catholic interpretation of the law. Repeatedly they asserted that existing laws gave the child only two options: he must attend either a public school or an approved private school. It was therefore the responsibility of local school committees to visit private schools and to approve such of them as might be found to be adequate, before granting children permits to work. These urgings of the State Board of Education did not satisfy the editor of the *Journal of Education*. The inspection of private schools was too important a matter to be left to the discretion of local school committees, he said. A state agency must be created for the express purpose of making "special examinations into the character of the teaching in every private school in the state."[20]

In its report, the special joint committee made several recommendations. All private schools should be required to register and submit lists of their students to the local school authorities (committees) monthly. The school committees should be required to examine each approved private school once a month with the possibility of withdrawing approval at any time. Local school committees were also to

19. Massachusetts, *Acts and Resolves*, chapter 279–1878.
20. "The Parochial School Question," *Journal of Education* 26 (3 November 1887): 264.

certify the programs of all private schools annually and to notify the State Board of Education of their actions. Finally, after 1 September 1889 all teachers in private schools would be required to have certification by the state. Private school teacher qualifications were to be the same as those of teachers in the public schools.[21] One member filed a dissenting report in which he asserted that the committee had been given no authority to consider non-public schools and that the parent's natural right to educate his child as he saw fit was guaranteed by the state constitution. The *Transcript* dismissed his arguments as "hollow and flimsy."[22]

In an atmosphere highly charged with emotion, five hearings were held at the State House between 6 and 29 March 1888 on the joint committee proposals, which had become popularly known as the "Bill for Inspection of Private Schools." Of the twelve witnesses who supported the bill, nine were Protestant clergymen. One of them asserted that he was "in favor of Massachusetts running all private schools" and opposed to "interference by any Pope or potentate."[23] At the final hearing, Rev. T. E. Leyden, evangelist and pastor of Clarendon Street Baptist Temple and purportedly a convert from Catholicism, flourished before the audience a number of Catholic emblems and declared that Catholics were carried away by such things to the exclusion of instruction in the doctrines of Christianity. Leyden's charges drew loud applause from those in attendance, and the joint committee voted to suppress all such demonstrations.[24]

The *Transcript*, meanwhile, insisted that the school inspection bill was not a product of bigotry, but rather was a protest against a few aggressive priests who threatened their flocks with damnation if they attempted to use the public schools. Thus, this anti-Catholic newspaper saw the struggle as a necessary attempt to help Catholic citizens to achieve the liberty to send their children to the public schools. There, their children might sit side by side with Protestant children as "unconscious of their parents' religious tenets as Baptist and Methodist children."[25]

---

21. Massachusetts, *General Court Hearings of Legislative Committee on Education in March, 1888: House Document No. 19* (Boston, 1888), pp. 43–46; *BET,* 19 January 1888, p. 4. *House Document No. 19,* cited here, is the official account of the hearings on the bill presented by the committee. The proceedings were reported in greater detail in the anti-Catholic *BET.* As seen from the Catholic point of view, the best source (and also the most complete account extant) is Katherine Conway and Mabel Ward Cameron, *Charles Francis Donnelly* (New York: James T. White and Co., 1909).

22. *BET,* 1 February 1888, p. 4; *House Document No. 19,* p. 50.

23. *House Document No. 19,* p. 22.

24. "Massachusetts School Legislation," *Journal of Education* 27 (5 April 1888): 216; *BET,* 28 March 1888, p. 5.

25. 7 March 1888, p. 4.

Ironically, the most effective testimony against the bill came from a number of well-known Protestants, including Rev. Edward Everett Hale, who appeared on behalf of certain non-Catholic private schools; Superintendent of Public Schools A. T. Marble of Worcester; Principal J. W. McDonald of the Stoneham High School; and Gen. Francis A. Walker, president of the Massachusetts Institute of Technology. Most impressive, no doubt, were the presentations by Pres. Charles A. Eliot of Harvard and Col. Thomas Wentworth Higginson. It was clearly President Eliot's hope to moderate the hostility concerning parochial schools. The measure under consideration would widen the breach between religious groups, he said, and it was "therefore hostile to the interests of the entire community." Speaking more specifically, Eliot was not willing to accept the joint committee's claim that the bill was a compulsory attendance measure to be applied impartially in all private schools. "We all understand," he said, "that although the term 'private school' is used in this bill, the bill is really directed solely to those private schools which receive large numbers of Catholic children belonging to the poorer classes . . . . " Although some might hope that the proposed legislation would result in an improvement of the private schools, he continued, others viewed it as a means to effect their "suppression." In a statement surely designed to prick the consciences of some of the bill's proponents, Eliot said:

> I suppose we all feel the warmest respect and admiration for the self-sacrificing spirit of the Roman Catholic population which supports the parochial schools. I do not see how the children of the Puritans can possibly feel other than respect and admiration for the sacrifices which the Roman Catholic population makes day by day for the schools which in their view are the only ones in which their conscientious belief concerning the education of their children is respected.

Wholly unimpressed, the editor of the *Transcript* charged that Eliot's view was, in effect, "that we shall get whipped if we try to oppose those who are digging at the cornerstone of our institutions; so let's look the other way and pretend not to see them."[26]

Colonel Higginson, in his statement to the committee, declared that his original intention had been to discuss the bill upon educational grounds and he had not expected to allude to the religious question. But the atmosphere pervading the hearing did not permit this, and he declared dramatically:

> Mr. Chairman, I took my first lesson in religious liberty when I stood by my mother's side and watched the burning of the Ursuline Convent in

26. *House Document No. 19*, pp. 7–8; Conroy and Cameron, *Charles Francis Donnelly*, pp. 35–37; *BET*, 7 March 1888, p. 4.

Charlestown, a Catholic convent burned by a Protestant mob; I took my second lesson when in the Know-Nothing days I saw procession after procession of Protestants march through the streets then occupied by Irish Catholics, with torchlights and waving every form of insulting banners in their hand . . . . I hope never to see the renewal of those questions for if those scenes were to be renewed, it would not be necessary to go further than this room to find who would lead the mob.[27]

Instead of attacking the private schools, said Higginson, local school committees should strive to improve the quality of the public schools and thereby to attract more students to them.

The proposed inspection bill had been thoroughly discredited. Although Fulton presented a petition containing one hundred forty signatures urging the committee to report out the bill as originally proposed, the committee did not do so. Miner of the State Board of Education was undaunted and continued to preach sermons in which he charged that the public would never know what went on behind the doors of the parochial schools until the state passed an adequate school inspection bill. The committee did report out a proposal that required the private schools to keep a register of their pupils and to send a copy of it every six months to the local school committee, but even this was defeated in the Senate.[28]

For a time, the tempo of the excitement slackened, but it did not disappear. Early in April 1888, an attempt was made by the *Boston Evening Transcript* to create a controversy over the harsh punishment allegedly meted out in parochial schools to recalcitrant students. At the meeting of the Boston School Committee on 10 April, one of the Catholic members introduced a motion that the subcommittee on manual training schools be given full power to permit children not attending the common schools to attend the public training schools and cooking schools whenever there were vacancies. He argued that the children of taxpayers were entitled to the benefit of any public school they wished to attend. Some committee members objected on the grounds that it might set a precedent that would lead to serious consequences. The motion died in committee.[29]

On 7 May, Augustus D. Small wrote an article for the *Boston Sunday Globe* defending the parochial schools and asserting that children received a thorough education in them. When it was discovered that Small was a teacher and administrator in the Lawrence School (a part of the Boston public school system), a former superintendent of

27. *House Document No. 19*, p. 21; Thomas Dwight, "The Attack on Freedom of Education in Massachusetts," *American Catholic Quarterly Review* 8 (April 1888): 552.
28. *Journal of Education* 27 (7 June 1888): 361; Dwight, "The Attack," p. 553; *BET*, 30 April 1888, p. 4.
29. *BET*, 2 April 1888, p. 6; 11 April 1888, p. 2.

schools in Salem, and a recent convert to Catholicism, the anti-Catholic press erupted again. Small's change of heart, said the *Transcript*, was clear evidence of the power that the Church had over individual members, and it was therefore obvious that Catholics should not be employed in the public schools.[30]

On the same date that Small's article appeared, Theodore A. Metcalf, pastor of the Gate of Heaven Catholic Church, sent a letter to the Boston School Committee that was soon to make the city forget Small's article. In the letter, the priest charged that Charles D. Travis, a history teacher in the Boston English High School for nineteen years, had in his classes described indulgences as payments made in advance to commit sin. Metcalf maintained that Travis had "trespassed on the forbidden ground of religion, and made statements which were an outrage to Catholics in his efforts to explain a question of Catholic doctrine."[31]

When Travis was questioned about the charge, he cited as authority for his statements the textbook used in the course, *Swinton's Outline of the World's History, Ancient, Medieval and Modern*. The School Committee immediately appointed a subcommittee to investigate the matter. At about the same time a countercomplaint was lodged against a textbook used in the Catholic schools on the grounds that it was biased in favor of the Catholic Church.[32]

The Boston School Committee waited some months before considering the Travis case in a regular meeting, probably in the hope that time would put the issue in better perspective. When it met on 19 June, it adopted its subcommittee's recommendation that "Any language . . . by our school teachers justly offensive to any . . . Catholic, Protestant, or Jew, white or colored, cannot be too severely censured." Swinton's book was removed from the official list of texts, and Travis was transferred to another teaching field.[33]

Now many thought the School Committee had gone too far. The report had been prepared by a committee of three Catholics and one Protestant. The *Boston Evening Transcript* cried: "This was a triumph for sacerdotalism . . . . It puts all teachers in the Boston public schools under a sort of terrorism." The School Committee action was vigorously opposed by the Evangelical Alliance of Boston, which submitted a petition requesting the restoration of Swinton's text. If the School Committee persisted in its decision, the alliance charged, it

30. Ibid., 8 May 1888, p. 4; 9 May 1888, p. 4; 10 May 1888, p. 7.

31. "Boston Letter," *Journal of Education* 28 (20 September 1888): 193; *BET*, 9 May 1888, p. 2.

32. *BET*, 16 May 1888, p. 6.

33. Ibid., 20 June 1888, p. 2; Massachusetts State Board of Education, *Report of the Board of Supervisors* (Boston: Rockwell and Churchhill, Printer, 1889), p. 8.

would then have allied itself with a religious sect: "It would plant sectarian strife in the cradle of American children."[34]

On the afternoon of 11 July, members of the Loyal Order of American Women, led by their national president, Mrs. Shepherd, held the first of a number of meetings in Tremont Temple to protest the committee's decision. The group adopted resolutions demanding that Swinton's book be restored to its proper place in the schools and that Travis be reinstated. Further, they resolved that no Catholic should ever again be elected to the School Committee, that no Catholic teachers should be employed in the public schools, and that Protestant teachers should be protected from Catholic intimidation. That same evening a mass meeting was held in the hot and oppressive atmosphere of Faneuil Hall. So many people appeared for the meeting that an overflow group had to be accommodated in Tremont Temple.

The meeting was called to order by a banker, Bryce S. Evans, and Rev. A. A. Miner was chosen chairman. At the beginning of the meeting, a few speakers attempted to urge moderation with the argument that a good Catholic could be a good citizen, but their efforts were greeted with hisses. Mrs. Caroline E. Hastings, a member of the Boston School Committee who had voted to retain Travis in his original position, was presented with an American flag. The audience was ecstatic.[35]

Steps were taken at the meeting to consolidate the Committee of One Hundred, an anonymous group under the leadership of Rev. J. B. Dunn, a Presbyterian clergyman, that was soon to become the coordinating agency for the anti-parochial school movement. The basic tenet of the Committee of One Hundred was simple and straightforward: "We charge the Papal hierarchy with being hostile to free education and seeking the destruction of the public school system."[36] After the meeting, the Committee of One Hundred exulted:

> Never did Boston witness such a spectacle as the grand old cradle of liberty presented on that night. The historic structure was packed to its utmost capacity, and a finer audience, or a more patriotic and enthusiastic one never gathered beneath a roof; and as the speakers one after the other avowed the determination of the people to defend at all hazards the public schools against Jesuitical intrigue, the famous old building fairly rocked with successive tempests of applause.[37]

For the remainder of 1888, voices calling for reason and understanding in Boston and other Massachusetts towns were drowned by

34. *BET*, 20 June 1888, p. 4.
35. *New York Times*, 13 July 1888, p. 1.
36. *The Great Victory in Boston* (Boston: Committee of One Hundred Series, 1889), 1:2.
37. *An Open Letter to the Friends of Free Schools and American Liberties* (Boston: Committee of One Hundred Series, 1888), 1:19.

the din of patriotic crusaders vying with each other to conquer once and for all the forces of Rome. Fulton and his Pauline Propaganda, the American Reformation Society, the Evangelical Alliance, the Loyal Women of American Liberty, the British American Association, a host of Protestant ministers, and one of the last of Mrs. Shepherd's creations—the recently formed British American Women's Association—were all in full cry. No activity or demonstration seemed beyond the bounds of reason and taste.

Evangelist Leyden assembled a group of "escaped priests" and presented a program in which at least one of the "priests" was exhibited in his "monastic costume." Fulton staged a Sunday show at Music Hall titled "High and Low Mass, A Roaring Farce; a Wafer Worshipped As God."[38] The incongruity of the charges made by the anti-Catholics seemed to escape notice. At least two Protestant clergymen accused the Jesuits of deeds performed long before that order was established, and a Protestant journal accused St. Thomas Aquinas of expressing hostility to the Constitution of the United States.[39] More than a few people called for mob action. Prof. Luther T. Townsend spoke to a group on the subject of "Jesuits" and urged his listeners to "wipe out Catholicism." In September, the Evangelical Alliance again presented a formal petition to the Boston School Committee protesting the removal of Swinton's textbook, but the committee refused to reconsider the matter.[40]

The Boston Election

By this time, many anti-Catholics had concluded that the School Committee was not responsive to the wishes of true Americans in the community and that the only effective remedy lay in the elective process. As early as June, the *Transcript* had called for women to vote in the next School Committee election to turn pro-Catholic members out of office.[41] (Women could vote only for School Committee members.) Despite the fact that the Catholics held the balance of political power in Boston, male voters were about equally divided between Protestants and Catholics.

Learning of the movement to inject the Swinton textbook affair into the next school election, Archbishop John F. Williams issued a stern admonition against pitting "class against class and creed against

38. Edwin Doak Mead, *The Roman Catholic Church and the School Question* (Boston: George H. Ellis, 1888), p. 3.
39. Lord et al., *Archdiocese*, 3:121–22.
40. *BET*, 20 June 1888, p. 4; 18 July 1888, p. 2; 26 September 1888, p. 2; *New York Times*, 11 September 1888, p. 1.
41. 20 June 1888, p. 4.

creed in Boston."[42] The statement by Williams led Protestants to believe that Catholic women would not register to vote. At least three Protestant women's associations were soon actively engaged in campaigns to register women and to provide instruction on voting procedures. Newspapers in other Massachusetts cities and towns took notice of this action and pointed out that similar measures could be used in their communities as well, should the occasion arise. But Catholic women were obviously aware of these developments. Whatever Archbishop Williams might have meant by his stern but rather general statement, a rally attended by several hundred Catholic women was held in Lyceum Hall in East Boston, and a committee was appointed to go from house to house urging the registration of all Catholic women who were eligible to vote.[43]

Less than five hundred women had registered to vote in the school election of 1887, but by 1 October 1888 (the deadline for registration) the newspapers reported that 25,149 women had registered. Veteran political observers felt that the anti-Catholic voter registration drive had defeated itself and that more Catholic than Protestant women had registered.[44] Perhaps the Boston School Committee thought so too, for on 9 October they reinstated Travis in his original position, although they replaced Swinton's book with another text.

Pleas for moderation were still present. Edwin D. Mead, a prominent Protestant, asked the Boston's Women's Suffrage League at a meeting on 1 October whether there was not some inconsistency in Protestants fighting bigotry with bigotry. The Massachusetts State School Suffrage Committee sent around the community two days before the election a list of recommended candidates for the School Committee, and at least two Catholics were on the list. The Citizen's Public School Union, composed mostly of women, also urged moderation. Its stated purpose was to "aid in securing for every child a suitable . . . education, free from the . . . influence of political and religious controversies." No one could be a member who refused to vote for a School Committee member solely because he was a Catholic.[45]

42. Lord et al., *Archdiocese*, 3:121; Alvin P. Stauffer, "Anti-Catholicism in American Politics" (Ph.D. diss., Harvard University, 1933), pp. 252–64. Both of these works maintain that the Catholic women did not vote in the election but, as is indicated later, it is evident that many of them did so.

43. *New York Times*, 23 September 1888, p. 4; 15 July 1888, p. 4; *BET*, 26 September 1888, p. 3.

44. *New York Times*, 23 September 1888, p. 4; 26 September 1888, p. 2; 2 October 1888.

45. *New York Times*, 2 October 1888, p. 1; *BET*, 10 December 1888, p. 1; Francis Parkman, *Our Common Schools* (Boston: Citizen's Public School Union, 1890), p. 1. Parkman, the eminent American historian, was himself not entirely free of the anti-Catholic sentiments of his time.

But the anti-Catholic leaders were not deterred. The *Transcript* complained bitterly that the Massachusetts Suffrage Committee was a statewide organization that had no business interfering in Boston affairs. A prominent university professor called upon all Protestants who had Catholic servants to inform them if they did not intend to vote for the "right" candidates in the forthcoming school election, they should look for work elsewhere. On the Sunday preceding the election, Miner and other clergymen urged their congregations to vote for the candidates recommended by the Committee of One Hundred. Rev. Louis A. Banks of St. Johns Methodist Church preached on "The Twin Leeches—Rum and Romanism," and Rev. J. H. Gunning, a Baptist, preached on "Religious Bigotry—Has It Advanced the Cause of Humanity?" His answer was yes, as long as Protestants were the bigots.[46]

In Boston, as elsewhere, the Republican party had a sympathetic ear for anti-Catholic causes. In November, the Republicans rejected the Democrats' proposal that they nominate a non-partisan ticket for the School Committee, as had been the custom in the past. Instead, Republicans nominated candidates favored by the Committee of One Hundred. With the Republicans and the Democrats unable to present a non-partisan ticket, the Committee of One Hundred became more aggressive. It insisted that "above one-half of the sentinels which have been placed about the cradle of our liberties are traitors." Catholic teachers must, therefore, be barred from teaching in the public schools.[47]

Election day was 11 December. The city awoke to a cold, drenching rain, which continued throughout the day. Despite the weather, more than eighty thousand citizens, including almost seventeen thousand women, braved the elements to give the Republicans and the Committee of One Hundred a victory at the polls. The Committee of One Hundred exulted: "It was a signal victory. It was a double and a treble victory; a victory over Jesuitical intrigue, over the elements, and over the basest kind of misrepresentations and forgeries . . . ."[48] The architects of the victory staged a "grand jubilee meeting" in Tremont Temple. Second to none in receiving the plaudits of the celebrants was Mrs. Shepherd—escaped nun, spiritual leader, and patriot.

Not all were so elated by the Republican victory. Nathan Matthews, Jr., a Protestant and later mayor of Boston, called the election "the most disgraceful page in the municipal history of the city of Boston." The *Andover Review* expressed regret about one group being

46. Mead, *The Roman Catholic Church*, p. 2; *BET*, 10 December 1888, p. 2.
47. "The Boston School Question," *Journal of Education* 28 (22 November 1888): 337.
48. *The Great Victory in Boston*, 1:4.

pitted against another on religious grounds. Gail Hamilton, one of the most vocal critics of the common schools, insisted that the difficulties between Catholics and Protestants were going to have to be worked out but that the public schools should not serve as the arena for contention.[49]

In fact, the victory of Dunn's Committee of One Hundred was not all that it seemed to be. Of the seventeen thousand women who voted, only about ten thousand voted the Republican ticket, and with one exception those supported by the committee won by comparatively small margins. The Catholic mayor, Hugh O'Brien, was defeated by only two thousand (out of more than eighty thousand) votes. Moreover, at least some of the candidates elected to the School Committee were neutral with respect to religious issues. W. A. Mowrey was a charter member of the Massachusetts Society for Promoting Good Citizenship and, although a strong proponent of the public schools, certainly no anti-Catholic. Also elected was Solomon Schindler, a Jewish rabbi. Schindler polled over eighty thousand votes, almost twice as many as any of the other successful candidates and almost the entire vote cast.[50]

After their initial elation had cooled, the Boston anti-Catholic organizations were strangely quiet for a time. On 13 January 1889, members of the Boston Evangelical Association held their monthly meeting and concerned themselves only with drawing up a petition protesting the serving of wine at President Harrison's inauguration. They also requested that the term *inaugural ball* be changed to *inaugural reception*.[51]

The Battle Resumes and Spreads, 1889

The results of the 1888 confrontations had been mixed: anti-Catholics exulted in the outcome of the Boston School Committee election, but their efforts to secure approval of a private school inspection bill had been thwarted. From an organizational point of view, the campaigns of 1888 had strengthened the anti-Catholic forces, and they were ready to resume the battle when the 1889 legislative session convened. Another attempt was made to put a private-school inspection bill on the Massachusetts statute books. And proposals for legis-

---

49. Lord et al., *Archdiocese*, 3:32; "The Public Schools and Roman Catholics," *Andover Review* 10 (December 1888): 620; Hamilton, "Catholicism and the Public Schools," *North American Review* 147 (November 1888): 572–80.

50. *New York Times*, 12 December 1888, p. 1; *BET*, 13 December 1888, p. 2. This is at variance with the conclusion of Lord et al., *Archdiocese*, 3:125–26, which claims that the elected slate contained neither any Catholics nor any persons who could be suspected of friendliness toward Catholics.

51. *BET*, 14 January 1889, p. 1.

lation concerning private schools now appeared in other states as well, as we shall see in the next chapter.

Meanwhile, in Boston, the Evangelical Alliance continued to insist that the state should control all education. The alliance also proposed to petition the United States Congress for such legislation as might be necessary to prohibit any religious group from interfering in the management of the public schools.[52] Moreover, the local elections in December 1888 had aroused controversy in many other Massachusetts communities as well as in Boston, among them Haverhill, Lynn, Lowell, Worcester, Springfield, and Peabody. In most of those places, Protestant clergymen led the anti-Catholic forces. Prominent among them was Rev. Isaiah J. Lansing of Worcester, whose *Romanism and the Republic* was heaped upon the growing pile of anti-Catholic literature.

A more or less typical controversy occurred in Dedham when a Catholic priest, Robert J. Johnson, objected to the use of the now-well-known textbook by Swinton in the public schools. Most of the heat in the ensuing controversy was generated through letters to the editor of the *Dedham Standard* by Johnson and a Protestant member of the Dedham School Committee, Rev. George Willis Cooke. The issue was never wholly resolved, but it went no further than the argument over the textbook and some grossly exaggerated charges by both Johnson and Cooke.[53]

A lengthy and more serious controversy in Haverhill, Massachusetts, was grounded in both nationalistic and religious beliefs. For some years, Haverhill had been experiencing an influx of French-Canadian immigrants. By January 1889 the *Boston Evening Transcript*, always on the alert for signs of Catholic and un-American plots, began to express alarm. The editor published a long criticism of the Canadian parochial schools and their alleged inability to aid in the assimilation of the French immigrants into Canadian life. He feared that a similar situation was likely to occur in Massachusetts. In fact, he charged, the French-Canadians who were immigrating to Massachusetts were determined to make all of New England a French province, and had started by urging the election of French-Canadians to local school committees.[54]

Others in Haverhill also saw the French-Canadian immigration as a clear and present danger. In September 1887, Catholics had opened St. James Parochial School for the English-speaking inhabitants of Haverhill, and six hundred fifty pupils withdrew from the public

52. *New York Times*, 11 September 1888, p. 1.

53. Johnson and Cooke, *Sectarian School Books* (Boston: Alfred Mudge and Son, 1889), pp. 12, 17, 60–61.

54. *BET*, 7 January 1889, p. 6; 13 February 1889, p. 4.

schools. In September of the following year, French-speaking Catholics of Haverhill opened St. Joseph Parochial School for their children, and an additional three hundred children were withdrawn from the common schools. Superintendent Albert L. Bartlett, a long-time teacher and administrator in the public schools and a native of Haverhill, expressed alarm over the fact that, in the course of one year, almost one-fourth of all of the children in the community had been withdrawn from the supervision of the local School Committee. The emergence of a parochial school system in Haverhill, said Bartlett, would be a direct threat to the continued existence of the common schools of that city. In a letter to the School Committee, he urged the committee to follow the spirit of the statutes of the state and to examine the parochial schools to ascertain whether they should be approved. Such visits were to be made at least quarterly.[55]

There is little doubt that Bartlett's views had been influenced by the annual report of the State Board of Education for the preceding year. The state board reviewed the statute regarding the employment of children that had been passed in 1886, but the board's conclusions were ambivalent. On the one hand, it said that the act clearly required the attendance of children in a public school or private school approved by the local school committee. Without such approval, work permits for employment of children between the ages of nine and fourteen could not be given. On the other hand, the board conceded, further legislation might be needed to clarify the meaning of the 1886 law.[56]

Most of the local school committees of the state were even more uncertain about the meaning of the law and had approved the parochial schools in their towns without inspecting them for the purpose of granting work permits. Nevertheless, urged on by Superintendent Bartlett, the Haverhill School Committee became convinced that they had a duty to inspect private schools in their town and to approve those found to be adequate. In the fall of 1888, the School Committee, after visiting St. James, approved it. On 18 December, however, apparently without visiting the school, they notified Rev. Oliver Boucher, director of the St. Joseph School, that the committee could not approve it "inasmuch as the teaching is not in the English language," and the School Committee therefore could not determine if the other conditions required by the statutes, as they interpreted them, were being carried out. The priest was informed that if the situation was not corrected by 10 January 1889, action would be taken

55. Haverhill School Committee, *Annual Report, 1888* (Haverhill: The Gazette Printing House, 1889), pp. 21–31, 33.
56. Massachusetts State Board of Education, *Annual Report, 1885–1886*, p. 16.

against the parents to compel them to enroll their children in the public schools.

Upon receipt of an invitation from Boucher, a subcommittee of the School Committee visited the St. Joseph School. The subcommittee reported that they found five teachers with more than two hundred fifty students. Three of the teachers taught in French and/or English as the occasion required, one teacher spoke only English, and one teacher spoke only French. American history was not taught in the upper grades, only a limited number of students received instruction in the English language, and only half of the school day was devoted to subjects required by law. After deliberation, the School Committee, on 16 January, refused to approve the school inasmuch as the instruction was not in English and some studies required by law were not being taught. Moreover, the School Committee insisted that the quality of instruction was not comparable to that of the public schools.[57]

Early in February 1889, six parents of children enrolled in St. Joseph's were taken into police court by the Haverhill School Committee on the charge of having illegally sent their children to an unapproved private school. Three parents pled guilty, and three parents contested the charge. In handing down his decision on 9 February, Judge Carter threw out the assumption that private schools must be approved: ". . . as I construe the statute, it is very clear indeed to my mind that the Legislature did not intend to make all schools subject to the approval of the committee; did not intend to take away the private judgment of parents from managing their own schools if they saw fit."[58]

The decision of Judge Carter caught the State Board of Education in an embarrassing position, and they expressed some confusion concerning the local school committee's responsibility to accredit private schools. When questioned about the Haverhill case on 10 February, John W. Dickinson, secretary of the board, reported ambiguously that the law was already adequate but that some clarification of the language regarding the responsibility of the local school committee as the accrediting agency was needed. Apparently the general feeling of the Board of Education was that any pressing of the issue at that time might awaken greater hostility from Catholics. Also, the board had reluctantly come to the conclusion that "to recognize the parochial establishment as state schools" could logically lead to a demand from the Catholics for a division of the school taxes in their favor.[59]

Although Superintendent Bartlett lost in his encounter with the court, he quickly became a favorite among patriots. In December

57. *BET*, 19 January 1889, p. 4.
58. Ibid., 11 February 1889, p. 4.
59. Ibid., 9 February 1889, p. 10; 11 February 1889, p. 1.

1889, a number of anti-Catholic organizations presented Bartlett with a total of twenty-six American flags, one for each school building in the Haverhill district. The years of 1889 and 1890 saw many of the schools in Massachusetts presented with American flags in an outburst of nationalistic fervor.[60]

On 6 February 1889, prior to Judge Carter's decision, State Rep. S. R. Gracey, a Methodist minister from Salem, introduced a new school-inspection bill into the House of Representatives. In most respects, the bill was similar to the legislation proposed the preceding year. The new measure, however, contained provisions in its last sections aimed at destroying what many Protestants believed was the real basis for parochial schools. Gracey, and perhaps most Protestants of the time, believed that many Catholic parents sent their children to parochial schools only under pressure from parish priests—and there was no doubt some justification for such a belief. Therefore, section five of the bill provided that any person influencing or attempting to influence a parent to withdraw a child from a public school would be liable to a fine not to exceed one hundred dollars. Section six provided further that anyone attempting to influence parents to send their children to a private school by "threats of social, moral, political, religious, or ecclesiastical disability or disabilities, or any punishment; or by any other threats or threatening acts of any kind" should be fined not less than three hundred dollars nor more than one thousand dollars for each offense. The Gracey bill had been prepared by the Evangelical Alliance and the Committee of One Hundred.[61] Such a bill, if enacted, could have exposed all Catholic officials to arrest and prosecution for obeying the explicit instructions laid down for them in the decrees of the Third Plenary Council.

The defense of the Catholic position was again placed in the hands of Charles F. Donnelly, and the proponents of the bill engaged the services of attorney Rodney Lund and of Congressman John D. Long, a former governor who would soon become secretary of the navy. A number of private schools, several of them Protestant, engaged the services of Nathan Matthews, Jr., to represent them. As with the earlier proposal, the battle was fought mainly in public hearings before the Joint Committee on Education of the General Court. While the committee also had before it a bill making the use of public school textbooks in the parochial schools obligatory, Gracey's bill aroused the most interest.[62] Sixteen hearings were held on the proposal between 20 March and 25 April. The Green Room in the State House

60. Haverhill, *Fifth Annual Report of the Superintendent of Public Schools, 1888* (Haverhill: Chase Brothers, Printers, 1890), p. 29.
61. Lord et al., *Archdiocese*, 3:12; *BET*, 12 April 1889, p. 4.
62. *BET*, 16 February 1889, p. 10.

was crowded to overflowing for all of the hearings, and on some days many who came to listen had to be turned away. The Committee of One Hundred reported, "Never was the Green Room at the State House filled with a more intelligent audience . . . ."[63] Not everyone present would have accepted this claim.

D. A. Buckley, publisher of the *Cambridge News*, was the first to appear before the joint committee. He immediately launched into an attack upon the pressure allegedly exerted upon parents by priests, and he flatly declared that loyalty to the Catholic Church was treason to the Commonwealth of Massachusetts. Buckley, purportedly an ex-Catholic, asserted that some Catholic priests had told their parishioners that women teaching in the Cambridge public schools were mistresses of the School Committee members.[64] Buckley's testimony seemed to set the tone for testimony in the bill's behalf.

Superintendent Bartlett, in his testimony, identified himself as the legal representative of the Haverhill community. He renewed his charge that there was a conspiracy afoot to make New England a province of Quebec, and he pointed to the rapid growth of the French population in various Massachusetts towns, among them Lowell, Lawrence, Fall River, and Haverhill. The attempt to use French as the language of instruction in the parochial schools was but one weapon being used to undermine the American way of life. Bartlett interrupted other witnesses throughout the hearings and on several occasions had to be called to order by the chairman. Other proponents of the bill also attempted to make an issue of un-Americanism by citing the use of a foreign language in parochial school instruction. When attorney Rodney Lund took the floor, he insisted that it was not his intent to antagonize anyone but that the safety of the republic depended upon education being common and general and in the English language. Ira A. Abbott, a member of the Haverhill school committee, supported Lund's position.[65]

In his testimony, Rev. Dr. Miner, a member of the State Board of Education, said that under the existing laws the local school committees were the "eyes" of the state, but unless the laws were strengthened and protected, the state would have absolutely no knowledge of what was going on in the parochial schools throughout the commonwealth. Miner was seemingly obsessed with the secrecy of the Catholic Church; the year before, in a sermon to his congregation, he had

63. *The Hearings at the State House, March 20 to April 25, 1889* (Boston: Committee of One Hundred Series, March-May 1889), 7:1. Both Lord et al., *Archdiocese*, and Conway and Cameron, *Charles Francis Donnelly*, report that there were fifteen hearings.

64. *BET*, 20 March 1889, p. 5; 21 March 1889, p. 5; 21 March 1889, p. 5; *The Hearings at the State House*, p. 2.

65. *BET*, 20 March 1889, p. 5.

maintained that only a good inspection bill could determine what really occurred behind the closed doors of the parochial school. Rev. T. E. Leyden, an ex-Catholic, testified, "I was taught that all Protestants were heretics; and I hold that any religion that teaches that my neighbor is a heretic is not a fit religion to have charge of education."[66]

On 3 April, Long concluded his introduction of evidence in favor of the bill, and the Committee of One Hundred moved five stenographers into the committee room to take down every word of what they believed would be the damaging admissions of the opponents of the bill. Meanwhile, Miner and Dunn continued to testify for the bill whenever they could inject themselves into the proceedings.

In his opening remarks for the parochial schools, Donnelly asked why the educated men of the state, the college presidents, were not at the hearings. The remark was satirical, but it went further than that. Donnelly was clearly aware that the measure did not have the broad support that had attended the hearings on the first school inspection bill. Neither did the proposed legislation arouse the general population emotionally as had the Boston School Committee election. Possibly a part of the reason for the lack of broad general interest in the matter was that Bostonians who had furnished much of the leadership for the anti-Catholic movement had read the annual report of that city issued in early April. The report noted a large increase in the enrollment in the public schools as evidence that the Catholic drive toward the construction of a parochial school system had been blunted. In addition, the anti-Catholic *Transcript* grudgingly conceded that the 1889 bill was badly framed, and even questioned the legality of sections five and six.[67]

Late in the hearings, Judge Carter, a Protestant, appeared to explain his decision in the Haverhill case. He related the threats that had been made against him after his decision, and he charged that the whole controversy was simply an effort to arouse hostility between Catholic and Protestant groups. Furthermore, he argued that if there were no Catholic Church to contend with, the Baptists and the Methodists would fight among themselves. Judge Carter's testimony was greeted with "repeated hisses," and only with considerable difficulty did the chairman of the committee maintain a semblance of order.[68]

Under conditions that seemed to be more favorable to the private school effort, Donnelly began a methodical hacking away at the Protestant argument. In his opening statement, he charged that "very often the Protestant minister is a great deal bigger pope than Pope

66. Ibid., 3 April 1889, p. 9; 30 April 1888, p. 4; *The Hearings at the State House*, p. 75.
67. *BET*, 10 April 1889, p. 1; 25 April 1889, p. 1.
68. Ibid., 2 April 1889, p. 9.

Leo is over the Catholic body."[69] As his first witness, Donnelly called Rev. Joshua P. Bodfish, a convert from Methodism to the Catholic faith. There now ensued one of the most bizarre episodes of the prolonged controversy. Miner had alleged on several occasions that there were subterranean cells and passageways under the cathedral in Boston where, hidden from the outside world, activities of an unknown nature were carried on. Father Bodfish, armed with plans and drawings of the entire cathedral area, described in detail the uses to which all the spaces in the building were devoted. Miner finally accepted Bodfish's explanation that there were no "cells" under the cathedral.[70] On both sides, the testimony often went far afield. Dr. Samuel Cote, a Catholic of Marlborough, testified against the bill on the grounds that the public schools allowed promiscuous mixing of the sexes. Edward Hamilton, also a Catholic, charged that the bill was a secret British plot to stir up dissension in the United States.[71]

On 17 April, Bodfish opened his testimony for the day with the charge that the proposed legislation should be retitled "a bill to suppress Catholic parochial schools." His charges were greeted with shouts of disapproval and demands from Dunn to have an opportunity to refute the charge. After some time order was restored, but Dunn was refused permission to speak and Colonel Higginson was granted the floor. In a calm and reasoned speech, he again viewed the proposed bill, as he had the earlier one, as essentially anti-Catholic legislation. More importantly, however, he argued that private schools had traditionally been experimental and had led to educational progress.[72]

Thomas J. Gargon, a Protestant, pointed out to the joint committee that Protestants were in a majority and might, if they so wished, force their will on the minority. However, said Gargon, Protestants should view such a solution with great caution. If the Catholics should achieve a majority in the state, as their birth rate indicated they might very well do within the lifetime of many of those attending the hearings, the existence of the common school could be threatened. Several Catholic parents from Haverhill took the stand to testify that no pressure had ever been brought to bear on them by Catholic authorities to have their children attend the parochial schools. And in support of their testimony, A. A. Hill, editor of the *Haverhill Gazette*, reported that there was no well-defined feeling against the Catholics or the parochial schools in that town.[73]

69. Ibid., 10 April 1889, p. 1.
70. Committee of One Hundred Series, nos. 6–8 (March, April, May 1889); *The Hearings at the State House*, p. 34.
71. *BET*, 11 April 1889, p. 1; Hamilton, *Socialism vs. Democracy* (Boston: Privately printed, 1889), p. 13.
72. *BET*, 17 April 1889, p. 4.
73. Ibid., 18 April 1889, p. 8; 23 April 1889, p. 8.

Nathan Matthews, Jr., serving as counsel for sixteen private schools, alleged that the Gracey bill was the "rankest kind of socialism," and went on to accuse Miner and the State Board of Education of socialistic utterances. More importantly, however, Matthews agreed with Higginson's earlier statements and argued that the private schools furnished the experimental work that the public schools could not do. Thus, they provided the stimulus of friendly competition for the common schools. Matthews cited the kindergarten as one example and predicted that the manual training school would soon be another. He summed up his arguments by saying, "The public school, gentlemen, was intended to supplement, not to supplant, the private school."[74]

During the hearings, Donnelly had been careful to present his arguments with calmness and reason, in the belief that the excesses of the proponents of the bill would discredit the proposal. But on the final day, he lashed out at the two principal supporters of the bill, asserting, "There are no two pulpits in Boston whence the Catholic body has been so much misrepresented and so often attacked as from the pulpits of Dr. Miner and Dr. Dunn." Further, he maintained that Superintendent Bartlett, who had testified at length on behalf of the bill, had been used by men more astute than he, and consequently "the people of Haverhill have been used as the monkey used the cat to get the chestnuts out of the fire." Even Long, in his closing statements, disclaimed any responsibility for some of the extreme statements made by proponents of the bill, although he warmly praised Dunn and Miner.[75]

As the hearings ended, it was clear that two years of effort by the opponents of the parochial schools had come to naught. Actually, the bill was discredited long before the hearings ended. Members of the Republican-dominated House of Representatives, somewhat more cautious than they had been in the past, refused to sponsor the bill in the legislature. They tried to extricate themselves from the dilemma by requesting the Massachusetts Supreme Court to give an official interpretation of the existing laws regarding private schools. The Republicans specifically requested clarification of the words *the means of education* and of whether all instruction had to be in the English language, or only that in those branches of learning required by law. The court refused to render an opinion since the procedure for the request was at variance with constitutional procedures.[76] While the House feigned anger and forwarded a rather sharp reply to the justices, it was more a face-saving gesture than anything else, and the matter

74. Ibid., 24 April 1889, p. 1; Matthews, *The Citizen and the State* (Boston: George H. Ellis, 1889), pp. 6, 8, 13.

75. Conway and Cameron, *Charles Francis Donnelly*, p. 187; BET, 25 April 1889, p. 1.

76. Massachusetts General Court, Untitled House Document 507, 19 April 1889, pp. 1–15.

was promptly dropped. Finally, the joint committee presented a less forceful version of the original bill; even this was defeated by the legislature.[77]

In June, a compromise measure was passed. The act provided that parents must send their children for twenty weeks each year to a public school or to an approved private school, for instruction "in the branches of learning taught in the public schools." The new attendance bill was said to be "the least objectionable, because it appeared to do the least," which made the law "about what it was supposed to be before the agitation in Haverhill last November." The law allowed two alternatives to attending a public school. One was attendance at a private school "approved by the school committee of such city or town." The other was the result of a clarification of the ambiguous phrase *means of education* found in the original compulsory attendance law of 1852 and reappearing in the laws of 1873 and 1878; that phrase now became ". . . or if such child has been otherwise instructed for a like period of time in the branches of learning required by law to be taught in the public schools . . . ."[78]

Catholics interpreted the new law to mean that parochial schools were now relieved of any necessity to seek approval from local school committees. But contemporary opponents of the parochial schools were not ready to concede victory to the Catholics. An editor of the *Journal of Education* predicted that the parochial school question would soon become the most important issue facing the country. A few clergymen continued to demand from their pulpits that parochial schools be banned and that Catholics be prohibited from serving on school boards or in the public schools as teachers. In November, the Committee of One Hundred again nominated a slate of candidates for the Boston School Committee. This time, six of the eight nominees of the committee were also nominated by the Republicans, and two by the Democrats. All of them, however, were more moderate than some of the candidates of the preceding year. Although Swinton's history textbook had been removed from use, controversies over the books adopted as replacements continued to arise.[79]

At the state level, no new legislation was proposed, and throughout the state the effectiveness of the "fighting parsons" declined. Part

77. "The Haverhill Case," *Journal of Education* 21 (9 May 1889), p. 296; and "The Parochial School Bill," *Journal of Education* 21 (13 June 1889): 337.

78. Massachusetts State Board of Education, *The Public Statutes of Massachusetts Relating to Public Instruction* (Boston: Wright and Potter Printing Company, 1892), p. 57; "Boston Letter," *Journal of Education* 29 (20 June 1889): 393.

79. "The Parochial School Issue," *Journal of Education* 30 (22 August 1889): 121; James B. Dunn, *The Second Great Victory in Boston* (Boston: Committee of One Hundred Series, 1890), 2:4; Boston School Committee, *Minority Report of the Committee on Textbooks* (Boston: Rockwell and Churchill, 1890), p. 3.

of the reason was that some of the zealots, such as Fulton, found greener pastures elsewhere, and Mrs. Shepherd was exposed as a fraud.[80] A part of the reason also lay in the fact that Protestants began to look more carefully at the results of previous agitations and saw that little had been accomplished. The only new argument offered in the 1889 hearings was presented by Protestants who testified against the bill. Colonel Higginson argued that private schools, including parochial schools, had been experimental, or at least had a freedom and latitude to experiment that the public schools did not have. The attorney for the non-Catholic private schools, Nathan Matthews, Jr., concurred in the argument and cited as specific examples the kindergarten and the manual training schools.

Had the proponents of the public schools been willing to consider the proposition that private schools could make a unique contribution to American society by sponsoring experimental approaches to learning, the School Question could have been lifted to a higher and more productive level of discussion. The merits of the proposition were soon to become clear. Much of the inspiration for the Progressive Movement in education was drawn from schools and theorists in the private sector. John Dewey opened his Laboratory School at the University of Chicago in 1906, and Marietta Johnson her Organic School in Alabama in 1907. The Progressive Movement in education drew upon developments in the larger society as well as upon specifically educational institutions, important among them the social settlements in the large cities.[81] In the main, however, public school proponents did not much credit the claim that private schools could serve as centers of innovation.

The temper of the times was not, in any event, conducive to accommodation. As the conflict was subsiding in Massachusetts, anti-Catholic fever was seizing other state legislatures, notably those of Illinois and Wisconsin, where legislation against private schools was enacted in 1889. Meanwhile, the excitement had spread to the national level as well. The question was mooted at a national convention in 1889, and in 1890 Archbishop John Ireland addressed members of the National Education Association on the topic "State Schools and Parish

---

80. Shepherd came to the United States from England, where she had given birth to an illegitimate child and had been jailed for swindling and theft. During periods of professed remorse she spent some time with the Salvation Army and also as a penitent in a refuge for fallen women in Bristol. Both associations eventually expelled her. See M. J. Brody, *A Fraud Unmasked; The Career of Mrs. Margaret L. Shepherd* (Woodstock, Ontario, Canada, 1893). The similarities to Maria Monk's career are evident, but the differences between the women were great. Monk was a simple creature, duped by others. Shepherd was a self-serving, crafty woman who lived by duping her admirers.

81. Lawrence A. Cremin, *The Transformation of the School: Progressivism in American Education 1876–1957* (New York: Alfred A. Knopf, 1961), chap. 6.

Schools." The controversy created by Ireland's speech was increased the following year by the appearance of a pamphlet by Prof. Thomas J. Bouquillon of the Catholic University of America, "Education: To Whom Does It Belong?" By this time the disagreements among Catholics had become so sharp that it was necessary to refer the question to Rome. These disputes within the Catholic fold need not concern us here, but we must examine the struggles waged in the political arena in Wisconsin and Illinois.

9

Anti–Parochial School Legislation
in Wisconsin and Illinois

Wisconsin's Bennett Law

Although defeated in Massachusetts, anti–parochial school legislation, in the guise of compulsory school-attendance measures, now appeared in several other states. There had been earlier attendance bills and laws providing for inspection of non-public schools. The U.S. commissioner of education, no doubt spurred on by the tempestuous and widely reported controversies in Massachusetts, reviewed several of these in his 1888–1889 *Report*. In most cases, these laws apparently caused no great stir, perhaps because little effort was made to enforce them. In New York, the Coon compulsory education bill of 1889 aroused more controversy. This bill required that teachers in both public and private schools must be approved by a public school commissioner and that instruction in the elementary branches must be in the English language. Private and church-related school authorities strenuously objected to these provisions, and although the bill was passed by both houses the governor refused to sign it.[1]

Particularly critical were the campaigns over the question in Wisconsin and Illinois. Like the attendance legislation proposed in Massachusetts (and, much later, in Oregon), the Wisconsin and Illinois measures served as a convenient umbrella under which to introduce requirements only peripherally related to attendance. Public school authorities had complained about truancy and absenteeism since the Common School Movement got underway in the 1830s, and with good reason. Child labor still existed on a large scale; many families needed the income their children could bring in, although the resulting absenteeism from school was often justified on other grounds. Compulsion, in the eyes of many, seemed to be at odds

---

1. *Report of the U.S. Commissioner of Education, 1888–1889*, pp. 157, 498–99, passim. Compulsory attendance bills were considered but not enacted in the late eighties in Ohio, Iowa, North and South Dakota, Nebraska, and Kansas.

with American ideas of freedom. As late as 1874 the state school superintendent of Wisconsin could declare, "I cannot help thinking that there is in a compulsory school law something essentially opposed to the genius of our free institutions—something essentially un-American."[2] As the evidence of irregular attendance, or complete non-attendance, was overwhelming, legislators often seemed ready to consider new laws, even when enforcement of existing laws would have done much to improve the situation. This provided an opportunity for special-interest groups to introduce provisions that went far beyond simple attendance requirements.

There was a remarkable similarity between Wisconsin and Illinois in the development and the outcome of the struggle over the compulsory-attendance legislation enacted in 1889.[3] In both cases the legislation was sponsored by the incumbent Republican administration and opposed by the Democrats. In both cases the legislation was adopted with little opposition, only to arouse a storm of opposition when its provisions became known. Both laws provided for compulsory school attendance of children between the ages of seven and fourteen. Both accepted attendance at private or parochial schools as fulfillment of this obligation, but they stipulated also that the child must attend a school in the district wherein he resided, which in itself would have made attendance at parochial school illegal for many children. They provided further that the attendance obligation could be fulfilled only by attendance at a school approved by the local public school board. Both laws also specified that instruction was to be in the English language. (Such a provision had been included in the Massachusetts bills as well, but the large German-born populations in the Midwest made it a more controversial issue there.) In both states the Republican-controlled administrations and legislatures were decisively defeated in subsequent elections, and the laws were promptly repealed. We look first at Wisconsin's Bennett Law.

Wisconsin did not seem to be at the time a particularly fertile field for nativist agitation. Its proportion of foreign-born residents was large, but they had been well-regarded by the migrants from New England and New York, who comprised the bulk of the state's population. There were in the state in 1890, in a total population of just under 1,700,000, some 275,000 persons of German birth and about

2. *Report of the State Superintendent, 1874*, p. 1. For additional expressions of this view, see Lloyd P. Jorgensen, *The Founding of Public Education in Wisconsin* (Madison: State Historical Society of Wisconsin, 1956), pp. 138–39.

3. These similarities were noted in the earliest systematic account of the event by Louise Phelps Kellogg, "The Bennett Law in Wisconsin," *Wisconsin Magazine of History* 2 (September 1918): 3–25. The most comprehensive account of the Bennett Law is Robert James Ulrich, "The Bennett Law of 1889: Education and Politics in Wisconsin" (Ph.D. diss., University of Wisconsin, 1965).

100,000 Scandinavians, two-thirds of them Norwegian. Germans had come to Wisconsin in larger numbers than to any other state in the Union. Like other immigrant groups, they tended to settle in homogeneous communities, and for a time they made Milwaukee virtually a German city. Those from northern Germany were mostly Lutheran, and those from the southern provinces largely Catholic. Both groups shared the ideal of reproducing in their new home the culture and customs they had known in their native land. This ideal, embodied in the term *Deutschtum*, was a potent factor in Wisconsin political and social life, and it had been present from the time of the earliest migrations. Bishop (later Archbishop) John Henni, German-born and a staunch proponent of *Deutschtum*, had assumed leadership of the Milwaukee diocese in 1844, four years before the state was admitted to the Union. Although most evident in Wisconsin, German churchmen were dominant in the Roman Church elsewhere in the Midwest as well. The "German Triangle of the West," as it was often called, comprising the areas bounded roughly by Milwaukee, Cincinnati, and St. Louis, constituted a powerful bloc within the American hierarchy. Arrayed against the German clergy at times, especially on educational questions, were many prelates who favored more rapid Americanization. Strong in the Northeast, this group nevertheless found its chief spokesman in the eloquent John Ireland, archbishop of St. Paul.

Until the 1850s, Germans had favored the Democratic party. But that party's stand on slavery alienated both Germans and Scandinavians, and they became an important and dependable bloc in the new Republican party and remained so well into the eighties. Although Know-Nothing elements had been present in Wisconsin in the 1850s, the party had not been able to establish itself as a political force of any consequence, and after the Civil War it seemed destined for extinction. The importance of immigrants in the building of the state was widely recognized. Industrial interests in the state encouraged immigration, and the state itself maintained an agent who worked both at the port of New York and in Europe to attract immigrants to Wisconsin. There were, however, signs of disquiet by the mid-eighties. Reverberations from the Haymarket Square riot in Chicago in 1886 were felt throughout the nation, and the fear was heightened in Wisconsin by the violence at the Illinois Steel Company in Milwaukee. Yet there were few overt manifestations of nativism in the state as yet, nor had nativism become synonymous with anti-Catholicism. The enactment of the Bennett Law was to change that abruptly.

William B. Hoard, editor of the widely circulated *Hoard's Dairyman*, had held no political office when he was nominated for the governorship of Wisconsin by the Republican State Convention in August 1888. In his acceptance speech, Hoard conceded his ignorance of political affairs, although he acknowledged the importance of the tariff question. Education was not an issue in the campaign, and Hoard had shown little interest in the public schools during his eighteen years as an editor. His own publications, however, were a major source of information on improved methods of dairying.[4]

The legislature convened on 9 January 1889 amidst predictions that, in the absence of any issues of great moment, the session would be short. In his message, otherwise routine, Hoard made a unexpected statement:

> It is to the little country school that we must look, in a great measure, for the inculcation of the true principles of American citizenship . . . . The child that is, the citizen that is to be, has a right to demand of the state that it be . . . provided with the ability to read and write the language of this country. In this connection I would recommend such legislation as would make it the duty of the county and city superintendents to inspect all schools for the purpose, and with the authority only, to require that reading and writing in English be daily taught therein.[5]

Early in the session, Michael John Bennett, a twenty-eight-year-old Republican member of the Assembly and chairman of the Committee on Education, introduced a number of bills, among them one "relative to the teaching of foreign languages in the common schools." The bill was approved unanimously and without debate in both houses, was signed by Governor Hoard on 28 April, and went into the books as chapter 519 of the Wisconsin Statutes of 1889, "An act concerning the employment of children." Scarcely noticed at the time, the act was soon to cause a furious political controversy in the state.

The authorship of the Bennett Law is uncertain. Bennett, a farmer and a teacher, was a Catholic in good standing. The *Wisconsin State Journal* attributed authorship of the measure to Governor Hoard, the *Milwaukee Journal* to the assistant city attorney of Milwaukee as a means of opposition to child labor. There can be no doubt that Superintendent of Public Instruction Jesse B. Thayer provided inspiration for those, including Hoard, who saw a need for instruction in English in all schools. Thayer had expressed this view before, and at the 1890 meeting of the National Education Association (see below) he was to deliver a searing attack on the Lutheran and Catholic clergy. But no one associated Bennett with the authorship, assuming instead that he routinely, and perhaps with little understanding of its implications,

---

4. Ulrich, "Bennett Law," pp. 133–44. It trivializes Hoard and his work to say, as Ulrich does, that Hoard's educational philosophy can be summed up in his slogan "Speak to a cow as you would to a lady."
5. Ibid., p. 154.

introduced the bill as chairman of the Assembly's Committee of Education.

Hoard's stubborn defense of the Bennett Law is puzzling. His own statements and actions, reported below, almost seem to paint him as a nativist, although this was certainly not the case. Son of a poor Methodist circuit rider and largely self-educated, Hoard became a leading figure in the founding of the modern dairy industry. An indefatigable author and publisher of articles on scientific methods of dairying, he arranged for the translation of many of these treatises into the German language.

A more likely explanation of Hoard's behavior during the Bennett controversy is that he was, in the first place, a thoroughgoing secularist. This fact alone might well have predisposed him to regard protests from church groups as a matter of no great consequence. But there was more: Hoard had become an admirer of Lester F. Ward's statist ideas. He was deeply committed to the improvement of society, and education was to be a major instrument in this process. But, true to Ward's philosophy, education at the lower levels was to be controlled by a beneficent state. In a letter to a clergyman, written during the controversy, Hoard expressed the optimistic belief that the use of a common language by all citizens would produce the "homogeneous moulding of all classes into a common stamp of American citizenship." It would also, said Hoard, twitting the clergyman, "secure a peaceful toleration of religious differences of belief."[6]

The legislature's uncritical approval of the measure can be explained in part by the existence of another bill, similar to Bennett's in some respects, which preempted the attention of legislators: Sen. Levy E. Pond's bill, listed as "requiring clerks of school districts to transmit to the town, city or village clerk certain statistical matters." The "certain statistical matters" were attendance records of parochial and private schools. Here, for the first time in Wisconsin, the issue of state inspection of non-public schools was raised, and the alarm was sounded immediately. The *Milwaukee Journal*, the leading Democratic newspaper in the state, sent a reporter to interview State Superintendent Thayer, who conceded that the bill probably had been inspired by comments made by both the governor and himself. The bill was designed, he said, to ascertain the number of children attending parochial and private schools and whether instruction in such schools was given in the English language. When asked whether he was in

6. Ibid., pp. 156–57, 232–35. These insights into Hoard's motivations (which have not been explored in the many earlier accounts of the Bennett controversy) have been provided to me in personal correspondence by Wilbur H. Glover, author of *Farm and Home: The College of Agriculture of the University of Wisconsin, A History* (Madison: University of Wisconsin Press, 1952).

favor of placing non-public schools under the supervision of public school authorities, Thayer replied that this was "not exactly" his intent. However, he continued, if the non-public schools, which are *"permitted* to care for the education of children," did not provide an adequate program, especially with regard to the teaching of English, then it would be the duty of the state to intervene.[7] Thayer's comment to the effect that non-public schools exist only by permission of the state was not to go unnoticed.

Soon remonstrances against the Pond bill reached the legislature. Christian Widule, a German-born Lutheran from Milwaukee and chairman of the Senate Education Committee, described the bill as an attack on the parochial schools. Senator Pond loudly proclaimed his respect for the family and the church as participants in the work of education, all the while insisting, however, that "the state has an abstract and complete right to control the secular education of its children . . . ." This did not satisfy opponents of the bill and, sensing defeat, Pond withdrew the measure. Meanwhile, virtually unnoticed, the Bennett measure had become law.[8]

Section one of the Bennett Law provided that children between the ages of seven and fourteen must attend some public or private school for a period of not less than twelve nor more than twenty-four weeks in the city, town, or district in which they resided. Sections two, three, and four contained administrative provisions, but section five provided that "No school shall be regarded as a school, unless there shall be taught therein, as part of the elementary education of children, reading, writing, arithmetic and United States history in the English language." The remaining sections dealt with enforcement, truancy, and child labor.

By mid-June 1889, organized opposition to the Bennett Law was developing rapidly. The leaders of two Lutheran bodies—the Missouri (Wisconsin District) and the Evangelical synods—were at that time in session. The approaches and emphases varied, but the message of the pastors in both synods was the same: the Bennett Law must go. It was "the duty of Lutherans to repel such an assault upon the German language and German schools," said one. The churchmen asserted again the historic rights of parents in education and expressed their fear of being "subjected to the tyranny of state school authorities." They affirmed their willingness to continue to support the public schools through taxation, as they had in the past. Then, speaking more directly, the Missouri Synod congregations in Wisconsin pledged themselves to support for election only those candidates

7. *Milwaukee Journal*, 1 March 1889. Italics added.
8. Ulrich, "Bennett Law," pp. 161–64.

committed to a repeal of the law. Committees were formed to direct the political action needed to accomplish this. Hardly a week later, the Wisconsin Synod launched its attack on the Bennett Law. Together, the three synods—the Wisconsin, the Missouri (in Wisconsin), and the Evangelical—represented close to seventy thousand voters.[9]

Within two months, therefore, and before any provisions had been made for its enforcement, Hoard found a majority of Lutherans in the state officially arrayed against the measure he had proposed and signed into law. He advised magnanimity and tolerance, but in the process he seemed to exacerbate the growing tension. In a Fourth of July speech he praised the public school, spoke with eloquence about the glory of the republic, and repeated the Republican slogan that the ignorance of the South had been responsible for the Civil War. Later in the year, Hoard made it clear that he would take his stand on the Bennett Law in the fall elections, and he insisted, "I want the little German boy and girl, the little Norwegian, the little Bohemian and the little Pole, the children of our foreign-born parents, to have the same chance in life as my children. Without a knowledge of the English language they cannot have this chance." German-American citizens considered Hoard's comments patronizing, and they resented his "Americanization program." How was it, they asked, that Germans could have lived in this country for two centuries as good citizens without the "compulsory patriotism" embodied in the Bennett Law?[10]

As in the Massachusetts controversies of 1888–1890 and the Know-Nothing battles of the 1850s, the struggle was carried on almost entirely by editors, politicians, and church leaders. Teachers remained silent for the most part. To be sure, the Wisconsin Education Association, meeting in December 1889, adopted a rather curious resolution. "We may entertain different views regarding the necessity or expediency of compulsory attendance laws," said the teachers, "yet we see . . . great benefits . . . from a just administration of the Bennett Law." The *Milwaukee Journal* expressed amazement. How could the teachers concede their inability to agree on the issue of compulsory school attendance and in the same paragraph solemnly support a compulsory attendance law? Sarcastically, the *Journal* remarked, "We trust 'the little German boy' will adopt this literary effort of the Teacher's Association as an example which he may profitably follow."[11] Early in 1890, a staunchly Republican Madison paper coined the phrase that

9. Ibid., pp. 173–76.
10. *Wisconsin State Journal*, 30 November 1889; 14 March 1890.
11. *Milwaukee Journal*, 3 January 1890.

was to become the slogan of the Republican party in its effort to preserve the Bennett Law. We must, said this paper, "stand by the little red schoolhouse."[12]

The torrent of opposition that had been precipitated by the Lutheran churchmen was only one of a series of setbacks that plagued the Republican party in the state. Equally disquieting was the defection of the German-language newspapers, which had been, with few if any exceptions, faithful supporters of the Republican cause. Municipal elections were scheduled throughout the state for April 1890, and a loss of support from the German editors would be a heavy blow. First to defect was the widely circulated *Der Herold* of Milwaukee. As the elections approached, most other German-language papers and a Polish newspaper as well went over to the Democratic cause.[13]

No less worrisome was the report that a statement by the Catholic bishops of the state was in process of formation. Although there had been articles on the Bennett Law in Catholic publications, there had been as yet no official pronouncement. Such a statement, promptly dubbed "The Bishops' Manifesto," appeared on 13 March 1890, and there was no mistaking its meaning:

> After calm and careful study of the Bennett Law, we hold that it interferes with the rights of the Church and of parents. We, moreover, conscientiously believe that the real object of this law is not so much to secure a greater amount of instruction in and knowledge of the English language as rather to bring our parochial and private schools under the control of the state [and] gradually to destroy the parochial school system altogether.[14]

The document was signed by Archbishop Michael Heiss of Milwaukee and Bishops Kilian C. Flasch of LaCrosse and Frederick X. Katzer of Green Bay, all of them German-born. Archbishop Ireland, on the other hand, supported that part of the Bennett Law which prescribed that instruction in the common branches of learning was to be conducted in the English language, although he objected to other features of the measure.[15]

The bishops went on to reject the claim, earlier voiced by State School Superintendent Thayer, that the parochial school existed by the grace and toleration of the state. It was, rather, a free and recognized institution as old as the state itself. They asserted that English was taught in all Catholic institutions in the state: 264 parochial schools, 14 colleges and academies, and 9 orphan asylums. They

12. *Wisconsin State Journal*, 18 January 1890.
13. Ulrich, "Bennett Law," pp. 211, 231.
14. Ibid., p. 214.
15. J. Coleman Barry, *The Catholic Church and German Americans* (Milwaukee: The Bruce Publishing Co., 1953), p. 185.

conceded that the use of the English language was at a low level in some Catholic schools, but they pointed out that this was as true of the public schools as of the parochial schools in some areas. They outlined the position of the Church on education, citing the decisions of the Third Plenary Council of Baltimore. The prelates gave particular attention to the section of the law that required attendance at a school within the public school district where the child resided. This requirement, they said, would often prevent attendance at parochial schools, which commonly drew their students from an area larger than one public school district. Moreover, there were many public districts within which no parochial school was located. They also objected to the provision that gave the local school board sole authority to determine whether or not a legal school existed. This in effect made the local school board both accuser and judge in determining the fitness of parochial schools. On the Sunday following its publication, the manifesto was read in most Catholic pulpits in the state. Republican newspapers were not cowed, however. The *Wisconsin State Journal* promptly characterized the manifesto as "a blow at our public school system." The *Milwaukee Sentinel* reprinted passages from a pamphlet issued by the Committee of One Hundred (Boston) and called upon all patriots to resist the encroachments of the Catholic Church.[16]

"The Bishops' Manifesto" appeared only two weeks before the 1 April 1890 municipal elections in Wisconsin. Republican politicians, clearly apprehensive, stoutly insisted that the Bennett Law controversy had no place in municipal contests; they knew that a setback in these elections would portend further trouble for them in the fall state elections. But their efforts to alleviate the problem were in vain. One scholar's examination of nearly one hundred Wisconsin newspapers for the last two weeks of March revealed that every one of them gave front-page coverage to the Bennett controversy. The principal contest was in Milwaukee, and the outcome was a disaster for the Republicans. The Common Council and all major administrative offices were captured by the Democrats. Election returns from other places revealed the full magnitude of the Republican defeat. Even Fort Atkinson, Governor Hoard's home town, had gone Democratic.[17]

Many Republican politicians realized the need to repair the damage, but Hoard's rash and doctrinaire statements were increasingly a source of embarrassment for them. Enemies of the Bennett Law, said Hoard in addressing a teachers' meeting, were enemies of the "poor, ignorant and defenseless little children." Even when Republican lead-

16. Ulrich, "Bennett Law," pp. 212–24.
17. Ibid., pp. 231, 255, 269.

ers talked directly to him, Governor Hoard remained adamant, confident that his "little red schoolhouse" slogan would arouse patriotic support. The recently defeated Republican mayoral candidate in Milwaukee let it be known that he had supported the Bennett Law during the campaign as a matter of party discipline, not as a matter of personal choice. U.S. Sen. John C. Spooner, visiting his home state, was appalled by Hoard's mismanagement of the issue and was reported to be "standing by the Bennett Law in public" and "swearing at Hoard in private."[18] Republicans were also embarrassed by the capricious enforcement of the law. A Catholic and two Lutherans were brought to court for sending their children to parochial schools, and one, a widow from Hoard's home county, was jailed; this was widely publicized as the "Shelbyville outrage."[19]

Newspaper editors were much less vulnerable to election returns, and the Republican editors seemed to grow bolder as the opposition mounted. Many of them now declared that the Bennett Law should be not only one issue but the only issue in the fall gubernatorial and legislative elections. They intensified their charge that the parochial school interests were un-American. But a German-language newspaper turned the charge around: "We are fighting the Bennett Law because we regard it as unnecessary, unjust, nativistic, and therefore an un-American measure."[20]

Late in May 1890 a mass meeting organized by a number of Catholic societies and attended by some three thousand people was held in Milwaukee. About a week later, an Anti-Bennett League was formed, the leadership coming in large part from German Lutheran pastors. The Norwegian-American Rasmus B. Anderson was prevailed upon to address the first meeting of the Anti-Bennett League. Anderson had earlier gained recognition as the leading proponent of Americanization and of the American public school in his own Norwegian Lutheran Synod. Again, he stressed the importance of the use of the English language in all schools, but he pointed out that this requirement was already present in the school law of 1879. The Bennett Law, so far from being necessary, was in fact punitive, said Anderson. Like Bishop Katzer, he pointed out the unfairness of making the local public school board the sole judge of what constituted a "legal school." Later, in his autobiography, Anderson remarked that the anti-Bennett campaign was the first time that "Lutherans and Catholics have

18. Ibid., pp. 273, 315–16, 426.
19. Peter DeBoer, "A History of the Early Compulsory School Attendance Legislation in the State of Illinois" (Ph.D. diss., University of Chicago, 1968), p. 279: Ulrich, "Bennett Law," p. 355.
20. *Wisconsin State Journal*, 3 April 1890; *Milwaukee Sentinel*, 12 April 1890; *Der Seebote*, 30 May 1890.

joined hands and been united in a common cause."[21] Lutheran synods in other states—Ohio, Michigan, Minnesota, and Iowa—also supported the efforts of their brethren in Wisconsin and Illinois to overthrow the Bennett and the Edwards Laws.[22]

Two incidents in the spring and summer of 1890, although independent of the Bennett controversy, further hardened the differences between parochial school advocates and opponents. On 18 March, in the Edgerton Bible case (*State ex. rel. Weiss v. the District Board*), the Wisconsin Supreme Court ruled unanimously that the reading of the King James version of the Bible in the public schools was a sectarian act and hence inadmissible. Predictably, Protestants charged that the court had succumbed to the demands of the "Romish hierarchy" in issuing this "un-American and pagan" doctrine, while Catholics saw the decision as further evidence that the public schools were fast becoming the godless creation of a godless society.[23]

A few months later, the public-parochial school question was debated on a national stage. John Ireland, archbishop of St. Paul, perhaps the Church's leading advocate of Americanization, was invited to address the annual convention of the National Education Association in St. Paul in mid-July. Association president James H. Canfield opposed this part of the program committee's plan and tried to cancel the invitation. When it became clear to him that such action would probably alienate so many Catholics that the convention itself might have to be canceled, Canfield traveled to St. Paul to issue a personal invitation to the archbishop, which was accepted.

Ireland opened his address by declaring his unbounded loyalty to the Constitution of the United States. He was, he insisted, a friend and advocate of the state school: "Free Schools! Blessed indeed is the nation whose vales and hillsides they adorn."[24] These reassuring words, however, could be understood properly only within their context. Ireland conceded and even asserted the right of the state school to exist. But this was a derivative right. The imparting of instruction, he explained, true to Catholic policy, is "primarily the function of the child's parent." But parents in most cases could not fully perform this duty. Therefore, without the intervention of the state, universal education would be impossible anywhere. Moreover, he favored compulsory education, but compulsory attendance at public schools was

21. *Wisconsin State Journal*, 23 May 1890; *Milwaukee Sentinel*, 5 June 1890; *Life Story of Rasmus B. Anderson, written by Himself with the Assistance of Albert O. Barton*, 2d ed. rev. (Madison, Wis.: N.p., 1917), p. 595.

22. Walter H. Beck, *Lutheran Elementary Schools in the United States* (St. Louis: Concordia Publishing House, 1939), pp. 237–40.

23. *Milwaukee Sentinel*, 10 April, 14 April 1890.

24. "State Schools and Parish Schools—Is Union Between Them Possible?" *National Education Association Proceedings* (Topeka: Kansas Publishing House, 1890), pp. 179–80.

justifiable only when children did not attend other schools known to be of equal quality. Thus, he identified himself as a supporter of compulsory education, but also as a supporter of the rights of parents to send their children to parochial schools. Then he turned to even more sensitive questions:

> Ought we not to have in connection with the schools religious instruction? . . . Secularists and unbelievers will interpose their rights. I allow them their rights. I will not impose upon them my religion which is Christianity. But let them not impose upon me and my fellow-Christians their religion which is secularism . . . .
>
> It is no honor to America that ten millions or more be compelled by law to pay taxes for the support of schools to which their conscience forbids access. It is no honor for the remaining fifty millions to profit for themselves of the taxes paid by the ten millions . . . . It is no honor to the American republic that she be more than any other nation foremost in efforts to divorce religion from the schools.

Ireland's solution was to "permeate the regular state schools with the religion of the majority of the children of the land, be it as Protestant as Protestantism can be." But he would also do as was done in England: the state should pay for the secular instruction provided in church-related schools.[25]

Such a solution was of course wholly unacceptable to public school leaders, as the next speaker on the program, State Superintendent of Public Instruction Jesse B. Thayer of Wisconsin, quickly made clear in language less temperate than Ireland had employed:

> When the German Catholic Bishops, the German Catholic priests, and the German Lutheran clergy of Wisconsin unite in a political organization [to secure repeal of The Bennett Law] I have a reason to suspect that there is something in the movement that is not exactly American, nor in harmony with the principles laid down by the fathers of this republic . . . . Unless the question which is now up for discussion is settled in harmony with the principles of this government there will be a conflict between the jesuitical hierarchy of the Vatican, armed with the syllabus, and the American people.[26]

Much as they needed allies, Republican leaders were not jubilant when the Prohibition party announced its support of the Bennett Law during the summer of 1890. The prospect of being seen arm-in-arm with them in a heavily German state was not reassuring. A more valued ally seemed about to falter, but the relapse was temporary. The Baptists, who had no experience with parochial schools, had been staunch and outspoken champions of the public schools from

25. Ibid., pp. 183–84.
26. *NEA Journal*, 1890, p. 197.

the outset, and had also contributed heavily to the anti-Romanism crusades. Now, unpredictably, the *Western Recorder*, a major journal of that denomination, declared that "the religious liberty of Lutherans in Wisconsin is dear to Baptist hearts everywhere" and asked whether the time had come when Baptists should renew their old battle for religious liberty. But Baptist hearts did not warm to this appeal. An earlier statement by another clergyman no doubt sensed the mood of the denomination more correctly: "We Baptists accept and subscribe for the platform adopted by the Republican party."[27]

Other Protestant spokesmen, as well, declined to come to the aid of Lutherans and Catholics in their quest for religious liberty as they saw it. A Congregationalist minister in Milwaukee cried, "Let us stand by the little school house, and God save the commonwealth of Wisconsin." The Methodists, in their annual meeting, asked, "Shall Roman Catholicism and Lutheranism maintain foreign ideas, customs, and languages, to the exclusion of what is distinctly American?" Unitarian and Episcopal clergymen had never been in the forefront of the crusades against Rome, but there were exceptions. A Unitarian minister strongly maintained that the intent of the Catholic hierarchy in opposing the Bennett Law was to destroy the public school. An Episcopal priest was even more aroused: "Imagine Uncle Sam kissing St. Peter's great toe at Rome . . . here stands this Romish church facing with stern and determined brow the common school of Wisconsin . . . have not people reason to suspect the Romish Church when it strikes at their school system?" Even a Lutheran publication in Philadelphia, speaking for a synod that had long since abandoned its parochial schools, considered the Lutheran-Catholic partnership in Wisconsin a strange and humiliating spectacle.[28]

The Republican State Convention met in Milwaukee on 20 August 1890. A declaration of support for the Bennett Law was the first plank in the platform adopted. Hoard was renominated and devoted his entire acceptance speech to a justification of that law, despite his awareness of misgivings within the party on the issue. A week later, the Democratic State Convention met, also in Milwaukee. The most influential Democratic leader in Wisconsin, William S. Vilas, hoped that the tariff would be the leading question in the campaign. The platform contained a declaration on the tariff and on several other issues as well. The Bennett Law was the last item considered, but the party's position on it was clear. The law constituted a needless interference with parental rights and freedom of conscience. The gubernatorial nominee, George Peck, promised in his acceptance speech

27. *Milwaukee Sentinel*, 24 March 1890.
28. *Wisconsin State Journal*, 13 September 1890.

that if elected the Democratic party would at once repeal the law.[29]

To the dismay of many of his fellow Republicans, Hoard conducted his campaign almost exclusively on the basis of the Bennett Law. Despite urgent appeals from their party headquarters, several Republican leaders refused to speak out for the Bennett Law. As the campaign progressed, religious groups intensified their activities. Incensed by this, the proponents of the law were drawn increasingly into an anti-ecclesiastical posture. The old anti-Catholic fulminations were rehearsed again, but now the Lutherans came in for their share of the abuse as well. That church groups as such had invaded the political arena was of course entirely true. Representatives of nearly all the Lutheran congregations in the state, meeting in Milwaukee as soon as the party conventions had completed their work, endorsed the Democratic party's stand on the Bennett Law and pledged to aid in the defeat of Governor Hoard. Pamphlets attacking the law were to be published in English, German, Polish, Norwegian, and Bohemian. On Sunday, 23 September, several of the Lutheran churches in Milwaukee took up anti–Bennett Law collections to aid in the cause.[30]

The Republican press pictured the fight against the Bennett Law as a manifestation of Romish hatred for the American public school and frequently reprinted comments allegedly made by Catholic priests in various places condemning the public schools. One Republican campaigner regained some of the fervor of the Know-Nothing spirit when he exclaimed, "If there is no hell, there ought to be . . . . And to that hell, followed by the execrations of mankind, should be consigned those intermeddling priests and political mischief makers who seek to destroy that great bulwark of American liberty, the common school."[31]

Nationalism as well as religious prejudice were at work in the campaign. One Republican paper alleged that instruction in a foreign tongue would "fit the pupils for becoming subjects of Kaiser Wilhelm, rather than loyal citizens of the United States." The young and never-reticent Theodore Roosevelt, at the time commissioner of the U.S. Civil Service, argued in a letter to a Republican newspaper that every good American, regardless of party, was obligated "to help the side which stands for true Americanism."[32]

In the state election of 4 November 1890, the Republicans lost the governorship and both houses of the legislature, and the event was heralded by newspapers throughout the country as a major political upset. Sen. John C. Spooner was outraged. The party, he wrote to a

29. Ulrich, "Bennett Law," pp. 402–12, 450.

30. *Milwaukee Journal*, 29 and 30 August 1890; *Milwaukee Sentinel*, 24 and 25 September 1890.

31. *Milwaukee Journal*, 20 October 1890.

32. *Milwaukee Sentinel*, 25 September 1890; *Wisconsin State Journal*, 18 October 1890.

friend, had "gone to hell through his [Hoard's] stupidity . . . . The school law did it—a silly, sentimental and damned useless abstraction, foisted upon us by a self-righteous demagogue." Elisha W. (Boss) Keyes of the state's Republican party machine exclaimed in dejection, "What a disastrous defeat . . . . It is worse than the first Bull Run." But editor Horace Rublee of the *Milwaukee Sentinel* seemed unrepentant, and he vowed that he would never bow down to the "foreign churches."[33]

In his message to the incoming legislature, Governor Peck recommended early repeal of the "unwise and unnecessary" Bennett Law, and the legislature promptly complied. Whether or not they were inwardly chastened, Republican leaders accepted this verdict. In their 1892 platform they said, "We regard the education issue of 1890 as permanently settled in this state . . . ."[34] It was an open admission that they had been unwise.

Although most political observers of the day held that the Bennett Law had cost the Republicans the election, this conclusion may be overdrawn. Democratic gains were made in several other states as well, and they were no doubt in part the result of resentment against the recently enacted McKinley Tariff, which was to figure so prominently in the Democratic national triumphs of 1892. Yet the large-scale exodus of Scandinavians and even more so of Germans from the Republican party in Wisconsin was clearly, in good part, a product of resentment against the Bennett Law.[35]

The Illinois Edwards Law

The Illinois counterpart of Wisconsin's Bennett Law was commonly called the Edwards Law because its chief architect was the state's superintendent of public instruction, Dr. Richard Edwards. The Illinois law was, in all major respects, very similar to the Wisconsin Bennett Law, as were the compulsory school attendance measures being promoted at the time in several other states. Communication among the numerous nativist societies was good; most of them published and distributed newsletters.[36]

Perhaps it was true, as Edwards said, that more than 250,000 school-age children in Illinois were not enrolled in any school, public

33. Ulrich, "Bennett Law," pp. 464–66.

34. Alexander M. Thompson, *A Political History of Wisconsin* (Milwaukee: E. C. Williams, 1900), p. 239.

35. A detailed analysis of the election returns is provided in Roger E. Wyman, "Wisconsin Ethnic Groups and the Election of 1890," *Wisconsin Magazine of History* 51 (Summer 1968): 269–93.

36. Extensive bibliographies of such newsletters are provided in Alvin P. Stauffer, "Anti-Catholicism in American Politics, 1865–1900" (Ph.D. diss., University of Washington, 1954).

or private.[37] But Edwards may have had other reasons as well for asserting that the state's existing compulsory attendance law (dating from 1883) was ineffective and in need of revision. Some years earlier he had announced that Roman Catholics were "known enemies of the common school" because the diffusion of knowledge weakened the power of the Church over its people.[38] The Edwards bill, which had been strongly supported by newly elected Republican Gov. John W. Fifer, quickly gained approval in both houses and was directly signed into law, to become effective on 1 July 1889. During the Christmas holidays in 1889, the Illinois State Teachers Association in annual session was told by State Superintendent Edwards that no "patriotic" parent could object to the requirement that instruction in all elementary schools, public and private, be in the English language, and the teachers dutifully adopted a resolution supporting the Edwards Law.[39]

As in Wisconsin, criticism of the compulsory attendance law, although slow in coming, gained in intensity as realization of its possible consequences increased, and it became a contested issue in the campaigns of both 1890 and 1892. Indeed, according to one historian, the Edwards Law was "the most controversial and explosive issue" of the 1890 campaign. As in Wisconsin, enforcement of the compulsory attendance law was sporadic, and the selection of cases to be prosecuted often proved unwise. Even though the office of the superintendent of public instruction issued advice to help school boards interpret the law, Edwards himself made the damaging admission that the law had been used in a few cases "as an instrument of persecution and a means of injuring the private schools."[40]

Although there were, in 1890, 254 Catholic parochial schools in Illinois with a total enrollment of 63,000 children, there was for some time no organized opposition to the Edwards Law by Roman Catholics in Illinois. Indeed, Bishop John L. Spalding of Peoria voiced support for this "necessary and good law," but he wanted it modified so that interference with church and private schools would be avoided.[41]

There were 292 Lutheran schools in the state in 1890. Lutheran

37. *17th Biennial Report of the Superintendent of Public Instruction of the State of Illinois, 1886–1888* (Springfield: Springfield Printing Co., 1889), pp. cxcii–cxciii.

38. "Shall the Public School Teach More Than the Alphabet?" *Schoolmaster* 5 (June 1872): 151–54.

39. DeBoer, "Compulsory School Attendance Legislation," p. 240; "Report on the Proceedings of the XXXVIth Annual Convention of the Illinois Teachers Association," *Journal of Education* 36 (9 January 1890): 28.

40. Bessie Louise Pierce, *History of Chicago: The Rise of the Modern City, 1871–1893*, 3 vols. (New York: Alfred A. Knopf, 1957), 2:367; *18th Biennial Report of the Superintendent of Public Instruction of the State of Illinois, 1888–1890*, pp. cii–cxi, lxxix.

41. DeBoer, "Compulsory School Attendance Legislation," p. 279.

leaders, convinced that the law had been "sent here from the East," were first to enter the fray. The Illinois district of the Missouri Synod of the Lutheran Church adopted a resolution that fully conceded the right of the state "to safeguard adolescents and promote the common welfare through compulsory attendance at schools." However, the resolution asserted, this did not include the right to "disturb and in some instances to destroy our schools, which are maintained in the interest of the state as well as of the church . . . ." The general body of the Missouri Synod met in 1890 for its triennial session and appointed a committee to direct the opposition to both the Bennett and Edwards laws. By midsummer 1890, the Missouri Synod's attack was well-organized and extensive. In May of that year, three thousand German Lutherans gathered at the Central Music Hall in Chicago to protest against the Edwards Law.[42]

Among the Protestants, the Lutherans stood virtually alone in their opposition to the law. The Quakers, who earlier had championed parental rights in education, now conceded the "unquestioned right of the state" to require that each child must be taught the primary branches of common school studies in the English language, although they added that such education might be provided "under parental control or otherwise." The Baptists were more outspoken. Charging that "some Lutheran and Roman Catholic Churches of our country have assumed an attitude hostile to our public schools," they resolved that "as the Baptist General Association of Illinois we boldly declare our faith in the Bible as God's word to men of all grades and races, our love for the public school as the nation's nursery and pride, our eternal allegiance to the free institutions of America, and to America's God, the One and Only Everlasting Father."[43]

Congregationalists and Methodists followed suit. The former resolved that "all attacks on the common school should be firmly resisted, and . . . our churches should spare no effort to promote public instruction." Delegates to the Methodist Annual Meeting declared, "There are elements in our midst which . . . repudiate our public school system, which is one of the strongest bulwarks of our civilization"; the delegates vowed, "We will stand by and for the public school."[44]

The Illinois State Convention of the Democratic party was held in June 1890. The platform called for a reduction in the tariff and declared, "The parental right to direct and control the education of the child shall remain forever inviolate and . . . the provisions of the

42. Beck, *Lutheran Elementary Schools*, pp. 232–33, 246; *Chicago Times*, 29 May 1890.
43. Daniel W. Kucera, *Church-State Relationships in Education in Illinois* (Washington: Catholic University of America Press, 1955), pp. 117–18.
44. Ibid., pp. 118–19.

[Edwards] Law of 1889 . . . impairing that inalienable right shall be at once repealed."[45] Only two state executive offices were up for election in November 1890, those of the state treasurer and the superintendent of public instruction. The Democrats won both, as well as control of the lower house of the legislature, but the governorship and the Senate remained in Republican hands. As a consequence, no agreement on amendment of the Edwards Law could be reached, and it continued in effect. In September 1892, the archbishop and the bishops of the province of Illinois belatedly broke their silence and issued a pastoral letter branding the Edwards Law as "insidious and unjust" and a violation of constitutional rights. One may speculate about the reasons for the tardy announcement of official Catholic opposition to the attendance laws in both Wisconsin and Illinois. A possible reason is that Catholic schools had been under attack during most of the century, and Catholic leaders were reluctant to enter new confrontations until the possibilities for compromise had been exhausted, whereas Lutherans, earlier accepted as welcome additions to Protestant America, were taken aback by this unexpected attack on their institutions.

Whatever the reasons, opposition to the Edwards Law was now clearly too extensive to disregard, and even the State Republican Party Committee called for a repeal of the law and the enactment of a new law. But it was too late; the Democrats captured the governorship and both houses of the legislature in 1892. The Edwards Law was repealed in February 1893 and replaced by a statute similar to the one of 1883, which simply required attendance at either a public or non-public school.[46]

Local controversies continued, but the major conflicts of the century over the School Question were now at an end. Paradoxically, although the School Question was for a time no longer a fertile field for agitation, nativism retained and even intensified its momentum in the early nineties under the sponsorship of the ferociously anti-Catholic American Protective Association.

45. *Chicago Times*, 6 June 1890.
46. DeBoer, "Compulsory School Attendance Legislation," pp. 400, 419.

10

The Oregon School Law of 1922

In 1922, the voters of Oregon approved an initiative petition requiring all children between the ages of eight and sixteen, with certain exceptions, to attend public schools. Similar legislation was under consideration in several other states. Masonic bodies claimed authorship of the measure, although members of the Ku Klux Klan became its most vocal proponents. From the time of its enactment, the law was under attack by Roman Catholic bodies, some Protestant groups, and the secular press. A Roman Catholic school and a private military academy secured an injunction against the law from a federal district court. Upon appeal to the U.S. Supreme Court, the law was struck down. In the court hearings, defenders of the law admitted that its purpose was the destruction of the non-public schools.[1]

We are now facing "the ultimate perpetuation or destruction of free institutions, based upon the perpetuation or destruction of the public schools," cried the "king kleagle" of the Pacific domain of the Knights of the Ku Klux Klan in 1922.[2] Grotesque as it might be to see the KKK as defenders of the common school, the Oregon adventure in education was in fact a reversion to the nativist alarms that wracked the country periodically during the nineteenth century. Like the nineteenth-century efforts to achieve a state monopoly in education, the Oregon law was also in part a product of religious prejudice. But patriotic fervor, accentuated by World War I, was now equally important. Uneasy patriots, determined to root out Darwinism, Bolshevism, and other heterodoxies, saw the public school as the first line of defense against pluralism.

---

1. The text of the law and a complete compilation of the legal proceedings are provided in *Oregon School Cases: Complete Record* (Baltimore: Belvedere Press, 1925). Prior to 1968, the best source on this subject was a brief article, "Oregon School Case," in the *New Catholic Encyclopedia*, 10:740ff. Later and more comprehensive articles are Lloyd P. Jorgenson, "The Oregon School Law of 1922: Passage and Sequel," *Catholic Historical Review* 54 (1968): 455–66; and David B. Tyack, "The Perils of Pluralism: The Background of the Pierce Case," *American Historical Review* 74 (1968): 74–98.

2. Luther Powell, preface to George Estes, *The Old Cedar School* (Portland: L. I. Powell, 1922), p. 9.

Initially, this sentiment had been manifested in the enactment of legislation in more than twenty states requiring that the English language alone be the medium of instruction in schools. None of these laws required attendance at public schools. But the prohibition of the use of another language created serious problems for the parochial schools, where the practice was more common. Under one of these laws, enacted in Nebraska in 1919, a Lutheran parochial school teacher was charged with, and convicted of, teaching a Bible-history lesson in German. This case was appealed, together with three similar cases, and reached the U.S. Supreme Court. The court in unmistakable language rejected the Nebraska law.[3]

Although the Nebraska case seemed to strengthen the position of the non-public schools, the hostility against them persisted. Determined but unsuccessful campaigns to secure legislation against them were waged in Washington, Ohio, California, Wisconsin, and Indiana. But the most dramatic precedent for the Oregon legislation was provided in Michigan. Here opponents of the non-public, and especially parochial, schools succeeded in gaining legislative approval for submission to the voters in 1920 (and again in 1924) of constitutional amendments designed to destroy parochial schools. The measures were defeated by sizable majorities.[4]

Although the Oregon anti–parochial school campaign resembled those of the nineteenth century in many respects, there were also some notable differences. The early-nineteenth-century anti-Catholic campaigns had been nurtured and led by acknowledged spokesmen for several of the major Protestant denominations, and often supported by resolutions of the denominational governing bodies. This is true even though the movements were captured by ruffians during the Know-Nothing period. By contrast, no major denominational body endorsed the Oregon law, nor were public school leaders in the forefront of the assault. Perhaps the shameless behavior of some of their predecessors during the 1888–1889 controversies lingered in their minds. The 1888–1889 measures had been supported by the Republican party, which for some years allowed itself to be seduced by anti-Catholic influences. The Oregon law had been endorsed by the Democratic candidate for governor, Walter M. Pierce, who had also solicited, and obtained, the support of the Klan during his gubernatorial campaign. But the Oregon law was not so much a product of

3. *Meyer v. State of Nebraska*, 262 U.S. 390 (1923). The same Nebraska legislature that passed the anti–foreign language law came within one vote of adopting a law compelling all children to attend public schools.

4. Some of these campaigns are related in Norman Weaver, "Knights of the Ku Klux Klan in Wisconsin, Indiana, Ohio and Michigan" (Ph.D. diss., University of Wisconsin, 1954).

partisan politics as of intense pressure by special-interest groups. Finally, whereas the nineteenth-century anti-parochial measures drew fervent praise in the press, the major newspapers and journals across the nation scorned the Oregon exercise.

At first glance, Oregon seemed to be an unlikely state in which to open a campaign for public monopoly in education. In 1920, only 8 percent of its inhabitants were Catholic, only 13 percent foreign-born, and only .3 percent black. Almost 95 percent of all children between the ages of seven and thirteen were in school, and more than 93 percent of these were in public schools. The major city, Portland, had few of the social problems of the crowded eastern centers, and outsiders (including the renowned Ellwood Cubberley) congratulated the city for its orderly, Americanized schoolchildren. There was certainly no threat to public education here. However, as Professor Tyack has commented, "Perhaps it was because Oregon did approximate the nativist ideal that partisans like the Klansmen chose it as a test case for compulsory public education, for there the majority of citizens might be persuaded to support a state monopoly . . . . If the Oregon campaign were to prove successful, a dozen other states were next in line."[5]

The crucial role of the Klan in the Oregon school campaign is clear. However, two Masonic bodies claimed credit for originating the campaign: the Grand Lodge of Oregon, A.F. & A.M., and the Imperial Council of the A.A.O. Nobles Mystic Shrine. The inspiration for their action, they said, was a resolution that had been adopted by the Supreme Council, A. & S. Rite, for the southern jurisdiction of the United States, in May 1920: "Resolved, that we recognize and proclaim our belief in the free and compulsory education of the children of our nation in public primary schools supported by public taxation, upon which all children shall attend and be instructed in the English language only without regard to race or creed as the only sure foundation for the perpetuation and preservation of our free institutions . . . ."[6]

The Oregon Masons were strongly supported in their effort by the major publication of the Scottish Rite, the *New Age*. This journal made known its support of the free public schools "against all opponents" and promised to do everything possible to exclude from the operation and control of these schools any who were not known to be their

5. Tyack, "Perils of Pluralism," p. 76.
6. *Oregon School Cases*, pp. 729–34. This policy was repeatedly reaffirmed by the Supreme Council. See *New York Times*, 3 December 1922, 2:8; *New Age* 31 (April 1923): 217. An advertisement in Oregon newspapers, prepared by P. S. Malcolm, inspector-general of Oregon Scottish Rite Masons, also proclaimed the Masonic origins of the measure. See *Catholic Sentinel*, 3 August 1922.

friends. Attendance of all children in the public schools was necessary if they were to get an equal start and an equal chance in life, "and this can best be done when they are all taught along standardized lines, which will enable them to acquire a uniform outlook on all national and patriotic questions . . . ." Alien and radical organizations were growing in the United States, and the free and compulsory public school was the only effective antidote. Citing alleged Bolshevist control of the education of Ukrainian citizens in Toronto, Canada, the *New Age* asked, "Does anyone need better evidence of the necessity of compelling all children to attend public schools . . . ?"[7]

Although the *New Age* insisted that its reasons for opposing non-public schools had nothing to do with religious issues, it nevertheless accused Catholics of trying to undermine the public school system. The journal quoted, without identifying, a Catholic bishop of Oregon as favoring the abolition of public schools and attributed (perhaps justly) to a Jesuit writer the declaration that "The first duty of every Catholic father to the public school is to keep his children out of it." Other agencies had also worked for passage of the measure. An organization calling itself the Federated Patriotic Society had supported the proposal, as had the Odd Fellows and the Knights of Pythias.[8]

Despite their official claim to authorship of the school bill and their loud professions of support for it, Scottish Rite Masons were not united on the issue. Some Masons, including two past grand masters, claimed that Masonic sponsorship of the measure had been endorsed at a special meeting called by two Masonic sympathizers of the Klan (one of them the "exalted cyclops" of a Portland klan) and attended only by hand-picked members. Infiltration of Masonic lodges by Klansmen was known to exist, and grand masters in a number of states had attacked the KKK and dissociated their orders from it. Yet, because of the secret membership and "invisible government" characteristic of the Klan, it is impossible to know the extent to which it influenced the Oregon Scottish Rite Masons or other groups allied in support of the school bill.[9]

The Oregon school measure, as submitted to the voters in the general election of 7 November 1922, required parents to send their children between the ages of eight and sixteen to public schools unless they were physically unable, lived too far from a school, had completed the eighth grade, or were allowed by the county superintendent to have private instruction. For each day of non-compliance, a parent would be subject to a fine of not less than five dollars nor more

7. *New Age* 30 (September 1922): 549; 31 (March 1923): 155; 30 (November 1922): 667.
8. *New Age* 30 (October 1922): 628; 31 (April 1923): 249; *Literary Digest* 85 (18 April 1925): 32; *New York Times*, 3 December 1922, sec. 2, p. 8.
9. Tyack, "Perils of Pluralism," p. 77.

than one hundred dollars, or to imprisonment in the county jail for not less than two nor more than thirty days, or by both such fine and imprisonment in the discretion of the court.[10] The measure was approved by a vote of 115,506 to 103,685.

The law was challenged by the Sisters of the Holy Names of Jesus and Mary, who maintained a number of schools in Oregon, and by the Hill Military Academy. On 22 December 1923, both filed in the federal district court of Oregon appeals for an injunction to restrain the state from putting the law into effect. In their request for an injunction, the sisters contended that the law would deprive them of property without due process of law; deprive parents of the right to control the education of their children and children of the right to acquire knowledge in private schools; deprive teachers of their right to engage in the useful occupation of teaching in private schools; impair the contract existing between the state of Oregon and the plaintiff inasmuch as the schools were organized under the corporation laws of the state; delegate arbitrary and unlimited authority to county school superintendents to determine when any child of the specified age must attend public schools; interfere with the free exercise of religious opinion and with the rights of conscience; and abridge the right of parents in the state of Oregon to send their children to private schools in other states.

The Domestic and Foreign Missionary Society of the Protestant Episcopal Church, the North Pacific Union Conference of the Seventh-Day Adventists, and the American Jewish Committee filed briefs *amici curiae*. The three-man district court found in favor of the plaintiffs, and on 31 March 1924 issued a preliminary injunction against enforcing the statute.[11] The attorney general of Oregon on 19 June 1924 appealed to the Supreme Court of the United States for reversal of the district court's opinion, and the Court's decision was issued on 1 June 1925.

From the time it was first aired in 1922 until final disposition of the issue by the Supreme Court, the compulsory attendance measure was the center of vigorous and often bitter controversy. Much of the criticism, naturally, came from Catholic quarters. Austin Dowling, archbishop of St. Paul and chairman of the Department of Education of the National Catholic Welfare Conference, compared the law to the "Soviet claim to invade the home and substitute communal for parental care." It was, he said, a denial of the right of the individual to engage in the profession of teaching in anything but a state school,

10. *Proposed Constitutional Amendments and Measures (with Arguments) to Be Submitted to the Voters at the General Election, Tuesday, November 7, 1922* (Salem, Ore., 1922), p. 22.
11. *Oregon School Cases*, pp. 7, 15–33, 54.

and an infringement of liberty of conscience. Constantine J. Smyth, chief justice of the court of appeals of the District of Columbia, speaking at the annual meeting of the National Council of Catholic Women, denounced as slanderous the allegation that parochial schools failed to inculcate devotion to American ideals. The contribution of Catholics to the war effort, he felt, should have been sufficient to disprove this. Archbishop Michael J. Curley of Baltimore declared, "The whole trend of such legislation is state socialism, setting up an omnipotent state . . . on the principles of Karl Marx." Others felt, as did Curley, that the existence of Catholic education was in danger. The Knights of Columbus were active in promoting opposition to the law.[12]

While Catholics actively opposed the law, they also made an effort to explain the value of church-related education. The National Catholic Welfare Conference's Department of Education, especially, made a vigorous effort to demonstrate that the Catholic schools provided sound education and graduated upright and moral men and citizens. Just as much as the public schools, it was argued, Catholic schools were American in their teachings, curriculum, language of instruction, and ideals. Several Catholic organizations were founded to help in the cause. A Civic Rights Association was launched, and the Catholic Truth Society of Oregon was organized by Alexander Christie, archbishop of Oregon City, for the purpose of offsetting the anti-Catholic publications being circulated. The Catholic School Defense League was founded to disseminate information, especially among non-Catholics, about the aims and spirit of Catholic education. Catholics in the state also utilized American Education Week as a means of promoting a better understanding of Catholic education.[13]

Lutherans and Seventh-Day Adventists had schools of their own, and both harshly criticized the law. A spokesman for the Adventists charged, "The government that turns its citizens into subjects, . . . without any rights of their own, is a government that is transforming itself into a tyranny." A Lutheran synodical chairman denounced the measure. The Lutheran Schools Committee of Portland, Oregon, asserted the rights and responsibilities of parents for the upbringing and education of their children and denounced the law as "an intolerable invasion of religious liberty."[14]

12. National Catholic Welfare Conference *Bulletin* (hereafter cited as NCWC *Bulletin*) 4 (December 1922): 16; 5 (October 1923): 23; 4 (January 1923): 26; *New York Times*, 12 December 1922, p. 7; 2 January 1923, p. 17; 21 January 1923, p. 22.

13. NCWC *Bulletin*, 3 (March 1922): 17; 4 (October 1922): 22; 4 (November 1923): 16–17; 5 (September 1924): 24–26.

14. *New York Times*, 3 December 1922, sec. 2, p. 8; *Literary Digest* 76 (6 January 1923): 34–35. The Lutheran Schools Committee kept a file of documents relating to the school bill controversy, including a full set of newspaper clippings and correspondence. This file, deposited with the Oregon Historical Society, is described by Tyack ("Perils of Pluralism," p. 76) as "the basic source of information available on the compulsory school bill."

Catholics, Lutherans, and Adventists were not alone. Spokesmen for denominations that had no schools also saw the dangers in the school act. Several Presbyterian ministers adjudged the law to be "inimical to the highest human welfare" and based on "the philosophy of autocracy that the child belongs primarily to the state . . . ." A leading Congregationalist posed a troublesome question: suppose the Catholic majority in Louisiana disregarded the rights of the Protestant minority in Louisiana; would we not call that tyranny? But if the Protestant majority in Oregon sets aside the rights of the Catholic minority, shall we call it patriotism?[15]

Proponents of the Oregon school measure used even more forceful language. Throughout the three-year controversy, the fulminations of Klansmen were unceasingly poured forth. Grand Dragon Fred Gifford, a chief sponsor of the school bill, extolled pure womanhood, white supremacy, the Constitution, uncorrupted religion, and "the American public school, non-partisan, non-sectarian, efficient, democratic, for all the children of all the people . . . ." But these American institutions must be protected from the baleful influence of immigrant and inferior peoples. Somehow, cried Gifford, "These mongrel hordes must be Americanized; failing that, deportation is the only remedy."[16] Professor Tyack points out a basic contradiction in the Klan's position on public education: the Klan believed in the inherent inferiority of aliens (especially those from southeastern Europe), blacks, Catholics, and Jews, yet if the children of these inherently inferior groups could be compelled to attend public schools, they would be transformed into true Americans. "Conflicting assumptions about heredity and environment sat side by side in mute antagonism."[17]

For all its stridence, the Klan rhetoric was little more than a repetition of nineteenth-century nativist fustian. Two specimens may suffice to convey the temper of its campaign. One, its chief propaganda piece, was the pamphlet *The Old Cedar School*. In this pamphlet the case for compulsory public education was buttressed by appeals to nostalgia, anti-clericalism, anti-intellectualism, and sheer paranoia. The author of the pamphlet cast his narrative in the form of a conflict between an old Oregon pioneer and his alienated and perverse children. Using the dialect of the common man, the pioneer recalled the building of a rural school so that "when it come time to votin' we'd know enuff to vote agin fool laws an' graftin' men." But the pioneer's children abandoned the humble country school and chose instead to send their children to parochial schools. One son, who had become a

15. *Proposed Constitutional Amendments*, p. 29; *New York Times*, 3 December 1922, sec. 2, p. 8; *Portland Telegram*, 21 October 1922.
16. Lem Dever, *Inside the Klan: Invisible Empire Revealed* (Portland, 1923), pp. 29–30. Dever was a leading Klan publicist until his break with the order in 1924.
17. Tyack, "Perils of Pluralism," pp. 79–80.

snob, wanted to send his children to Oxford Towers, an Episcopal school, "where there's a hull lot of big bishops and fellers who wear their collars an' vests buttoned in the back . . . ." The two daughters had married, respectively, a Seventh-Day Adventist and a Methodist, and they too did not think the Old Cedar School good enough for their children. But the real apostate was John, for he had married a Catholic and was going to send his children to the Academy of St. Gregory's Holy Toe Nail, where they would master "Histomorphology, the Petrine Supremacy, Transubstantiation and . . . the beatification of Saint Caviar."[18]

Saddened by his family's apostasy, the old pioneer concluded his story with a dark prophecy:

> At the three corners of the old school house . . . stood a 'Piscopalyun bishop, an' a Seventh Day Adventist Minister, an' a Methodist Presiding Elder . . . a knockin' out the foundations from under our Cedar School House; an' there was a Roman Catholic Bishop runnin' out from the fir grove toward the school house, a wearin' a long black robe an' a manicurist's lace shirt. He was holdin' up the crucifix high above his head in one hand an' carryin' a flamin' torch in the other.

Then the lights went out, and a new picture appeared:

> Our Old Cedar School House, next in my heart to Mother's grave, was tumblin' to the ground, in flames, the crushed an' shriveled form of old Silas Parker, its teacher for more'n fifty years, lay dead with his snow-white head hangin' out of the open front door, his thin, bony old hand aholdin' tight to the bell rope, the swayin' bell pealin' its final call, and the burnin' flag on the tall spire, THE LAST TORCH OF LIBERTY, FADIN' FROM THE WORLD.[19]

Although the charge that parochial schools constituted a grave menace to the republic was as old as American nativism itself, the old pioneer's dramatic presentation of the charge contained an element of originality. Not so with the Klan's revival of the favorite nativist weapon against the Roman Church, the "escaped nun." Sister Lucretia was paraded about the state, sometimes appearing in public school auditoriums, to vilify Catholicism in general and St. Vincent's Hospital in particular. A Catholic organization commented bitterly that Klansmen were seeking to veil their "moral leprosy" under the cloak of patriotism and religion. Styling themselves champions of truth and purity, "in reality they were peddlers of lies, vendors of filth, disseminators of hate and enmity."[20]

18. George Estes, *The Old Cedar School* (Portland: Powell, 1922), pp. 12, 16, 22–26, 32–39. Estes was also the author of the bitterly anti-Catholic *The Katholic Kingdom and the Ku Klux Klan*.
19. Ibid., pp. 40–43.
20. Tyack, "Perils of Pluralism," p. 85.

Several nationally known friends of public education spoke out against the measure. Philander P. Claxton, a former U.S. commissioner of education, declared that the public school system had been the salvation of democracy, but that the private schools have been "the salvation of our public schools," preventing them from becoming "autocratic and arbitrary." Nicholas Murray Butler, president of Columbia University, expressed dismay that one hundred thirty-five years after the adoption of the Constitution of the United States with its Bill of Rights, the people of the state of Oregon could enact by popular vote a statute that would make elementary education a government monopoly. "If Samuel Adams and Benjamin Franklin and Patrick Henry and Thomas Jefferson turn in their graves on learning this news, there need no surprise," he said.[21] John Dewey made no effort to hide his sentiments: "We have a constitutional amendment passed in Oregon a short time ago which to some of us who thought we were good Americans seems to strike at the root of American toleration and trust and good faith between various elements of the population and in each other."[22]

The courts spoke decisively on the measure. In the district court hearings, John Kavanaugh, the attorney for the sisters, enlarged upon the arguments contained in the briefs and presented the views of well-known educational leaders to support his case. The counsel for the state of Oregon, on the other hand, repeated virtually all the charges that had been made against non-public schools in the long controversies of preceding generations. He insisted that the increase of attendance at non-public schools had been accompanied by an increase in juvenile delinquency, that compulsory attendance at public schools was a necessary "precautionary measure against the moral pestilence of paupers, vagabonds, and possibly convicts," that children educated in non-public schools would fall prey to the doctrines of "bolshevists, syndicalists, and communists," and that "the great centers of population in our country will be dotted with elementary schools which instead of being red on the outside will be red on the inside." If any one denomination were permitted to conduct schools, he declared, other denominations would also want to do so, and the result would be destruction of the public school system. That the intent of the law was to destroy non-public schools was freely admitted by the state in both its briefs and its oral presentations. "The necessity for any other kind of school than that provided by the State has ceased to exist," the state's counsel declared.[23]

21. *Oregon School Cases*, pp. 273, 283–84.
22. "The School as a Means of Developing a Social Consciousness and Social Ideas in Children," *Journal of Social Forces* 1 (September 1923): 515.
23. *Oregon School Cases*, pp. 97–103, 200.

In its injunction restraining the state from putting the law into effect, the district court declared in stern language: "The Act could not be more effective for utterly destroying the business and occupation of complainants' schools . . . if it had been entitled 'An Act to prevent parochial and private schools from teaching the grammar grades . . . .'"[24]

The attorney general of Oregon, on 19 June 1924, appealed to the U.S. Supreme Court for reversal of the district court's opinion. Constitutional questions involving property rights, personal liberty, guarantees of religious freedom, and parents' rights over children's education were considered in the hearings before the Supreme Court on 16 and 17 March 1925. There was, again, no doubt about the intent of the law. Justice McReynolds asked the counsel for the state of Oregon, "Well, we know, do we not, and are we not bound to know, that this act, if it is put in force, will shut up every parochial . . . and . . . every private school . . . ?" To this direct query, the counsel replied simply, "Yes."[25]

In its decision, issued on 1 June 1925, the Supreme Court explained:

> No question is raised concerning the power of the State reasonably to regulate all schools, to inspect, supervise, and examine their teachers and pupils; to require that all children of proper age attend some school, that teachers shall be of good moral character and patriotic disposition, that certain studies plainly essential to good citizenship must be taught, and that nothing be taught which is manifestly inimical to the public welfare.

But, said the court, the Oregon law went much further than mere regulation. The inevitable result of enforcing the act under consideration would be the destruction of parochial and non-public schools. There was no warrant for such action, declared the court, because the non-public schools were engaged "in a kind of undertaking not inherently harmful but long regarded as useful and meritorious." Then, in a clear affirmation of the rights of parents, the court declared:

> The fundamental theory of liberty upon which all governments in this Union repose excludes any general power of the state to standardize its children by forcing them to accept instruction from public teachers only. The child is not the mere creature of the state; those who nurture him and direct his destiny have the right coupled with the high duty to recognize and prepare him for additional obligations.[26]

The press, with rare exceptions, had been hostile to the compulsory school legislation from the beginning and now hailed the Supreme Court's decision with jubilation. The *New York Times* denounced the

24. Ibid., p. 52.
25. Ibid., p. 646.
26. *Pierce v. Society of Sisters of Holy Names of Jesus and Mary*, 268 U.S. 510 (1925).

law as "one of the most hateful by-products of the Ku Klux Klan." The *Chicago Tribune*, which had reviled the parochial schools during the Wisconsin and Illinois campaigns of 1888–1889, now conceded that "there are still principles of individual liberties which our legislators are bound to respect." The *Boston Transcript*, which had campaigned savagely against the Catholic schools during the 1888–1889 Massachusetts struggles, now affirmed that a blow had been struck against intolerance and bigotry. The *Philadelphia Public Ledger* rejoiced, "Standardized education has been defeated."[27]

Almost alone, the *New Age* held out against the decision. As this Masonic journal had presented itself as a champion of true Americanism, it seemed necessary to pay homage to the ruling of the highest court of the land. "Now that the decision has been firmly and finally reached and the highest court of justice has expressed itself unreservedly . . . it will become the duty of all loyal Americans to adhere to the law as it stands." But having made this obeisance to the court, the *New Age* proceeded at once to reaffirm its original position. The real purpose of the parochial schools, said the journal, was to turn out "a separate class of citizens, inbred with a different set of ideas [than those] which had been inculcated in our public schools." Therefore, "the development of the parochial school along present lines must make it the greatest single disruptive force in . . . our American democracy." Proponents of the law should not admit defeat, in spite of the Supreme Court decision, said the *New Age*. "Let us reorganize our campaign, revise our methods and resolve to 'carry on' until the full objective has been obtained." Parents must be convinced of their patriotic duty to send their children to public schools. A few months later the *New Age* returned to the attack, alleging that the truly American concept of education seemed to be "beyond the Roman understanding."[28] Until well into the 1930s this journal represented the Masons as protectors of, and indeed as the originators of, the public schools.

But it was all in vain. The first of the many major crusades to destroy the non-public (and especially the Catholic) schools had been launched in 1855 by the Massachusetts Know-Nothings, aided by many Protestant clergymen and public school leaders. Now, seventy years later, the Supreme Court had dealt a fatal blow to the proponents of state monopoly in education. Many problems remained, to be sure, and the non-public schools were long to remain outside the pale of officially recognized educational enterprise. But they had survived.

27. A large collection of newspaper and journal articles on the reversal of the Oregon law may be found in Jorgenson, "Oregon Case," pp. 463–65.
28. *New Age* 33 (July 1925): 389–401; (October 1925): 581.

11

Epilogue

American public education is pervaded by the myth that prohibition of public aid to non-public schools is a policy of constitutional origin. In fact, that policy was well established at the state level by 1860, a good century before the U.S. Supreme Court gave it constitutional status. As originally established by the leaders of the Common School Movement, the policy was not justified by any appeal to the abstract principle of separation of church and state. The argument of the common school leaders was simple and blunt: the growth of Catholicism was a menace to republican institutions and must be curbed. Catholic schools, as a contributing factor to the growth of the Church, must also be restricted and, if possible, suppressed.

Similarly, the policy of excluding religious observances from the public schools is also pervaded by some confusion. Many conservative Protestants now denounce such exclusion as a plot devised by secularist educators and liberal jurists. Secularism, gaining strength in the late nineteenth century, did indeed contribute to the decline of religious observances in the schools. But a more fundamental cause was the reaction against the excesses of the leaders of the (Protestant) Common School Movement, who aggressively sought to impose their brand of religious beliefs and practices upon all children by persuasion, by legislation and judicial proceedings, by punishment of non-complying students, and, if all else failed, by violence.

Educational leaders in other Western nations were meanwhile learning that it was possible both to provide public financial aid to non-public (mostly church-related) schools and to include religious observances in state school programs, if only provisions were made to accommodate differences in—or absence of—religious beliefs. But accommodation was not a part of the outlook and policy of the leaders of the Common School Movement and their successors. Conformity was their watchword and, unyielding to the end, they pursued their objectives. The results were mixed. Their efforts to reverse the traditional public policy of granting public funds to non-public schools met with sweeping success, and for a time the common school leaders were also able to impose Protestant religious instruction on all children in public schools. But this was a pyrrhic victory. In the end, their excesses led to the exclusion of all religious observances in the public schools, a policy at the time abhorrent to Catholics and Protestants alike.

The termination of public aid to non-public schools and the exclusion of religious observances from the public schools (the two major elements in the long-disputed School Question) were both sharp reversals of traditional policies in American education. Yet, despite the fact that the U.S. Supreme Court has spoken repeatedly on both issues, no one would pretend that anything approaching a consensus of opinion has been reached in this country. The dimensions of the problem are all too clear. With the exception of desegregation, no other school topic has contributed cases as frequently to the U.S. Supreme Court docket as have church-state issues.[1]

Other issues also entered into the school controversies, among them attempts to tax church properties, including schools, and to bar Catholics from serving on school boards/committees or from teaching in the public schools. In a broader sense, however, the controversies over the School Question were much more than a series of struggles over specific school-related issues. Catholic (and other church-related) schools were not designed merely to *educate* children, as that term is commonly used. They were designed to socialize children into a specific value system, the core of which consisted of the faith and teachings of the Church. Both Catholics and the Protestant leaders of the Common School Movement understood this. What many Protestants did not understand was that the "common" school system had been established for precisely the same reason—to inculcate a specific (not a common) set of values.

Hundreds of books and articles on the School Question, most of them polemical, appear every year. As stated earlier, it is not the purpose of this work to discuss and analyze the legal intricacies of the School Question, but rather to review the political, social, and economic conditions that gave birth to our current public policies. It may be useful, however, to take note of some other problems that have arisen, unintentionally, as a result of the policies adopted. One is that the non-public schools in this country operate with a minimum of public supervision. Another is that when any change in public policy related to the non-public schools is proposed, sober consideration of the proposal is usually stifled by charges that it is unconstitutional.

Historically, the state's interest in requiring universal education has

1. Martha M. McCarthy, *A Delicate Balance: Church, State, and the Schools* (Bloomington, Ind.: Phi Delta Kappan Educational Foundation, 1983), p. 15.

been based on the collective welfare of the state rather than on the individual interests or needs of the child. The Oregon case verdict made it abundantly clear that the states have the legal authority "reasonably to regulate *all* schools, to inspect, supervise, and examine them, their teachers and pupils; to require that all children of proper age attend some school, that teachers shall be of good moral character and patriotic disposition, that certain studies plainly essential to good citizenship must be taught, and that nothing be taught which is manifestly inimical to the public welfare."[2]

Yet, sixty years later, the large majority of non-public schools in the United States function with virtually no state supervision. It is impossible to calculate with any degree of certainty the number of non-public schools in the country. Data-gathering machinery for schools in the non-public sector is inadequate, and the task is further complicated by the rapid growth of Christian fundamentalist schools since about 1975. A recent study puts the number of non-public schools at roughly 20,000, although the number is probably larger than that. As of the school year 1980–1981, however, only 5,378 of these were accredited by state departments of education and 313 by other agencies including two non-public ("independent") school associations. (The term *accreditation* is used broadly here, to describe governmental relations with the non-public schools, however denominated. Twenty-nine states use the term *accreditation*, fifteen the term *approval*, three the term *classification*, and one each the terms *basic approval*, *chartering*, and *standardization*.)[3]

Moreover, such state supervisory influence as exists is exercised unevenly. Of the 5,378 state-accredited schools reported in 1980–1981, 3,486 were located in only eight states. Fifteen states reported that they had no records of non-public schools within their boundaries in 1980–1981! Further, the standards established by the states vary widely. Three states have stringent requirements that must be met by all non-public schools, whereas, at the other extreme, three states require only that non-public schools comply with all health, fire, and safety regulations.

Whether a more uniform exercise of state jurisdiction over non-public schools would confer significant benefits on society should be the focal point of any discussion of such jurisdiction, and the answer

2. *Pierce v. Society of Sisters of the Holy Names of Jesus and Mary*, 268 US 510 (1925). Italics added.

3. Paul A. Kinder and Robert C. Shaw, "Regulations and Accreditation Standards for Non-Public Schools in the United States" (unpublished paper, University of Missouri–Columbia, no date, 8 pp.). This paper is based on Paul A. Kinder, "The Regulation and Accreditation of Non-Public Schools in the United States" (Ph.D. diss., University of Missouri–Columbia, 1982).

to this question is by no means self-evident. Some church-related schools, notably those sponsored by Catholic and Lutheran bodies, long pre-date the appearance of public schools in this country. These church bodies have their own educational infrastructures including teacher-training institutions, educational associations, and publishing houses. There is much evidence to indicate that the quality of the education provided in these schools equals, if not surpasses, that provided in the state schools.

True, Catholic and Lutheran bodies have been the most adamant and effective opponents of state surveillance over their schools, and with good cause. Too often in the past, efforts to extend state jurisdiction over the non-public schools have been pretenses, the real objective being to destroy such schools. An intelligent exercise of the limited type of state jurisdiction allowable under the Oregon case decision, if that is possible, should not create any problems in well-conducted non-public school systems.

Whatever may be the case among the long-established non-public school systems, the dramatic growth of church-related schools during recent years has been among religious bodies, themselves of relatively recent origin, that have no tradition of school sponsorship and only scanty educational infrastructures to support their efforts. The vast majority of states exercise no jurisdiction over these schools and know very little about them. As noted above, several states—officially, at least—are unaware of the existence of any non-public schools within their boundaries. Yet most states accept attendance at such schools as compliance with their compulsory attendance laws. This is an anomalous situation, but it is one of the unforeseen outcomes of the cleavage of American education into public and non-public sectors brought about by the Common School Movement.

Why have most of the states not exercised the limited jurisdictional rights over non-public schools that the U.S. Supreme Court has made available to them? One reason may be that the divisions of opinion on church-state relations are so deep and volatile that state legislatures often become immobilized when confronted by such questions. It must also be admitted that the high court pronouncements on church-state relations in education, numerous though they are, have established very few general principles applicable to a wider range of specific situations. The Court has admitted as much: in 1947, it referred to the wall of separation as "high and impregnable," whereas in 1977 it saw the wall as "a blurred, indistinct, and variable barrier." Chief Justice Burger captured the judicial dilemma in 1971 when he observed that courts "can only dimly perceive the lines of demarcation in this extraordinarily sensitive area of constitutional law." Further, added Burger, "The language of the Religion Clauses of the First Amendment is at best opaque."[4]

A more dramatic example of judicial uncertainty about church-state relationships in education occurred when a federal district court (in *Wallace v. Jaffree*, 1985) upheld certain Alabama requirements for prayer or moments of silence as part of the daily exercises in public schools. The district court directly challenged the Supreme Court's "incorporation theory," which holds that the Fourteenth Amendment made the provisions of the First Amendment binding upon the states. (See the section "Fourteenth Amendment and Interpretations Thereof" in Chapter 6 above.) Had this decision been upheld, the federal constitutional basis for prohibition of public aid to non-public schools and exclusion of religious observances in the public schools would have been severely eroded. But the U.S. Eleventh Circuit Court of Appeals overturned this portion of the district court's ruling, and this decision was summarily affirmed by the Supreme Court in 1985.[5] *Wallace v. Jaffree* revealed that there are serious misgivings even in some judicial quarters about the soundness of the Supreme Court's interpretation of the Fourteenth Amendment. On the other hand, by again reaffirming its support of the incorporation theory, the Supreme Court closed the door even more tightly against further challenges of this type.

A secondary reason for the inability of the states thus far to deal constructively with the non-public schools is that when they discontinued the policy of providing financial assistance for such schools they also lost a valuable instrument for exercising influence over them. Even in the public schools, state supervision is exercised as much by incorporating stipulations into financial disbursement formulae as by statutory or regulatory provisions. (There are, in fact, eight states in which accreditation of public schools is neither authorized nor mandated by law.)

But there is a more fundamental, although more subtle, effect of our current policies. It was perhaps inevitable, but it was also in one sense unfortunate, that our current policies on the School Question were enshrined by the Supreme Court as a part of the law of the land. Now, whenever a proposal is made to change a policy, the specter of constitutionality is always raised, and the debate becomes an endless recital of legal precedents and technicalities. Arguments on the merits of the proposal are in effect shouted down.

Constitutional questions must of course be taken into account. But we should remind ourselves again—if that is necessary—that our

4. *Everson v. Board of Education*, 330 U.S. 1, 18 (1947); *Wolman v. Walter* 433 U.S. 229, 236 (1977); *Lemon v. Kurtzman*, 403 U.S. 602, 612 (1971).
5. George C. Wallace et al. v. Ishmael Jaffree et al., 105 S. Ct. 2479 (1985).

current policies were the product of discrimination against minority groups by a still-dominant but fearful Protestant majority. It is ironic that policies born of religious intolerance should today be regarded with reverence.

The formation of sound social policy should have first priority in any discussions of the School Question. In providing secular education, do the non-public schools render a valuable civic service, and if so should the state bear some share of the cost of that service? Is pluralism in education a potential source of strength and should it be encouraged? Should the state respect the wishes of those parents of public school children who consider religious observances or instruction an essential part of schooling? Should we continue to have the most thoroughly secularized public schools in the Western world, excepting only those of the U.S.S.R.? These are still relevant questions, and mere reliance upon legal precedents will not provide adequate answers. To smother discussion of these and similar questions by assertions that any departure from the status quo would be unconstitutional is to do a grave disservice to American education, both public and non-public.

Bibliographical Essay

General

Some of the topics considered in this work have already been studied and the findings recorded in scholarly books, journals, and dissertations. Where such secondary sources exist, they are cited as such, giving the reader ready access to more detailed information, and also to a wealth of primary sources. Primary sources are used and cited for topics not heretofore explored in secondary accounts.

In a striking departure from the traditional practice of equating education with formal schooling, Lawrence A. Cremin looks at all social institutions that influence—and so educate—people in his two-volume *American Education*, subtitled *The Colonial Experience, 1783–1896* and *The National Experience, 1783–1896* (New York: Harper & Row, 1970, 1980). A less comprehensive but also useful work is Robert L. Church and Michael W. Sedlak, *Education in the United States, An Interpretation* (New York: The Free Press, 1976). Cremin, *The Wonderful World of Ellwood Patterson Cubberley: An Essay on the Historiography of American Education* (New York: Teachers College, Columbia University, 1965) is, for the most part, an examination of the work of the early school historians. Among the bibliographies, the old work by William W. Brickman, *A Guide to Research in American Educational History* (New York: New York University Bookstore, 1949), is still very useful. Subsequently, at least until 1979, Brickman periodically published bibliographical essays on the history and philosophy of education, many of them in *School and Society*. Joe Park, *The Rise of American Education: An Annotated Bibliography* (Evanston: Northwestern University Press, 1965), is a helpful reference, as is Jurgen Herbst, *The History of American Education* (Northbrook, Ill.: AHM Publishing Corp., 1973). There are some useful entries in Lloyd P. Jorgenson, "Materials on the History of Education in State Historical Journals" (in four parts), *History of Education Quarterly 7–9* (Summer, Fall 1967; Winter 1968; Spring 1969).

1. The American State-Aided Voluntary School

The conventional view that American public education was an indigenous development with its origins in the colonial period was fashioned in good part by works such as George H. Martin, *The Evolution of the Massachusetts School System* (Boston: D. Appleton & Co., 1894); William H. Kilpatrick, *The Dutch Schools of New Netherland and Colonial New York* (U.S. Bureau of Education *Bulletin*, no. 12, 1912); and Ellwood P. Cubberley, *Public Education in the United States* (Boston: Houghton Mifflin Co., 1919). The then (1937) novel view that public monies were distributed more or less evenhandedly to church-related as well as "public" schools during the colonial and early national periods was presented in great detail in Richard J. Gabel, *Public Funds for Church and Private Schools* (Washington, D.C.: Catholic University of America Press, 1937). There are serviceable histories of the major educational movements of the colonial and early national periods, as listed in the footnotes.

2. The Protestant Common School Movement

As a comprehensive treatment of pre–Civil War nativism, Ray A. Billington, *The Protestant Crusade, 1800–1860: A Study of the Origins of American Nativism* (New York: Macmillan, 1938), remains the standard work, even though it focuses largely on anti-Catholicism and overlooks the social and economic causes of the movement. John Higham, *Strangers in the Land: Patterns of American Nativism, 1860–1925* (New Brunswick, N.J.: Rutgers University Press, 1955), is the definitive work on postbellum nativism. Sydney E. Ahlstrom, *A Religious History of the American People* (New Haven: Yale University Press, 1972), is a comprehensive treatment acutely sensitive to the heavy dependence of the Common School Movement upon the Second Awakening. It is a major thesis of the present work that the Common School Movement, the Second Awakening, and the nativist/anti-Catholic crusade intermingled with and reinforced each other, in the process profoundly altering the course of American education, both public and non-public. There is to date no comprehensive examination of this thesis. There are a very few excellent local studies such as those by David Tyack and Timothy Smith, cited below.

3. Protestant Clergy and the Common School Movement

Two brilliant articles on the prodigious educational labors of Protestant clergyman in local areas are David Tyack, "The Kingdom of God and the Common School: Protestant Ministers and the Educational Awakening in the West," *Harvard Educational Review* 36 (Fall 1966); and Timothy Smith, "Protestant Schooling and American Nationality, 1800–1850," *Journal of American History* 53 (March 1967). But these are exceptions and, as Tyack says, "Ministers have not won recognition for their contribution to public education, nor has the Protestant coloration of the common school been examined sufficiently" (p. 448). One reason for this neglect, Tyack continues, is that the earlier historical accounts were essentially "house histories" written by school administrators or education professors who chose to disregard ministers because they were outside the profession of teaching and did not share the educationists' view of schooling as a purely civil enterprise.

Earlier state histories of education (predating Cubberley et al.) and contemporary state journals of education are often fruitful sources. Dissertations on church-state relationships in education in specific states, many of them done at Catholic University of America, are useful. A few state biographical histories have been used here, and a further search of such compilations would probably be fruitful. Area, state, and local histories of nativism, often in the form of dissertations, should not be overlooked.

4. The Clergy, Teacher Training, and Textbooks

Nowhere is the symbiotic relationship between teaching and preaching in nineteenth-century America more sensitively portrayed than in Paul H. Mattingly, *The Classless Profession: American Schoolmen in the Nineteenth Century* (New York: New York University Press, 1975). It is strange that such a work had not appeared earlier, for the literature of the Common School Movement is suffused with pious affirmations of this relationship. The *Wisconsin Journal of Education*, founded in 1856, is used here to provide local color and substance to the theme of clerical/pedagogical collaboration; other state educational journals would have served equally well. *Reports* of the U.S. commissioner of education are useful on this topic, as on other phases of nineteenth-century American education. On nineteenth-century textbooks, the most scholarly and perceptive work is Ruth Miller Elson, *Guardians of American Tradition: American Textbooks of the Nineteenth Century* (Lincoln: University of Nebraska Press, 1964). Elson is fully aware of the extent of anti-Catholic sentiment in those textbooks, but does not develop the thesis. This is done in Marie Leonore Fell, *The Foundations of Nativism in American Textbooks, 1783–1860* (Washington, D.C.: Catholic University of America Press, 1941). The above works provide an excellent introduction to a study of the textbooks themselves. Some bibliographical information on textbooks is provided in the footnotes to this chapter. There is a sizable collection of nineteenth-century textbooks in the Elmer Ellis Library of the University of Missouri–Columbia.

5. The Know-Nothings and Education

As mentioned above, Ray A. Billington, *The Protestant Crusade*, is still an essential part of the background reading on antebellum nativism. Regional and state histories of nativism often provide a good deal of information on school controversies. Diocesan and archdiocesan histories almost invariably devote some attention to the School Question, as do biographies of American Catholic prelates. Several are cited in the footnotes. Robert H. Lord, John E. Sexton, and Edward T. Harrington, *The History of the Archdiocese of Boston in the Various States of Its Development*, 3 vols. (Boston: Pilot Publishing Co., 1944–1945), is an excellent example. James A. Burns, *Growth and Development of the Catholic School System in the United States* (1912; rpt. New York: Arno Press, 1969), is still useful but should be supplemented by Edward J. Power, *The Transit of Learning: A Social and Cultural Interpretation of American Educational History* (New York: Alfred Publishing Co., 1979). The fulminations of many of the early state superintendents of education against the Catholic Church and its schools should be regarded as essential documents in the history of American education. Among them are Ira Mayhew, *Popular Education: For the Use of Parents and Teachers and for Young Persons of Both Sexes*, 2d ed. (New York: Daniel Burgess & Company, 1852); and Edward D. Neill, *The Nature and Importance of the American System of Public Instruction* (St. Paul: Owens & Moore, 1853). The papers and reports of other state school superintendents, especially those of Robert J. Breckinridge of Kentucky, clergyman and nativist sympathizer, should be examined further.

6. Catholics and Protestants Consolidate Their Positions, 1865–1885

Again, diocesan and archdiocesan histories, biographies, and autobiographies of Catholic prelates and collections of official church documents are useful. Among them, as listed in the footnotes, are Hynes, *Diocese of Cleveland*; Lamott, *Archdiocese of Cincinnati*; Guilday, *John England* and also *National Pastorals*; Ireland, *Lectures and Addresses*; Gibbon, *Retrospect*; and Ellis, *Documents*. Alvin P. Stauffer, "Anti-Catholicism in American Politics, 1865–1900" (Ph.D. diss., Harvard University, 1933), is valuable not only for its wealth of detail but also for its extensive bibliography. "The Education of the People: A Symposium," *The Independent* 42 (September 1890) is an excellent collection of opinions, pro and con, on the public-parochial school experiments. Father Isaac Hecker as editor of the *Catholic World* frequently and forcefully presented the Catholic view on education, as he saw it. The National Education Association *Addresses and Proceedings* of the period are tinged with anti-Catholic sentiment. Works such as those by Barnum, Hawkins, Hartwell, and other anti-Romanists (footnote 5) are vitriolic attacks against Catholicism. Some of the topics included in this chapter have already been treated in a systematic manner in earlier journal articles, as indicated in the footnotes. Chief among these are John Pratt, "Boss Tweed's Public Welfare Program"; Harold M. Helfman, "The Cincinnati 'Bible War'"; John Whitney Evans, "Catholics and the Blair Education Bill"; and F. William O'Brien, "The States and 'No Establishment' Proposed Amendments to the Constitution since 1789." The main thesis of the last-named article anticipated by twenty years (and possibly provided the basis for) the argument for the defense of the Alabama school prayer (or "moment of silence") law in *Wallace v. Jaffree* (1985). In effect, the Supreme Court ignored the defense contention that historical evidence did not support the Court's "incorporation theory."

7. Background of the School Controversies of 1888–1890

Higham, *Strangers in the Land*, cited above, is indispensable for the exploration of post–Civil War nativism. Lester F. Ward, *Dynamic Sociology* (New York: D. Appleton Co., 1883), is a landmark in the transition from religious to secular values as the basis for moral instruction in the public schools. The voluminous writings of U.S. Commissioner of Education William Torrey Harris on moral instruction carried much weight. Emerson E. White, *School Management* (New York: American Book Co., 1894), is a classic example of the late-nineteenth-century normal school's preoccupation with moral instruction.

8. The School Question in Massachusetts, 1888–1889

In this chapter, with the author's permission, I have drawn rather heavily on a Ph.D. dissertation completed under my supervision: James M. Benjamin, "The School Question in Massachusetts, 1870–1900: Its Background and Influence on Public Education" (University of Missouri–Columbia, 1968). Prior to the appearance of this dissertation, the most comprehensive account of the 1888–1889 Massachusetts disturbances may well have been volume 3 of Robert H. Lord, John E. Sexton, and Edward T. Harrington, *The History of the Archdiocese of Boston*, 3 vols. (Boston: Pilot Publishing Company, 1945). The official account of the 1888 legislative hearings is *General Court Hearings of Legislative Committee on Education in March, 1888: House Document No. 19* (Boston, 1888). The proceedings were reported in greater detail in the anti-Catholic *Boston Evening Transcript*. As seen from the Catholic point of view, the best source (and also the most complete account extant) is Katherine Conway and Mabel Ward Cameron, *Charles Francis Donnelly* (New York: James T. White and Co., 1909). The *Annual Reports* of the Massachusetts State Board of Education are important. Justin D. Fulton, *Why Priests Should Wed* (Boston: Rand Avery Co., 1888), is beyond doubt one of the most obscene and scurrilous anti-Catholic tirades ever published in this country.

9. Anti-Parochial School Legislation in Wisconsin and Illinois

The most comprehensive accounts of the 1889 Wisconsin and Illinois compulsory school attendance laws are Robert James Ulrich,

"The Bennett Law of 1889: Education and Politics in Wisconsin" (Ph.D. diss., University of Wisconsin, 1965); and Peter DeBoer, "A History of the Early Compulsory School Attendance Legislation in the State of Illinois" (Ph.D. diss., University of Chicago, 1968). The newspapers reported the controversies aroused by these laws in great detail. A random sampling of the newspaper files yields little information of any consequence not included in the dissertations. Ulrich's interpretation of Governor Hoard's role in the controversy is, however, inadequate, as mentioned in footnotes 4 and 6. The review of compulsory attendance bills contained in the 1888–1889 *Report of the U.S. Commissioner of Education* is useful.

10. The Oregon School Law of 1922

The text of the law and a complete compilation of the legal proceedings that arose are provided in *Oregon School Cases: Complete Record* (Baltimore: Belvedere Press, 1925). Prior to 1968, the best source on this subject was a brief article, "Oregon School Case," in the *New Catholic Encyclopedia*, 10:740ff. Two more comprehensive articles, independently prepared, appeared in October 1968. One, by the present author and bearing the title given to this chapter, was published in the *Catholic Historical Review* 54: 455–66. The other was David B. Tyack, "The Perils of Pluralism: The Background of the Pierce Case," *American Historical Review* 74: 74–98. The former article, which focuses primarily on the Masonic role in the controversy, is used as the basis for this chapter, with permission from the editor of the *Catholic Historical Review*. Borrowings from the latter article, which assigns a larger role in the developments to the Klan, are acknowledged in the footnotes.

Index